COGNITIVE DEVELOPMENT

The Child's Acquisition of Diagonality

THE CHILD PSYCHOLOGY SERIES
EXPERIMENTAL AND THEORETICAL ANALYSES OF CHILD BEHAVIOR

EDITOR
DAVID S. PALERMO
DEPARTMENT OF PSYCHOLOGY
THE PENNSYLVANIA STATE UNIVERSITY
UNIVERSITY PARK, PENNSYLVANIA

The Perception of Stimulus Relations: Discrimination Learning and Transposition, HAYNE W. REESE, 1968

Cognitive Development: The Child's Acquisition of Diagonality, DAVID R. OLSON, 1970

COGNITIVE DEVELOPMENT

The Child's Acquisition of Diagonality

DAVID R. OLSON

ONTARIO INSTITUTE FOR STUDIES IN EDUCATION
TORONTO, CANADA

ACADEMIC PRESS   New York and London   1970

ACADEMIC PRESS, INC.
111 Fifth Avenue, New York, New York 10003

United Kingdom Edition published by
ACADEMIC PRESS, INC. (LONDON) LTD.
Berkeley Square House, London W1X 6BA

LIBRARY OF CONGRESS CATALOG CARD NUMBER: 72-127694

PRINTED IN THE UNITED STATES OF AMERICA

To all of the children,
including Joan, Bradley, and Ellen,
who were willing to suspend their own curiosity
in order to satisfy mine.

CONTENTS

FOREWORD

There are several ways to read this admirable book. My own recommendation is that the reader start with the last chapter, the author's conclusions and conjectures, and then sample chapters according to his interest in their substantive content.

It is not that the book does not have an order that carries one from beginning to end. To the contrary, it has several such forms of order that reinforce each other. Rather, it is that the book also is something like the log of a journey, a kind of odyssey in which a persistent question is asked, and asked again in a different form calling for different data and even a different mood. Or perhaps it is not so much a log, which implies a record of a continuous voyage. Better to think of it as a record of battles in behalf of clearing up a conjecture—some of the battles being waged in the domain of philosophy, some in the subtle recesses of intellectual history, some in the closed spaces of psychological experiments with children.

The question that drives Dr. Olson in this odyssey, drives him from the study of eye movements and problem solving as far afield as East Africa to considerations of McLuhan's media and how, really, did Massacio hit on a way of representing on canvas the "natural" drape of hanging cloth, is a powerfully simple one. How is it that though a child can *discriminate* one diagonal from another or either from a horizontal or a vertical line, he may not be able to *construct* a diagonal on, say, a checkerboard? How do perception and performance differ? What is their kinship to "intelligence" and in what sense does "representation" of the perceptual world require shaping to the requirements of action?

Although Dr. Olson did not intend it so, he also has managed to write an autobiography of five years of hard experiment and conjecture, beginning with a "little thing," the child's difficulty with diagonals, and ending with intractable questions about the nature of spatial knowledge, its relation to action, to language, and to culture.

There is one thing more about this work that should be pointed out, a particularly estimable feature. Dr. Olson, in pursuit of the elusive spatial diagonal and what it may reveal about the growth of cognitive processes, quite properly takes seriously his own advice about cultural conventionalism. Is the phenomenon, the child's difficulty in constructing conceptually in two dimensions, a reflection of cultural conventions? Or better, does the growth of the capacity to handle such "two-requirement" designs depend in some measure upon transmitted conventions? Or should the problem be more properly stated or extended in terms of the demands that different cultures place on their members to see and to construct certain features of their environment rather than others? Working within the context of West African culture, the author shows the way in which, in fact, convention and demand interact with each other. It is an interesting facet of the book.

David Olson, whatever else he is, is also an educator. He is preoccupied in later chapters of the book with the kinds of experience from which children learn how to deal with spatial–geometric concepts. He hits on the medium of the "educational toy," and to the best of my knowledge there is no analysis of the impact of a toy on intellectual functioning of comparable depth to the one we are offered here. The book must be treated as an essay into educational theory.

It was an architect who coined the phrase "Less is more." This book, by its use of a particular phenomenon—the author speaks of the "method of the representative anecdote"—is a proof that less may be more even in a study of the spatial–conceptual life of the child. Egon Brunswik argued for "representativeness" in the design of our psychological studies. But perhaps one of the fruitful ways in which representativeness can be achieved is precisely by looking deeply at the varied manifestations of a single phenomenon.

It is a courageous book to the very last sentence: "It becomes obvious that we are now equipped with a whole new set of conjectures about the nature of intellectual development, conjectures that would probably serve better to introduce a volume than to conclude one." And so my advice finds an ally in the author himself. Try the final chapter first, then begin the book and read it through.

J. S. BRUNER

London, England

PREFACE

This book is an empirical and rational enquiry into the formation of a small set of spatial or geometrical concepts in young children. There are several general considerations that influenced the nature of this study and the direction it has taken.

The first is that I have attempted to introduce a new approach to the psychological account of intellectual development. The traditional approach involves the review of all studies that may be construed as relating to the general questions under study, even if they in fact deal with different problems and use different methods. The evidence is then pulled together to find general trends and to make summary statements. The approach taken here involves rather the use of a "representative anecdote," a conception taken from Kenneth Burke. He points out that one can, if one chooses carefully, select one event which gives a fair representation of the essence of the whole domain. This approach is used frequently in literature and history where the range of possible facts is practically infinite. An example of this can be found in W. S. Allen's portrayal of the Nazi rise to power by attending faithfully to the activities in one small German town. This monograph has utilized the perspective of the representative anecdote by attempting to specify intellectual growth in one particular area in such a way as to be representative, that is, to give a clear portrayal of conceptual growth in general. In order to show that the problem studied in this book, namely, the development of children's early spatial concepts, is representative of cognitive development in general, I have found it useful to examine the problem from the more general perspectives offered by such related disciplines as art, epistomology, linguistics, and the history of science. I have tried to show how the contributions of such nonpsychologists as Gombrich, Cassirer, Kuhn, and McLuhan are important for the formulation of a psychological theory of human cognition. It may be hoped that such an approach will reduce the current intellectual isolation of psychology from the other disciplines that concern themselves with man's intellectual functioning.

The second is the recent flurry of interest by both psychologists and educators into the process of conceptual development that was launched by Piaget's extensive work in this field. More recently, Bruner's stimulating efforts to specify intellectual development in such a way that it could be related to the educational process has added to the general concern. Considerable progress has been made in describing the different processes of perceptual development, some aspects of intellectual development, and language development. The effects of age and the cultural setting have also been considered in different studies. The approach of this monograph is to consider the relation of several aspects of development as they relate to one specific problem. In the context of this problem, three major theoretical problems come in for closer scrutiny. One of these is the role of language in conceptual development, an issue that deeply splits Piaget and his co-workers from Bruner and his associates. Another is the question of the relation between perceptual information and performatory action, a relationship that is usually hidden by the simple assertion of a link between an S and an R. Another is the question of "What is a concept?" and "How do concepts develop?" For adults it appears that concepts are formed by linking other concepts or attributes to form the new concepts. But can this hold for the formation of early concepts in children? It would appear not, for where would the child get the concepts and the conceptual attributes to hook together? A fourth, concerned with another theme of this book, is the effects of instruction on the formation of early concepts.

The third concern of this monograph is the problem faced by practical educators and, especially, educational theorists of building school programs and curricula in such a way as to complement the intellectual development of the child rather than to ignore it. Dewey was not the first to cogently argue the position, based on the "growth" metaphor, that schools should provide a learning environment such that the child could take from it whatever was suited to his "needs." In our own time, because we are not as optimistic that children will be able to choose what is best for them, we have specified more precisely what the criteria or goals for learning must be. However, within the context of these specific educational goals, it is assumed that some ways of organizing and presenting information are more compatible with the manner in which children process information at a particular stage of development than are other ways. For this reason, educational theorists turn to the research on intellectual development with unprecedented enthusiasm. Descriptions of stages hardly satisfy their needs, however. What is required is a description of development complemented by an account of the process involved in the child's selection and utilization of the information he encounters in his experience and in instruction. This aspect necessarily involves an account of the nature and effects of instruction on this development. Instruction is one of the major concerns of this monograph, as well as one of the major research tools used in elucidating the process of intellectual development. As well as formal instruction, the effects of educational toys and out-of-school contexts are examined in terms of this development.

The fourth emphasis of this monograph is to expose the process of psychological and educational research to show that it is not necessarily dull. Library shelves are not barren of books on how to do research. They concern themselves primarily, however, with the technical and procedural problems of framing a null hypothesis, or the making of objective judgments, or the running of a t-test, and not with the substantive issues of asking an interesting question, reflecting on possible solutions to the question, and devising experimental techniques that will yield an answer to the question. The latter is the attempt of this monograph. Research is best taught in the context of doing research. I have attempted not only to present the results of some research but to expose the conducting of the enquiry itself, how the questions were asked, how one answer leads to the next question, and how each question relates to the more general psychological and educational questions. This concern with the process of research gives this book some of the qualities of a personal odyssey, a long wandering marked by many changes of fortune.

The odyssey would not have taken the direction it did and certainly would not have been as enjoyable without the interest and suggestions of my colleagues to whom I am deeply grateful. Jerome Bruner's written and informally presented views coupled with his enthusiasm strongly influenced the choice of the questions I considered to be worthy of attack as well as some aspects of how they actually were attacked. Mrs. Joanne Byrne was responsible for planning and executing the first instruction study reported in the book. Robert Lee Munroe was responsible for the collection of the data in East Africa and for innumerable suggestions in its interpretation. The generosity of Norman H. Mackworth, both with his equipment and his time, made possible the research reported in the chapter on eye movement. A substantial amount of the experimental work was done by Jane Millikan, Susan Pagliuso, Nancy Johnson, Donna Crossan, and Susan Yamaguchi. I also benefited from countless discussions with Frank Smith, Douglass Carmichael, Al Bregman, Mary Potter, Janellen Huttenlocher, Clifford Christensen, Edmund Sullivan, and many others. Valuable editorial assistance was provided by David Palermo, Nikola Filby, Carolyn

Csongradi, and Academic Press; clerical help was competently provided by Diane Hansen, Unarose Thompson, and Peg Bander.

This research was begun at the Harvard Center for Cognitive Studies in 1965–1966. That research was in part performed pursuant to a contract with the U.S. Department of Health, Education, and Welfare, Office of Education (Contract 6-10-043 under the provisions of the Cooperative Research Program) to the Center for Cognitive studies and in part by a Leave Fellowship from The Canada Council. A large part of the research reported was supported by my home institution, the Department of Applied Psychology of the Ontario Institute of Studies in Education. The book was completed in the pleasant, intellectual, and physical environment of Stanford University at the Center for Research and Development in Teaching, again with the support of a Leave Fellowship from the Canada Council. Needless to say I am deeply grateful to these agencies and institutions.

Finally, I am grateful to my wife, Fran, and our children who were the ones who had to adjust to the fact that even an intellectual odyssey involves, at least in this case, a good deal of wandering about the continent.

DAVID R. OLSON

Stanford, California

COGNITIVE DEVELOPMENT

The Child's Acquisition of Diagonality

1

INTRODUCTION

For centuries men have been looking at the stars. Some appeared to be fixed relative to one another; others appeared to move, sometimes quickly, other times slowly. Besides simply admiring the stars, men have framed hypotheses about their apparent motion. It was long assumed to be a simple perceptual fact that the earth was fixed and at the center of the universe. It was conjectured that stars that formed the well-known stable configurations were farther away than those that appeared to move. Perhaps even those stars moved independently and at high speeds; they just looked fixed because of their great distance from the earth. The theorizing ranged widely from the three-layered dome of Thales to the spheres within spheres of Anaxamander and Aristarchus, and to the geocentric theory of planetary rotation advanced by Ptolemy. We now feel relatively comfortable with the heliocentric system articulated by Copernicus, Galileo, and Kepler, provided that we amend the theory to admit that all motion is relative. We consider all this theorizing to be the gradual discovery of the nature and motion of the planetary bodies, the stars out there that attracted man's attention.

But such a point of view obscures one of the most interesting things about man's contemplations. At least to a psychologist, the really note-worthy aspects of man's theories are not the facts pertaining to the stars, but are rather man's cognitive activities in the process of creating theories about things, including the stars. As Kepler noted, "The roads by which men arrive at their insight into celestial matters seems to me almost as worthy of wonder as those matters in themselves" (Koestler, 1959, p. 263). In my estimation, this is a fundamental psychological fact that an account of the cognitive processes must explain.

The manner in which children arrive at their insights into the structure of the universe is no less worthy of concern. How children formulate their conceptions of themselves and the world around them, and how they continuously revise these conceptions in light of further experience and the tutoring of adults is one of the concerns of this book. For example,

1

what is the form of the child's knowledge that permits him to deal with a diagonal pattern, and how was that knowledge acquired or developed?

But it is not at all clear how to describe man's intellectual contributions to his theories—either the processes involved in the formulation of such theories or those involved in the comprehension of the theories formulated by others. The behaviorist suggestion that the psychological world consists of behavior or responses that are simply selected by their consequences somehow seems inadequate to account for the origin and transmission of knowledge. That a theoretical idea, such as the hypothesis that the earth is in motion, would be simply a low-probability response seems neither to be adequate to the facts nor to excite the imagination of this generation of psychologists. Progressive abandonment of a response model of psychology is more or less obvious in such areas of psychology as perception, psycholinguistics, and intellectual functioning.

If we abandon the older response model of knowledge we are left with the problem of trying to provide a credible alternative. Since our concern is with theoretical ideas, we may expect to receive some help from those whose problem it is to characterize the development of ideas in general; such an account is provided by T. S. Kuhn's "The Structure of Scientific Revolutions."

Kuhn has developed a historical account of the formulation, testing, and ultimate rejection of scientific models. A scientific model or theory that is accepted at some point in time he calls a *paradigm*. A paradigm gains acceptance because it is more successful than its competitors in solving a few problems that the members of the discipline have recognized as acute. Most of the empirical work of normal science is within such a paradigm, an enterprise that "... seems an attempt to force nature into the pre-formed and relatively inflexible box that the paradigm supplies" (Kuhn, 1962, p. 24). The product of that research is to articulate the paradigm, examine its implications, increase its precision, and reduce its ambiguities. The paradigm involves a set of expectancies that indicates what to look for and what kinds of solutions to expect—and, by implication, what to ignore (for example, such questions as why do like charges repel, what is force, what is a man that he can invent theories about the world). But, often because of the very precision of the paradigm, new and unexpected phenomena occur.

> Discovery commences with the awareness of anomaly, i.e., with the recognition that nature has somehow violated the paradigm-induced expectations that govern normal science. It then continues with more or less extended exploration in the area of the anomaly. And it closes only when the paradigm theory has

been adjusted so that the anomalous has become the expected
(Kuhn, 1962, p. 53).

Kuhn documents the feverish activity and channeled attention that
accompanies this detection of an anomaly—Roentgen rarely left his laboratory over a period of seven weeks after he accidentally noticed a nearby
barium screen light up when he was studying cathode rays; it turned out
to be caused by invisible x-rays. The cycle closes with the invention of a
new paradigm, which amounts to a scientific revolution, that can handle
the anomaly.

Science is replete with theoretical developments that fit this model.
The early study of static electricity and its accounts illustrate this (Kuhn,
1962). It was early noticed that a glass rod that was "excited" by rubbing
it on silk attracted small bits of paper to itself. The theory that was
elaborated to account for this phenomenon postulated "affluvia," qualities
or properties that resided in varying degrees in materials which, in an
excited state, reached out and captured small objects. The paradigm
worked so well (one could predict the distance the affluvia would reach
out on the basis of the degree of rubbing it had received) that it was unnoticed that some bits of paper first approached and then "bounced"
away. Finally, when one scientist built a rod capable of holding a large
charge, the rebound was so obvious that it could no longer be ignored.
The observation presented an anomaly; affluvia could hardly be expected
to reach out and attract, change their "minds" and repel. The recalcitrance
of the anomaly prepared the way and provided the occasion for invention
of the theory of positive and negative charges that defined the new paradigm.

This account from the history of science may provide the alternative
paradigm for viewing cognitive development that we have been seeking.
The child either begins with a model or *constructs* a model to deal with
the events to which he is exposed. The model or *schema* is articulated
through subsequent encounters; at first, mild anomalies are not noticed.
Upon consolidation of the schema, the anomaly stands out in bold relief.
The paradigm ruptures and a new schema capable of dealing with the
anomaly replaces it. Some start has already been made in showing that
this constructive process applies to all knowing or "cognition," both
perceptual and conceptual. Neisser (1967) has recently developed a coherent statement of this cognitive perspective primarily in regard to visual
and auditory perception. Piaget (1960), Bruner *et al.* (1966), Werner
(1948), and Sokolov (1969) have been most ambitious in applying this
perspective to conceptual or intellectual development.

The study of the evolution and transmission of theoretical knowledge may then provide a paradigm for our viewing the elaboration of the child's conceptual or intellectual world in terms of such basic processes as theory formation, hypothesis testing, detection of anomalies, and the like. While I have not attempted to work out the implications of this paradigm, it is obvious that it is radically different from the "individual differences" model, or paradigm of human intelligence that has been dominant perhaps since the time of Galton, and certainly since the time of Binet. In that paradigm, the word "intelligence" was preempted to refer exclusively to the differences between people, and not to the accomplishment of skills that are common to the species. Thus, the simple recall of digits could be considered an aspect of intelligence because people differed in their performance, but the acquisition of language, or skills of locomotion, being common to the species, could not be considered intelligent—only variance between people is examined in an individual difference paradigm.

The difference in focus of these paradigms may be indicated by the different questions that they generate. Consider one of the observations on which this book hinges: young children cannot construct a diagonal. The older paradigm would lead one to ask if some children can reach that achievement earlier than others. That variance would then be taken to define "intelligence." The paradigm offered here would lead one to ask why young children have difficulty with such a problem. What happens in or to a child that subsequently makes it possible for him to succeed on such a task? The concern is not with rank ordering children but with uncovering the mechanisms by which all children become "intelligent."

In order to study intensely the nature of intellectual development from any perspective, it is essential to restrict the field of study. In this book, I have narrowed the problem by studying only a limited age range, primarily three to six years, and a very limited set of problems, primarily, the diagonal. As to the first of these constraints, several respected psychologists, including Piaget (1960), Bruner (1966), Luria (1961), and White (1965) have presented a wide range of evidence strongly suggesting that some fundamental change occurs in the child's organization of his experience around the time that the child enters school, a shift we may call the development of conceptual or operational thought. For this reason, the studies in this book examine intensively the intellectual development of children at this age.

The second of these constraints, the choice of the problem, is more difficult and warrants some discussion.

Whenever a psychologist selects a problem to administer to a group of children he makes the assumption that that problem is "representative" of either some target set of problems or of some underlying ability. This is usually described as the problem of validity. An item on an intelligence test is not created because it's interesting in its own right, but only because it can be shown that this item is representative, that it is a valid estimate of some underlying ability. An experimental psychologist is in a more difficult position. It usually cannot be shown that the task the experimenter is exposing his children to is representative of anything at all. Examples of this could be taken from virtually any branch of psychology, but the situation in regard to concept formation is typical. One group of psychologists (Kendler, 1961) studies how a child comes to make one response to two dissimilar stimuli and takes this problem to be representative of the formation of concepts, while another (Piaget, 1960) studies how a child comes to establish a set of logical relations, including class inclusion, and takes this problem as representative of the formation of a concept. It is clear from Kuhn's analysis that the experimental findings are due more to the paradigm than to the "structure of the world," but as each task defines its own paradigm, and since there are an infinite number of tasks, it becomes critical to select for critical study tasks that can be judged or construed as "representative" of the domain of intellectual development. Alternatively, the representativeness of the problem may be indicated by examining the empirical findings in context of the general and basic questions that led to the psychological study in the first place. This informs the present study, because an attempt was made to examine and describe one aspect of development in such a way as to show the nature of cognitive development in general.

The focus of this book, then, is the theoretical and empirical study of the child's development of a conceptual system relating to the concept of the diagonal during the age range three to six years. A detailed examination will be made of why a young child has difficulty with such a problem, and what occurs during development that removes this difficulty. In the context of these empirical arguments, we shall be examining such theoretical questions as the nature of intellectual skills and conceptual or symbolic knowledge, as well as the role of experience and instruction in their development. The study will conclude with a description of the child's reconstruction of the diagonal in terms of what at least poses as a general model of perceptual and intellectual development, and accounts for, among other things, man's increasing ability to apprehend and theorize about the motion of the stars.

While the relevance of our account of intellectual development in terms of the child's acquisition of the concept of the diagonal must be judged according to a relatively strict criterion of "representativeness," the selection of the problem was not formally dictated by that criterion. It was

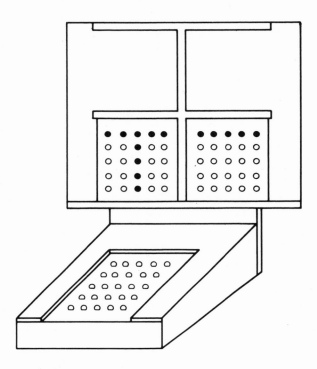

Fig. 1–1. Apparatus used in the experiments. (From Bruner, J. S., *et al. Studies in cognitive growth.* New York: Wiley, 1966.)

selected because it appeared interesting and puzzling, an anomalous observation that failed to fit into (at least my own) prevailing cognitive theory. As part of the pilot work in connection with an experiment on conceptual strategies (Olson, 1966), a series of models or patterns of various geometric shapes were constructed. These patterns were formed by an array of red dots arranged on a gray sheet of paper to form a pattern such as a line, a square, an E, a diagonal, and various other patterns or models. These models were then to be used as a guide to 5- and 6-year-old children who were to press the bulbs on the "bulb-board" that corresponded to the array of dots on the models. The bulb-board, which is shown in Fig. 1–1, shall be described more fully later. The first child that we tried with these materials, Jeff M., a bright 5-year old, looked at the patterns on the model, then went and directly pressed the corresponding bulbs on the bulb-board. He did this with patterns such as a simple top row, or more complex patterns such as the entire outside edges of the bulb-board, or patterns of an E or an H. It then came as a surprise to us that when we showed the child a simple 5-bulb pattern of the diagonal, he looked at the pattern and then pressed bulbs, apparently at random. It was as if he had not looked at the model. We then had the child look back at the model, run his finger over the pattern on the model, and try again. It made no difference; he continued to press almost randomly. What was there about the diagonal that constituted such a problem for the child? Within a week it was clearly established that 7- and 8-year-old children had no difficulty with the diagonal. What happened in the meantime that made the problem so easy for the older children? Our young but persistent child continued in his attempt to copy the diagonal, but with little improvement. When the child did manage to hit one of the diagonal bulbs, thus causing it to light up, he appeared not to notice that it was part of a sequence of the diagonal bulbs, part of a pattern. On one occasion we interrupted the child long enough to press down all five of the correct bulbs simultaneously. The child appeared delighted and quickly began pressing each of five diagonal bulbs in sequence. His success was short lived; as the memory of the bright visual configuration faded, so did his ability to press the diagonal bulbs. After about 15 seconds, he was back to where he had been at the beginning.

About a year or so later the child was able to look at the pattern and copy it much as an adult does with little recollection that such a problem could ever have been difficult. But what has happened in the mind of the child that makes this later success possible? It is that transformation over that year or two interval that has been our primary concern.

The purpose of this study then, is to accumulate and examine some evidence that will permit us to refine our conception of the nature of intelligence of the child and its transformation over the ages of four to seven years. This development, which may be described as the beginnings of operational or conceptual thought, will be examined by reference to the child's developing ability to copy a diagonal pattern. The study is programatic, if that is not too exalted a term for the gropings reported herein, in that the original hypotheses were somewhat vague, and that each subsequent study was designed to refine the conclusions and to eliminate alternative explanations of the results.

In the process of this study we have given the diagonal problem to almost 1000 children in the contexts to be described presently. The picture one gets of the child and his apprehension of the world resembles that described by Gombrich (1960) of what an artist sees when he looks at the world:

> The individual visual information . . . [is] entered, as it were, upon a pre-existing blank or formulary. And, as often happens

> with blanks, if they have no provision for certain kinds of in-
> formation we consider essential, it is just too bad for the in-
> formation (p. 73).

The more critical kind of question is why does that blank or formulary change to receive certain kinds of new information? More specifically, the primary questions which have been the focus of the studies reported here were the following:

> When do children come to construct the diagonal?
> Why is the problem difficult?
> What do children subsequently know that permits them to construct the diagonal?
> How do they come to have that piece or form of knowledge?
> What is the relation between perception and a performatory act such as that of constructing the diagonal?
> What is the role of experience and instruction in this development?
> How is language related to this process of development?
> What is the nature of instruction?

In the concluding chapter, I shall try to show that it is the elaboration of the child's perceptual knowledge in the context of his performatory attempts in such cultural media as language and geometry that accounts for his ability to copy a diagonal in particular and his intellectual development in general.

The plan of the book is most easily gathered by looking at the chapter headings and the brief abstracts that appear there. In my estimation, the most important theoretical developments of the book appear in the final chapter. However, I reached the conclusions presented there by means of the preceding nine chapters; most readers will find the high points raised there most accessible by the same means.

2

CONCEPTUALIZING CONCEPTUALIZING: THE DIAGONAL AS AN INTERESTING PROBLEM

> . . . in which we see that the construction of the diagonal is interesting not only because it appears to be anomalous but also because it can be viewed in a larger theoretical context of the nature of perception and its relation to language, of the origins of concrete operational thought, of the development of symbolic systems of thought and the development of forms of representation in art.

Having established a point of view or a perspective for viewing intellectual development in general, it becomes important to examine more specifically what is known about the psychological processes involved in the child's copying a visual form such as the diagonal. This literature has at least three relevant components that shall be reviewed in turn. First, the perception of orientation—why do oblique lines appear to be more difficult to discriminate than horizontal or vertical lines? Second, the child's conception of space and of geometry—how does the child come to know about the properties of spatial and geometric forms and how is that knowledge related to that involved in his simple discrimination? And third, the problem of visual representation—what is the relation between what we make or draw and the perceptual event that serves as a model?

The other aspect of this problem, the nature of intelligence and the role of the culture in its development, particularly as systematized in instruction, will not be reviewed here, but will be dealt with in the contexts of the relevant chapters. (See Chapters 5, 6, and 7.)

PERCEPTUAL SPACE

First, consider the perception of orientation. Not all orientations are equally easily discriminated. Lashley (1938) found that rats could

9

learn to discriminate an upright U from an inverted U more easily than similar U's opening to the right and to the left. In general, the ordering for difficulty of discrimination problems was similar for rats and men. Sutherland (1960, 1969) found that the octopus could discriminate a vertical from a horizontal rectangle but could not discriminate one oblique rectangle from another inclined in the opposite direction. From this, and from the fact that this invertebrate has a radically different visual system, Sutherland inferred that the octopus used different kinds of cues in their discrimination. Rudel and Teuber (1963) applied and extended this approach to children. They found that like the octopus, the child can readily discriminate horizontal from vertical lines, but the same figures are virtually indiscriminable if they are obliquely oriented. Moreover, they found that training on one oblique transferred completely to the opposite oblique, and that it was easier to learn to discriminate an oblique from a horizontal line than from a vertical line. Like Sutherland and Lashley they also found that U shapes oriented up and down were more easily discriminated than those same shapes oriented to the right and to the left. Similarly Benton (1959) presented considerable evidence that children have difficulty remembering the orientation of objects, particularly orientations involving left–right differences such as in the letters "b" and "d." Huttenlocher (1967b) showed that the account is somewhat more complicated than had been realized. Both up–down and left–right discriminations were easy or difficult depending on the relative position of the alternatives. If up–down alternatives are arranged vertically they become almost as difficult as left–right alternatives arranged horizontally, mirror image alternatives being the most difficult to distinguish.

Now, consider the status of an obliquely oriented line from this point of view. For both a vertical and a horizontal line, one mirror image is identical to the model, the other reversed; for the oblique, neither mirror image is identical, that is, there are more ways to go wrong. These relations are shown in Fig. 2–1.

The perception of the diagonal may therefore be expected to be more complex than the perception of lines having other orientations. That is, if children have difficulty differentiating mirror images, the oblique, for which both mirror images are different from the model, will be more difficult for them than either horizontally or vertically oriented lines for which only one mirror image differs from the model.

This presumed perceptual difficulty is exactly parallel in the structure of our language. The forms which are readily perceptually differentiated are matched by a word in English. The forms that are virtually indistinguishable (at least for octopus, rats, and young children) are not marked

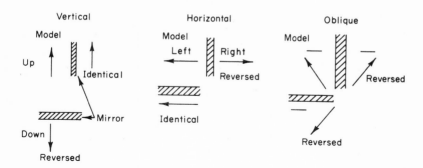

Fig. 2–1. For a horizontal and vertical line one mirror image is identical and the other is reversed; the reversed one has a distinctive name. For the oblique, both mirror images are reversed and neither can be named.

by a word. Thus either of the words *horizontal* or *vertical* will differentiate the horizontal–vertical perceptual alternatives. The oblique alternatives cannot be differentiated by a vocabulary item. In the same way, the mirror images that are to be distinguished have a corresponding lexical entry for horizontal and vertical lines; for oblique lines they do not. These latter vocabulary items are also shown in Fig. 2–1. A Whorfian view would lead us to expect that humans would have more difficulty discriminating oblique lines than vertical and horizontal lines because of these asymmetries of the language. It would have less success in accounting for the difficulties of octopus and rats!

It seems more reasonable to conclude that language reflects the perceptual cues to which the human organism is most receptive and those cues which are most useful in differentiating important alternatives.

As we shall see in the following chapter, the order of difficulty in perceptual discrimination roughly parallels that in the reproduction of similar forms; it is easier to copy a row or a column than it is to copy a diagonal. But it is not clear how these perceptual discriminations are related to the copying of forms. The latter is essentially human and late developmentally; hence the copying of forms is quite different from simple discrimination. But what is this difference?

REPRESENTATIONAL SPACE

Piaget and Inhelder (1956) deal with this problem by differentiating perceptual from representational space, the former being almost immediate and occurring in the presence of the physical stimulus, the latter being more dependent on perceptual activity and occurring in the absence of the object by means of an image. Mental representation of space is analyzed through several means, the most prominent of which are, first, the recognition of visual forms on the basis of haptic exploration and, second, the drawing of visual forms; both of these presumably involve the reconstruction of visual images.

> A drawing is a representation, which means that it implies the construction of an image, which is something altogether different from perception itself, and there is no evidence that the spatial relationships of which this image is composed are on the same plane as those revealed by the corresponding perception (p. 47).

The nature and development of "representations" or mental images is somewhat problematical. Piaget has elsewhere argued that "representations" are the basis of symbolic processes in general in that they provide for the differentiation of the signifier, a sign or a symbol, and the things signified, the meanings or thoughts themselves. Although the theoretical basis for this distinction is not completely convincing, at least to me, and although it has been argued that the concept of representation is no advance over the older concept of idea, Piaget's distinction is an important one in at least two ways. First, it reflects the fact that children's perception, at least in terms of visual recognition, far outstrips the child's ability both to copy such forms and to recognize them through active touch, that is haptically. Second, it leads to Piaget and Inhelder's (1956) observation that the types of cues or features utilized first in perception and later in the childs representation of space, develop progressively from topological cues such as proximity, separation, order, and enclosure to projective and Euclidean cues such as geometric shape, dimensionality, and position in terms of a set of reference axis.

Consider some of the evidence they have assembled on the development of these representations. In regard to tactual recognition, Piaget and Inhelder (1956) found that 3- and 4-year-old children could distinguish shapes such as open from closed circles, and independent from entwined forms, a differentiation involving typological features; it was not until around 5 or 6 years of age that they differentiated Euclidean forms, such as squares from rectangles and other more complex forms. This ability was related to the method of haptic exploration utilized, the older subjects exploring contours and corners much more actively than the younger. These findings were greatly extended and refined by Zaphorozhets (1965) and by Abravanel (1968); the latter found that younger children engaged in gross palping and clutching, or passively holding the object in their palms. Older children actively explored with their fingertips those aspects of the object relevant to the subsequent task, for example, spanning the rod if they were to make length estimates.

While thus confirming the developmental priority of features pertaining to topological space over those pertaining to Euclidean space, the transition is not abrupt or complete. For example, Abravanel (1968) reports that young children made accurate diameter estimates well before they made accurate length estimates, both of which involve Euclidean concepts. This observation was traced back to the fact that young children automatically grasped the diameter in picking up the object, while length could not be apprehended without active search. In general, it appears that the topological–Euclidean distinction generally characterizes the types of cues that young children tend to hit upon. When the materials were such that an Euclidean cue was more accessible, that feature influenced the child's performance. Further, it may be that it is the child's knowledge of the alternatives to be differentiated that comes to regulate his tactual search; presumably young children haptically search a block in the same way when they are to choose between a tall and a short block as they do when they are to choose between a thick and a thin block. This question begs for further research.

Piaget and Inhelder's hypothesis about the developmental priority of topological relations is also applicable to the child's copying of visual forms. As Binet had earlier found, Piaget and Inhelder demonstrate that the child could copy the square at about four years of age, but not until considerably later could he copy a rhombus. Piaget and Inhelder (1956, p. 74) conclude, "The fact that at least two years work is required . . . in order to pass from copying the square to copying the rhombus . . . shows pretty clearly that to construct an euclidean shape, something more than a correct visual impression is required." They attribute the difficulty not to mere skill in drawing, but to the abstraction of shape in general, straight sides, angular symmetry, and primarily that of slope. One child is quoted as saying, "It must be like the top, but I can't manage it." The child must slowly acquire the representational schemata primarily through his own activity before he can construct the rhombus, even if his perception of it is well developed.

Another means of assessing the child's spatial representation is through the child's constructions. Consider Piaget and Inhelder's treatment of the straight line. The child begins to perceive a straight line very early in life, but it is only much later that he can picture it in his imagination. Children are given the task of arranging a straight row of "telegraph poles" between two given end points. Children aged four to seven years can form a straight line more or less correctly when it runs parallel to the edge of the table, but they are unable to when it lies at an angle to the sides. Piaget concludes that the child is unable to break away from the perceptual influence of the table edge. Finally, the child of about seven years can consistently make the straight lines by sighting along or aiming down the row of posts. It is this physical activity which, when it is internalized, becomes the conceptual operation or representation of a projective straight line.

While Piaget's distinction between perception and thought is quite clear and readily grasped, the essential nature of this difference is not clear, at least to me. What does a child know about an event when it is recognized (perception) as opposed to what he knows when he forms an image of it in his mind or his drawing (representation)? Recent studies of perception by Neisser (1967) and Garner (1966) show quite convincingly that perception is both a selective and constructive act that is strongly influenced by expectancies, properties that could be taken to characterize representation. Moreover, the hypothesis that what is being constructed is an image seems equally troublesome. How would the image, for example, be differentiated from a perceptual scheme that is involved in recognition?

The view that guided at least the early stages of the present studies was the opinion that Piaget's distinction was very important. How else could one account for the fact that perceptual knowledge of space is years ahead of the child's conceptualization of space? On the other hand, the account of the relation between these two systems is a problem that recurs frequently in the chapters that follow. In the concluding chapter it is hypothesized that both perception and representation are perceptual forms; they differ primarily in terms of what is perceived in the two cases. But that is to get ahead of our story.

No matter how that question is answered, it is the case that the forms of the knowledge that permit the copying of a model or the reconstruction of a straight line are described by Piaget and Inhelder (1956) as concrete operations; however, they do distinguish logical from infralogical operations. While these two are formally equivalent and are acquired at about the same time, Flavell (1963) and Piaget and Inhelder (1956) have pointed out several features that separate them. Just as a class is composed of class objects as the basis for the logical concrete operation of classification, so, too, the object can be considered in terms of parts. One can perform the operation of combining the parts into the whole, and the reverse operation of breaking the whole back into the parts. Piaget calls these reversible part–whole relations "infralogical" operations. This position makes the class and class–object relation completely analogous to the part–whole relation. The adjective "infralogical" seems well chosen to indicate the contrast with "superordinate" or "classification" in that one could assume the child's representation of the world to begin in the middle of these two types of operations, that is with the objects themselves, the hierarchical organization of the classificatory system being the inverse of the hierarchical organization of the infralogical part–whole system. The reason Piaget expects them to occur at the same time is that the same conditions for equilibrium, the conditions of combinativity, reversibility, associativity, and identity, hold in both cases.

It follows that the study of the child's ability to copy a diagonal, involving infralogical operations, is ipso facto a study of the origins of concrete operational thought.

Concepts and Conceptual Space

Most of this literature will be considered in the context of the relevant empirical arguments, but some orientation may be necessary. For reasons we shall see later, the diagonal is a concept that is related to a set of other concepts such as square, corner, and straight line. Although there is no universally or even widely accepted theory that specifies what a concept is and how it is developed, there is fairly wide agreement that percepts must be differentiated from concepts; the hallmark of the latter is their association with language. Thus Humboldt [cited by Cassirer (1957, p. 15)], argued that the knowledge we have of objects is exclusively that shown to us through the medium of language. Cassirer (1957) extends this argument to state that a world of symbols intervenes between perceptual and performatory worlds. It is this knowledge of symbols, theoretical knowledge, which is responsible both for the development of culture and for the development of the higher level of thought in an individual. To show that perception does not account for differentiated, organized symbolic knowledge, Cassirer (1957) says

> . . . the phenomenon of perception, taken in its basic and primary form, in its purity and immediacy, shows no such division. It presents itself as an undivided whole, as a total experience, which is, to be sure, articulated in some way but whose articulation by no means comprises a breakdown into disparate sensory elements. This breakdown occurs only when the perception is no longer considered in its simple content but is viewed from a definite intellectual standpoint and judged accordingly . . . (p. 27).

That is, knowledge is not immediately given in perception, or by the concrete data, but is postulated in a symbolic system. Reflecting what Cassirer calls the revolution in 20th century physics, natural science no longer looks for the fundamental laws of nature by inductively looking at nature itself but, rather, is devoted to the construction of symbolic systems thus:

> . . . Heinrich Hertz is the first modern scientist to have effected a decisive turn from the copy theory of physical knowledge to a purely symbolic theory. The basic concepts of natural science no longer appear as mere copies and reproductions of immediate material data; rather, they are represented as constructive projects of physical thinking—and the only condition of their theoretical validity and significance is that their logical consequences must always accord with the observable data . . . (p. 20).

Concepts are therefore to be thought of in terms of a conceptual or symbolic system that arises through such "spiritual" activities as analysis and reflection and are not given directly by viewing nature; rather, their meanings must be "wrested from the world of language."

In regard to the conception of space which may be assumed to be more relevant to the concept of the diagonal, Cassirer again argues that spatial knowledge does not reflect concrete perceptual data but reflects, instead, the process of symbol formation. The concrete knowledge of space, "the space of action" is replaced by the symbolization or representation of space "the space of intuition" which breaks up the stream of successive experiences and organizes it into conceptual systems. The conceptual system one employs to represent space depends upon which spatial determinations and relations one postulates as invariant. Thus according to Felix Klein [cited by Cassirer (1957, p. 157)] every special geometry is a theory of invariants which is valid in reference to a set of transformations. Thus whether a square and a rectangle are considered as similar or different depends on which transformations you choose to admit. In any case the fact that we appear to have one perception of square and any number of theories of square is used as evidence for the difference between perceptive space and abstract geometric space.

Cassirer cites another interesting piece of evidence. Primitive peoples' knowledge of space is generally known to be restricted to specific concrete knowledge. Though they may exactly know every bend in a river, they will be unable to draw a map of a river, to organize that knowledge into a spatial schema. It is this transition that marks the development of the pure representation of spatial relations.

To indicate the relevance of this description to the studies which follow it seems reasonable that while recognition of a diagonal may involve only perceptual space, reconstruction of the geometric form would require a knowledge of abstract or conceptual space. We may expect therefore, that a conceptual revolution must occur, a "crisis of spatial consciousness" as Cassirer calls it, before the child could represent and reconstruct the diagonal.

The similarity of Cassirer's views on this development to those of Piaget is obvious. Both make a clear distinction between perception and representation, the latter of which is the primary component of thought and intelligence. They differ primarily in that Cassirer attributes the development to the culture while Piaget attributes it to the internalization of the child's actions. Since the views of Cassirer are similar to and underlie the more specifically psychological accounts of Whorf, Vygotsky, and Bruner, the theoretical views of these latter will be considered in more specific contexts.

VISUAL REPRESENTATION

At least one other line of theoretical and empirical literature is relevant to our problem; it is the problem of "representation" in art to which outstanding contributions have been made by Gombrich (1960) and Arnheim (1954). The account is helpful because it begins essentially where those considered above end. In art there is no doubt that there is a difference between one's perceptions of nature and one's representations of nature. The question then becomes what is the relation between what one sees and what one draws or constructs.

Gombrich's (1960) conclusion is quite compatible with the views presented above:

> . . . the correct portrait, like the useful map, is an end product
> on a long road through schema and correction. It is not a faith-
> ful record of a visual experience but the faithful construction of
> a relational model (p. 90).

Consider the arguments and the evidence in more detail. Alain's cartoon (Fig. 2–2) which Gombrich cites considers the possibility that the reason Egyptian painting looks so strange to us today is that their models really looked like that. Is it the case that the perception of events have remained relatively invariant across the ages and only the systems for representing things in art change? Or is it possible that as the forms of representation change, ones perceptions of the world actually change?

Fig. 2–2. Do you draw what you see? (Drawing by Alain, *The New Yorker*, 1955.)

Gombrich (1960) states that in order to describe or portray the visible world in art one needs a developed system of schemata. The schemata is compared to a questionnaire or formulary which selects information from the visual world; only those aspects of information that are judged to be relevant or useful are registered in the schemata. The objective of the artist, that is, his conception of what he is trying to do, together with the constraints of the medium in which he is working and the visual forms that he already knows or can portray, will determine what information he gains from his perceptions of the world. Gombrich provides interesting illustrations of the important effects of an artist's schemata on what he sees in nature. Garland assumed that the Cathedral of Notre Dame was a Gothic structure so although he was "drawing it from nature" he gave it pointed arches when in fact it had rounded windows (Gombrich, 1960). Similarly, Goltzius, a master of Dutch realism, in portraying a whale washed ashore, apparently mistook the flipper for an ear and hence made it look remarkably like a cow's ear and placed it much too close to the eye. In both cases the artist's schema or conception or expectancies regarding the event influenced both his perception of the event and its subsequent portrayal. The act of portrayal itself involves the choice or guess of an appropriate schema and corrections in the light of viewing the production in terms of that schemata.

Gombrich points out, moreover, that these schemata are invented, not discovered simply by looking intensively at nature. Two further examples drawn from Gombrich document this point. An early art historian had described how Masaccio had "loved to paint drapery with few folds and an easy fall just as they are in natural life." Before Masaccio no one did; after Masaccio many artists did. Gombrich then asks, "What difficulty could there have been in this simple portrayal which prevented artists before Masaccio from looking at drapery for themselves (1960, p. 12)?" A second example comes from Constable's experiments with color, such as his use of yellow paint to represent sunlit green grass, which, although it at first looked odd, was adopted by a whole generation of artists. Art develops by the progressive development of "a vocabulary of forms;" what you can see in nature and what you can "say" in art depends on the limitations of your vocabulary or schemata. That vocabulary is expanded by such inventions as we have mentioned above and it is transmitted primarily from looking at the record of these inventions, that is, other paintings, not directly at nature. It is because of this invented, conceptual property that art has a history at all.

To relate this to the problem at hand, it should be clear that the copying of a visual form or its construction in any other medium reflects not a simple "printout" of a perceptual input but, rather, a conceptual schemata that has been constructed by the child's reflection upon his own activities and by the influence of the culture through the pictorial record of past inventions.

Arnheim's (1954) account of the development of children's art is quite compatible with the view of the representations being determined by the vocabulary of forms described above. What the child draws is not any print out of the real world, but the visual world recast in terms of the schema that the child has learned. While there is a discontinuity between perception and representation, Arnheim points out several parallels between the perceptual development of children and the progressive elaboration of their drawings. For example, despite the similar visual projections, a six-foot man at ten feet looks larger than a three-foot child at five feet, and children's drawings tend to preserve this fact. Similarly there is a corresponding pattern of progressive differentiation in the child's perceptual world and the pattern of differentiation in a child's drawing. However, children undoubtedly see more than they draw. To account for this Arnheim also relies on the concept of representation. "Representation never produces a replica of the object but it's structural equivalent in a given medium (p. 162)." The evolved system for representing objects or events depends on the medium in which the artist is working. But within any medium the "vocabulary of forms" demonstrates a continuous evolution. For children's drawings it involves differentiation and integration of simple

Fig. 2–3. Child's drawing of a man and a saw. (From Arnheim, R. *Art and visual perception: a psychology of the creative eye*. Berkeley: University of California Press, 1954.

lines to circles, to angles, to obliques, and so on. Whatever the child draws will be constructed out of the forms available to the child at the time. Arnheim presents a convincing set of drawings composed entirely of straight lines and circles made by preschool children where the same set of elements, or forms, are rearranged to represent such diverse objects as a hand with figures, a flower, a face, and a sun, or even the teeth of a saw as shown in Fig. 2–3. The evidence is compelling that the child's drawings proceed, as Arnheim and Gombrich suggest; any object is represented by, or within, the set of elements, operations, or "schema" available. Improvements in drawing occur by virtue of refinements and precision in the use of these schemata or forms, and innovation occurs through the development of alternative sets of forms. It should not be assumed that the "knowledge of forms" is any more explicit than the child's knowledge of grammar. The parallels are intriguing but too tenuous to be pursued here.

Two points of divergence between Gombrich and Arnheim may be mentioned. First, Gombrich criticizes Arnheim for assuming that the relation between perception and representation in art is so close that once we are sufficiently exposed to such revolutionary works as those by Picasso and Klee we see that they "look exactly like the things they represent." Rather, Gombrich emphasizes the varying objectives an artist may have in his portrayals, and the inventiveness he may use in achieving these objectives.

The second concerns the factors involved in the origins and cultural transmission of these forms. When a child draws a circle, has he learned it from looking at balls, moons, and wheels, or from experimenting with his own pencil drawings, or from looking at other people's portrayals or representations of a circle? Only (some) psychologists believe the first; Arnheim favors the second, and Gombrich emphasizes the third. Arnheim (1954) says

> The young child spontaneously discovers and accepts the fact that a visual object on paper can stand for an enormously different one in nature, provided it is its structural equivalent in a given medium (p. 162).

Gombrich, on the other hand, emphasizes the role of the culture, that is the effects of looking at other artists' works on the development of representation. In regard to the development of a child's ability to represent things in art there is some anecdotal evidence that childrens' drawings of houses are markedly facilitated by looking at other children's drawings, as opposed to looking at the houses themselves. It is also a well documented fact that it is easier to copy a painting than to paint the original scene. The implication is that in copying the painting, the biggest part of the work is done by the previous artist, namely that of providing, or at least suggesting, the appropriate schemata for representation. On both counts it follows that one learns to represent nature in art more by looking at art than at nature.

The divergencies between these views reflect the fact that Gombrich as an historian is attempting to find the continuity in the culture whereas Arnheim is more interested in the origin of forms themselves. The relative emphasis given to self discovery and to learning from the culture would then be a single case of the more general argument between the proponents of discovery and expository learning (Bruner, 1960; Ausubel, 1963).

The extent to which a cultural medium is involved in one's ability to use such pictorial forms as drawings and maps has been indicated by McLuhan (1964):

> The art of making pictorial statements in a precise and repeatable form is one that we have long taken for granted in the West. But it is usually forgotten that without prints and blueprints, without maps and geometry, the world of modern sciences and technologies would hardly exist.
>
> In the time of Ferdinand and Isabella and other maritime monarchs, maps were top-secret, like new electronic discoveries today. When the captains returned from their voyages, every effort was made by the officers of the crown to obtain both

originals and copies of the maps made during the voyage. The result was a lucrative black-market trade, and secret maps were widely sold. The sort of maps in question had nothing in common with those of later design, being in fact more like diaries of different adventures and experiences. For the later perception of space as uniform and continuous was unknown to the medieval cartographer, whose efforts resembled modern nonobjective art. The shock of the new Renaissance space is still felt by natives who encounter it today for the first time. Prince Modupe tells in his autobiography, *I Was a Savage*, how he had learned to read maps at school, and how he had taken back home to his village a map of a river his father had traveled for years as a trader.

. . . my father, thought the whole idea was absurd. He refused to identify the stream he had crossed at Bomako, where it is no deeper, he said, than a man is high, with the great widespread waters of the vast Niger delta. Distances as measured in miles had no meaning for him. . . . Maps are liars, he told me briefly. From his tone of vocie I could tell that I had offended him in some way not known to me at the time. The things that hurt one do not show on a map. The truth of a place is in the joy and the hurt that come from it. I had best not put my trust in anything as inadequate as a map, he counseled. . . . I understand now, although I did not at the time, that my airy and easy sweep of map-traced staggering distances belittled the journeys he had measured on tired feet. With my big map-talk, I had effaced the magnitude of his cargo-laden, heat-weighted treks (pp. 145–146).

In all of the theoretical contexts we have considered, systems of representation of an abstract, conceptual, or symbolic nature have been postulated as mediating perception and overt behavior. It is these representations that are used to account for the possibility of thinking or intelligence, and for the influence and development of human culture. It is important to notice, however, the slightly different meanings of "representation" in two contexts. For Gombrich and Arnheim, representation is the performance in a medium such as pencil, paint, or clay. For Piaget and Cassirer, on the other hand, representation is a conceptual, imagined, or internal event that lies behind these performatory behaviors. Although the research reported in this book was not influenced by this difference, it will come up again in the conclusion where it provides the basis for a conjecture about the nature of intelligence; intelligence is skill in a cultural medium.

Finally, to distinguish perception from representation is not to solve the problem of how they are related. Although this problem arises repeatedly in this book, we shall gradually come around to a suggestion made by Arnheim (1968, p. 206). "The difference then is not primarily between perception and representation, but between perception of effect and perception of form, the latter being needed for representation."

Through what may be a literary slight of hand, I have made the theoretical concerns of this review, and this study in general, almost cosmically proportioned, and relevant to the great questions of the nature, development, and transmission of knowledge. In the light of the scope and sophistication of these theories, our first attempts at experimentally studying how a child comes to construct a simple geometric pattern, the diagonal, will appear crude indeed. The emphasis on these theoretical considerations may be somewhat justified by reference to Popper's (1962) dictum: "The significance of observations depends entirely upon whether or not they may be used to criticize theories." Consider now the observations and their use in refining some of our conjectures.

3

THE NATURE OF THE DIFFICULTY

... in which we show that the diagonal is indeed more difficult than comparable problems in the same medium and that these relative difficulties fit well within the established Gestalt laws of perceptual organization,

... and in which we show that these laws account *only* for the nonoccurrence of these events, and that an account of the occurrence of these events requires a substantial reorientation to the problem and an addition to the theory.

Just how difficult is the diagonal and why is it so difficult? Our original conjecture about the child's difficulty with the reconstruction of the diagonal was that the problem required some skill or knowledge that the child at that early stage of development did not possess. But what skills or what knowledge? How are we to examine and refine this conjecture? We may be able to find out what skills are required for the construction of the diagonal by comparing it to other related problems. It may then be possible to find a limited number of factors that account for this difficulty. For example, is it diagonality per se that is involved, or is it slope, or straightness, or some factor in the perceptual organization of the pattern? If we succeed in this first task, we will still have to face the problem of where this knowledge or skill came from—the problem of development.

The first of these questions, namely the nature of the difficulty as determined by the comparison of the diagonal problem to related problems, was examined through two experiments with somewhat different designs; hence, they shall be reported separately.

Fig. 3–1. Original square checkerboard.

PROBLEM DIFFICULTY COMPARISON I

Method

Materials. Although our original observations were made on the bulb-board, and one further study was conducted using it, at this point our methodology changed to the use of the "checkerboard" for this part, and most of the subsequent studies.[1] The checkerboard is a 7-inch square wooden board with 25 recessed holes cut into the surface so as to make five rows and five columns of equally spaced holes into which standard 1-inch checkers could be placed to make a pattern. This checkerboard is shown in Fig. 3–1. For any single problem, two such checkerboards were used; on the first, the Experimenter constructed a model; on the second, the child attempted to construct a pattern identical to the one shown him by the Experimenter with some of the 15 checkers placed in front of him.

---

[1] The checkerboard was originally "invented" by J. S. Bruner as an alternative to the "bulb-board" employed in an earilier study (see Olson, D.R. "On Conceptual Strategies" in Bruner, J.S. *et al.*, *Studies in cognitive growth.* New York: Wiley, 1966.

The advantage of this piece of equipment over the bulb-board was that it was more portable, the data were more directly transcribed, and more importantly, the child could see more easily the correspondence between the model presented and the board on which he was attempting his production. This was so for two reasons: first, the model was just a paper representation in the case of the bulb-board, while it was composed of identical materials for the checkerboard; second, for the bulb-board the model was set above the place where the child would make his copy, while for the checkerboard the model was set in the same place. This fact will be made more clear in the description of the procedure. Finally, it was possible to build alternative checkerboards that would permit us to make a better assessment of the problem difficulty.

The Gestalt laws of perceptual organization suggest that such factors as edgedness and proximity may serve as a perceptual support or a distractor in the reproduction of such visual patterns as we have presented to the child (Werner, 1948; Hertz, 1956; Kohler, 1929). On the checker-

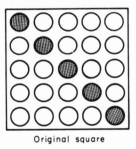

Original square

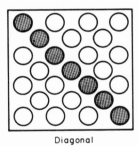

Diagonal

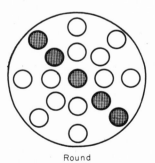

Round

Fig. 3-2. The three types of checkerboards used.

board we have been describing, these factors are highly correlated. For example, a pattern consisting of the top row has both edgedness and relative proximity between the checkers, while the diagonal has neither. In order to untangle these factors other checkerboards were developed. First, the relative distance (proximity) between row and column holes (which were originally closer together), and the diagonal holes (which were originally farther apart), were simply reversed; the diagonal holes now being brought closer together.[2] Second, a round board with equal distance between the holes constituting the horizontal and vertical and sloped arrays was constructed. These boards are all shown in Fig. 3–2. We shall refer to the original checkerboards as the "Square Boards" and the others as the "Diagonal Boards," and the "Round Boards," respectively.

Procedures. It is important to make one general point about the methodology used all through this study and for research with children in general. It is generally assumed that keeping conditions constant means that the children must all be told exactly the same thing in exactly the same way. This, however, runs counter to the central point in a theory of intellectual development; that is, one cannot assume that constant input corresponds to a constant interpretation or constant understanding by the child. The interpretation he assigns to some instruction is a function of his set, background experience, and stage of development. To employ standard instructions therefore, immediately introduces considerable "noise" or even bias into the results of the experiment. Much more critical for an experiment with young children is to make the child's comprehension of the instructions as comparable as possible. This relationship may be shown as follows:

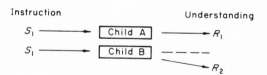

That is, constant instructions to different children may yield differing comprehension of those instructions.

$$S_1 \longrightarrow \boxed{\text{Child A}} \longrightarrow R_1$$
$$S_2 \longrightarrow \boxed{\text{Child B}} \longrightarrow R_2$$

---

[2] I am indebted to Dr. Mary C. Potter for this suggestion.

Similarly, different instructions to different children may yield similar comprehension. In experiments with children, it is much more critical to see that the comprehension of the task, R_1, is comparable across Ss than it is to keep S_1 constant. To achieve this, it may and frequently will be necessary to modify the instructions from child to child or to engage in a short training session in order to clarify the requirements of the task to the child. That is why, for example, Piaget's "clinical method" is quite appropriate. While he is frequently criticized for imprecise methodology, the opposite is the case. American investigators are usually the ones who make the naive assumptions about constant input (instruction) yielding constant understanding across children. In the experiments reported in this monograph, we have attempted to make the child's understanding of the task somewhat constant as assessed by the warm-up problems, even if it has meant introducing some variability into the instructions and handling of the child.

In this specific experiment, the child is first given a checkerboard and some checkers and asked if he would like to put some checkers into the holes in the board. After a minute or two, E asks him to take them all out again. E constructs a pattern on his checkerboard without letting the child see what he is making, and then displays the pattern by putting the board directly in front of the child, thus covering up the child's board. E says: "See the picture I made? Could you make a picture like that?" The child is then requested to run his finger over the pattern (in order to guarantee that he is, in fact, visually attending to it). E then removes the model and, pointing to the child's checkerboard, says: "Here is your checkerboard, see if you can make a picture exactly like mine." E's board is hidden from the child while he is attempting his construction. The child's construction is recorded on a score sheet. The child is told "good" or "fine" and then asked to remove his checkers from the board. During this time the experimenter is constructing the next pattern to display. It was sometimes necessary to repeat the instructions or modify them slightly in order to make sure the child grasped the idea of correspondence between the model and his construction, and the requirements of the task.

The warm-up patterns the child was asked to copy consisted of the top row, and if necessary, one or more of the four corners of the board. The warmup tasks employed a correction procedure whereas the experimental tasks did not involve telling the Ss of the correctness of their productions.

Subjects. Children employed as subjects (Ss) in this part of the study were 29 Cambridge Nursery School children aged 3 to 5 years, drawn from the Nursery School at Peabody Terrace, the graduate student resi-

dence of Harvard University. From this fact it may be inferred that these
*S*s are somewhat above average in ability.

Design. Following the warm-up problems, each child was given at least
two problems of each type (edge, interior row, and diagonal) on both
the Square and Diagonal Boards, a total of twelve problems. The specific
problems were as follows: edge-top and right edge; interior row (the
second column from the right and the middle row); diagonal (left oriented
and right oriented). For data analysis the two problems of each type were
treated together. The order of the presentation of the problems was not
counterbalanced, that is, there was no assurance that each problem occurred equally often at each position in the sequence. Rather the order
was made contingent on the child's performance on any particular problem.
The objective of this procedure was to arrange the problems hierarchically
to permit us to make and test hypotheses of the form: if a child can solve
a problem at any level of difficulty in the hierarchy, can he also solve all
the problems lower in the hierarchy?

The method involved is a modified paired comparison technique similar
to that which Gagné (1962) employed to determine which skills were a
prerequisite for the learning of other skills. The complication in the experiment reported here involves the fact that the level of performance generally
improves somewhat over the testing period as a result of practice. (We
shall subsequently have to account for this effect as well.) For example,
if a child failed to copy an interior row but later successfully copied the
diagonal, two explanations are possible. Either the interior row is more
difficult, or the practice has improved his performance to the level that
he is now able to solve problems higher in the hierarchy. This latter
alternative may be examined by repeating the first problem; if he fails
the interior row again, the interior row is indeed more difficult; if he now
succeeds on the interior row, no inference may be drawn. On the other
hand, if the child succeeds in copying the interior row and subsequently
fails to copy the diagonal, since the practice effects are staggered against
the inference we may infer that the diagonal is, in fact, more difficult
than the interior row. The method employed was therefore cyclic in that
each problem was revisited after every other problem, with the limitation
that once the child got a problem correct twice in a row, it was simply
assumed he would continue to get it correct, and he was not re-tested on
it.

The three problems on the round board were administered two and
three days after the testing on the other problems. Since practice on the

other boards may have inflated the scores, they were not calculated in with the paired-comparison data.

Results and Discussion

First a rough index of problem difficulty was made by calculating the percentage of correct constructions on each of the types of problem on each of the three checkerboards. This data is presented in Fig. 3–3. For

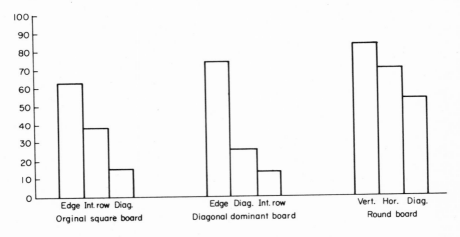

Fig. 3–3. Percent of correct reconstructions on each problem on three checkerboards ($N = 29$).

both the Square and the Diagonal Boards, problems involving the reconstruction of the edges remain the easiest. On problems involving nonedge patterns, there is a complete reversal between the two boards, the pattern based on proximity (the interior row on the Square Board and the diagonal row on the Diagonal Board) being easier. In other words, proximity becomes critical. Finally, for the Round Board, where both edgedness and proximity are removed, the vertical and horizontal rows produce slightly fewer errors than the sloped row ($Z = 2.12$, $Z = 2.56$, $p < .05$). In any case, slope accounts for a small part of the difficulty, compared to the presence or absence of proximity. (Consider that the nonsloping interior row on the Diagonal Board leads to only 29% success, while the sloping array on the Round Board leads to 65% success.)

More important are the results from the paired comparisons of the problems on the Square Board with those on the Diagonal Board. Data for these comparisons were obtained by scoring children's constructions into three categories: first, correct, second, configuration correct (but the pattern displaced, e.g., left column, may be reconstructed on the right, or row second from the top may be displaced to the middle row), and third, configuration incorrect. The resulting data were analyzed by calculating the percentage of children who could perform on one type of problem better than they could perform on another type of problem. More simply, could children who could solve problem A also solve problem B? For example, what percentage of the children who could construct an edge could also construct a diagonal? These percentages are presented in Table 3–1.

From this table we see that on the Square Board, 18% of those who succeed with the edge could also construct the diagonal; on the other hand, 100% of those who could construct the diagonal could also construct the edge. All other pairs of comparisons are listed in the Table. To determine if one problem is more difficult than the other, a series of z tests for the significance of the difference between two correlated proportions was carried out. The resulting z is recorded under the more difficult of the pair compared. Notice, for example, if the child could construct the diagonal on the Square Board, it can be seen by reading down the column that it was almost certain that he could solve the other problems. Since the Table is symmetrical, the appropriate pair for each comparison can be found symmetrically displaced around the diagonal entries. The entries in the diagonal cells give some indication of the stability of the performance on each of the problems as calculated on the repeated measures. As was pointed out earlier, since the overall performance tended to be improving, these figures were calculated by determining the proportion of cases in which performance on the repeated item was identical or improved, as opposed to the proportion of cases that indicated a regression. The resulting values ranged from .77 to .92. The value .92, for example, means that of the 25 Ss for whom we have two measures on the edge pattern of the Diagonal Board (measures separated by various alternative problems), 92% obtained the same or an improved score on the second attempt at that item; only 8% showed a regression.

This data may now be used to determine the hierarchy of tasks and the extent of their overlap, and to infer the factors that give rise to problem difficulty. If the child can construct the diagonal on the Square Board, the probability is very high ($p = .96$) that he can make the diagonal on the Diagonal Board. In the opposite direction, however, if the child can construct the diagonal on the Diagonal Board, the probability that he

TABLE 3-1

PROBLEM DIFFICULTY COMPARISONS

If a child can solve this problem:	Original (Square) Board (B)			Modified (Diagonal) Board (A)		
The obtained probability that he can subsequently solve this problem is:	Edge	Internal row	Diagonal	Edge	Diagonal	Internal row
Original (Square) Board (B)						
Edge	.83[1]	1.00**[2] $z = 4.35$	1.00** $z = 4.41$	.95 $z = 0.00$	1.00** $z = 3.60$	1.00** $z = 4.12$
Internal row	.23	.85	1.00** $z = 4.12$	.25	.68 $z = 0.24$	.90 $z = 1.90$
Diagonal	.18	.37	.81	.15	.31	.35
Modified (Diagonal) Board (A)						
Edge	.95 $z = 0.00$	1.00** $z = 4.24$	1.00** $z = 4.80$	.92	1.00** $z = 4.12$	1.00** $z = 3.87$
Diagonal	.48	.64	.96** $z = 4.03$	.37	.77	.86 $z = 1.74$
Internal row	.29	.62	.90** $z = .305$	.29	.57	.85

[1] N ranged from 21 to 27.
[2] Asterisks mark the more difficult of the pair compared—** $p < .001$

can do the diagonal on the Square Board is significantly lower ($p = .31$). Since the two problems are identical in slope, lack a reference axis, and differ only in proximity between adjacent checkers, we may conclude that relative proximity is the crucial variable. Similarly, the effect of the presence of a reference axis, such as the edge of the board, parallel to the pattern can be seen by comparing the internal row on the Diagonal Board with the diagonal on the Square Board. There again, the proportions are significantly different ($p = .90$, compared to $p = .35$). That is, when relative proximity is held constant, a pattern that is parallel to some reference axis is consistently easier for the child to copy. However, this factor may be more appropriately interpreted as the oblique orientation of the array rather than as parallel to a reference axis because these two factors are not independent. It may be possible to differentiate them by setting the board at various orientations. Although this was not done systematically in the present study, preliminary observations indicated that when the board was set on a corner to make a diamond shape, the child either used the table and his body as reference axis or else he tilted his head to match the orientation of the board. There is some evidence that slope is an independent factor in that on the Round Board there were significantly more errors on the oblique array than on the other arrays; but, again, the reference axis may be related to this effect.

These comparisons show that not only do the problems vary in relative difficulty, but that there is a relatively rigid ordering of the problem types that appears to be attributable to the features or cues that the child is utilizing to regulate his productions. It is possible therefore to represent these problems hierarchically and to infer the feature of the problem that accounts for the gap between it and the other problems in the hierarchy. This hierarchical representation and the underlying factors responsible are presented in Fig. 3–4.

An examination of Fig. 3–4 shows that the most primitive or the lowest in the hierarchy in the copying of these patterns is "edgedness." This factor corresponds to the empirical fact that the highest proportion of these young children could copy a pattern along an edge. Even then, some edges are more difficult than others; top and bottom seem to be easier than left and right side, but this is complicated by the effects of the position of the Experimenter's model checkerboard relative to the child's checkerboard. For example, if the boards are set side by side, left–right errors predominate; if the boards are set one above the other, top–bottom errors predominate. This phenomenon has already received some considerable attention in the psychological literature. Benton (1959) and Rudel and Teuber (1963) found that children have difficulty discriminating and

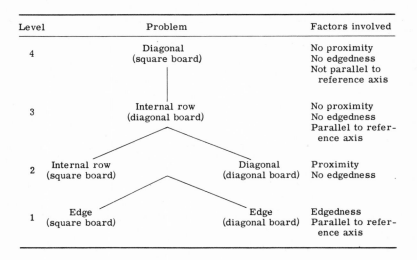

Level	Problem	Factors involved
4	Diagonal (square board)	No proximity No edgedness Not parallel to reference axis
3	Internal row (diagonal board)	No proximity No edgedness Parallel to reference axis
2	Internal row (square board) Diagonal (diagonal board)	Proximity No edgedness
1	Edge (square board) Edge (diagonal board)	Edgedness Parallel to reference axis

Fig. 3–4. Problem difficulty comparisons.

copying figures that are identical, but are oriented to the right or to the left (such as a "b" versus a "d"), while they have little difficulty when the differences are in the up–down orientation (such as a "b" versus a "p"). Huttenlocher (1967b) has confirmed this, but has shown, in addition, that the errors are more strongly affected by the relative position of the model and copy. Thus, if the model is above, up–down errors predominate; if the model is to the side, left–right errors predominate. This is precisely what was observed in the present study. To minimize these factors, the model and copy were shown in exactly the same positions.

At the next level in the hierarchy, relative proximity becomes critical. Patterns formed using the holes that are closest together constitute the "figure" while other holes constitute the "ground." For children at this second level or below, the checkerboard is an irreversible figure-ground; hence, they can deal with any pattern for which the figure is provided either by the salient edge or the proximity of the checkers.

The third level in the hierarchy involves problems which are neither at an edge nor grouped by proximity. They are problems which are parallel to a reference axis provided by the board or the room or perhaps even the person's body. Patterns parallel to such a reference axis, such as up–down, left–right, are easier to reproduce than those that are not.

At the top level in the hierarchy is the diagonal problem which has none of the factors that aided in the child's reconstruction, neither proximity, edgedness, nor supporting reference axis.

Of these three factors, that of proximity is the most significant, both in terms of the amount of variance accounted for, and in terms of relevance to the understanding of mental development. The significance of proximity (the figure-ground properties of the board) is shown in three ways. First, when everything else is constant, as the comparison of the Diagonal on the Square Board with that on the Diagonal Board, the nonproximate is substantially more difficult. Second, when proximity is held constant, as on the Round Board, all the problems are relatively easy. Third, it is the figure-ground factor that is overcome at about Kindergarten age, just at that point when Piaget, Werner, Bruner, and Luria expect a transition from perceptual to operational thought; but that point requires extended discussion as it is essentially the central point of this whole monograph.

PROBLEM DIFFICULTY COMPARISONS II

The problem difficulty comparisons experiment was repeated because of a limitation inherent in the cyclic procedure utilized in the study. There is no assurance that the problem orders were counterbalanced, that is that every problem occurred equally often at each position in the sequence. This could not be done because of our assumption about a declining baseline or threshold. On the other hand, this replication ignored the problem of the changing baseline and simply presented the six problems we have been comparing in a completely randomized order. While these results will not enable us to make such precise estimates of the probabilities of success on one problem given success on another one, they do conform more closely to the measurement assumptions of the paired-comparisons model.

Method

Subjects. Subjects for this study were 68 Nursery School children from St. Catharines, Ontario, ranging in age from 2 to 5 years, who were being pre-tested for an educational toy experiment that is reported in a later chapter.

Design. Three problems on each of the two checkerboards were presented in a completely randomized order. Specifically, the problems on the Square Board were the right edge, the second row from the top and the right-oriented diagonal; the problems on the Diagonal Board were the left edge, the second row from the bottom, and the right-oriented diagonal. Each problem was presented twice in the series. A small candy reinforcer was given to the child at the completion of each trial. Other than that, the same procedure was used here as in the first study, in that E showed the child the model, had him run his finger over the pattern, removed the model, and then asked the child to try to reproduce it.

Results and Discussion

Problem difficulty was assessed by comparing the percentage of children who made at least one errorless construction of the pattern in the two tries on each pattern. These percentages are shown graphically in the white portions of Fig. 3–5. Again, the pattern at the edge is easiest for both checkerboards and, again, there is a reversal between the interior row and the diagonal for the two boards. Thus, the diagonal is more difficult than the interior row on the Square Board, while the interior row is more difficult than the diagonal on the Diagonal Board. The one part of the results that appears anomalous is the finding that slightly more children made errors on the interior row on the Diagonal Board than they did on the Diagonal of the Square Board. In the first study, we found very few instances of a child who could construct the Diagonal who could not construct the interior row (which was, accordingly, represented higher in the hierarchy). This apparent discrepancy is resolved if we consider a secondary source of evidence, namely the seriousness of the errors. If we use the three category scoring system utilized in the previous study, and assign two points for a correct answer, one for a displacement error, and zero if neither configuration nor displacement are correct, and if we convert these to percentages, we obtain the results shown in the black portions of Fig. 3–5. From this portion of the figure it becomes clear that the errors made on the diagonal are at least more grave than those made on the other problems because, for the diagonal, errors are not only displacements, but the basic configuration is also incorrect.

Hence, our analysis of the problem hierarchy may be tentatively considered to be correct. Accordingly, this analysis confirms the importance of the Gestalt principle of perceptual organization or Pragnanz, including proximity, closure, and good continuation, used earlier to account for the difficulty children have with these problems. However, as we shall see presently, such an account is also extremely limited.

Further research should be conducted to determine more exhaustively the set of cues utilized in such productions and the order in which they

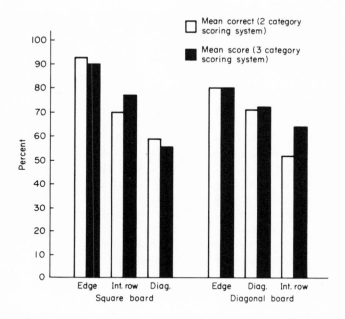

Fig. 3–5. Percentage of *S*s getting one or more trials correct on each of six problems (*N* = 68).

appear developmentally. Recent studies of distinguishing feature analysis, such as that devised by Johnson (1967), may help to get at such a set of features; compare Kinsbourne and Hartley (1969) and Spring (1969).

General Discussion and Conclusions

It would appear that we have come to the end of our search. We have found that the child in copying patterns of this sort is critically dependent on the perceptual organization of the visual field in which he is to make his construction. The most salient perceptual properties that account for the child's success or failure have been isolated and described as proximity, edgedness, and presence of a perceptual reference axis; all are quite compatible with Gestalt theory. We could, moreover, go on to describe the children's difficulty with these problems as an illustration of what Werner (1948) has called their "figure-ground deficit." It would appear then, that we have succeeded in doing what J. L. Austin (1962) says philosophers regularly do, namely "to bog, by logical stages, down."

However, there are several strong reasons why such an account cannot be considered adequate; before we point to its limitations, it is necessary to examine the theory more carefully. A student of Werner's, Witkin, and his associates (Witkin, Dyk, Faterson, Goodenough, and Karp, 1962) have presented this point of view very clearly. They describe cognitive development as a process of psychological differentiation, a progressive analysis or articulation and structuring of the child's knowledge of himself and the world. Development is best indicated by a shift from a person's dependence upon external frames of reference towards a reliance upon internal ones that can be imposed on the stimulus events by the person himself. Their best demonstration of this is the rod-and-frame test. A subject sits in a dark room facing a luminous rod surrounded by a luminous frame; the rod and the frame can be moved independently. He first sees them both tilted and he is required to move the rod to a position that is true vertical, ignoring the position of the frame. Some people, labeled "field-dependent" are more influenced by the frame, i.e., by the visual field surrounding the rod, in their estimation of the true vertical. Others, the "field-independent," are able to bring the rod close to the true vertical, presumably because of their internalized frame of reference based on body position, while paying relatively little attention to the visual field. This "field-independence" is found to relate to performance on a wide range of tasks such as imposing a structure on ambiguous stimuli and locating familiar patterns in a complex design.

More critical to our present purpose is the fact that development proceeds primarily in the direction of greater field-independence, less reliance on external frames of reference, and more reliance on internal frames of reference which may be imposed upon ambiguous stimuli.

Such an account permits us to discuss development by specifying the structure or embedding contexts in the visual field and to describe their salience or effects in terms of the well-known laws of perceptual organization. Thus, the following dots are more easily seen as two sets of three than as three groups of two.

· · ·   · · ·

However, as the child develops he becomes less field dependent; he relies more heavily on conceptual structures not explicit in the perceptual array. It is at this level that our earlier analysis and that of Witkin *et al.* (1962) fail to provide an account. We have described the perceptual field factors and their effect on behavior; moreover, as they are withdrawn, we can infer that the behavior is regulated by some internalized conceptual structures. But the nature and development of these latter structures is omitted and, perhaps, inaccessible within that mode of enquiry. To

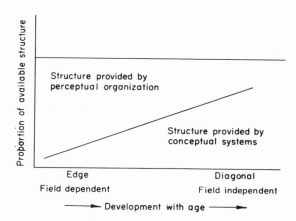

Fig. 3–6. Proportion of the structure provided by the perceptual field and by the child's conceptual knowledge.

repeat, we can and have specified the factors in the visual field, proximity, edgedness, and the presence of a reference axis, and their relative effects on a child's copying of a figure, but when a child no longer relies on these factors, we have no comparable description of the internal conceptual structure that serves as an alternative to these perceptual factors. The relation between these two types of account is shown in Fig. 3–6 which indicates that our description thus far involves the factors above the sloping line. Thus, in our account of the diagonal, we have provided an account of why children fail in their attempted reproductions but we have not given any account of why they succeed. For example, the diagonal involves neither proximity, edgedness, nor the presence of a parallel reference axis. These factors, therefore, account for why children do not construct it but not for why they do construct it. This account does not specify what the child is relying on or what is serving to structure or organize his behavior when he succeeds in the construction. This then becomes the focus of our enquiry. What does a child know, that is, what is the conceptual structure that a child relies on that makes the construction of the diagonal possible?

It should be noticed that the distinction drawn here corresponds to one widely honored in the child development literature. Piaget (1960) carefully distinguishes perception from thought in a manner somewhat similar to that developed here. Bruner et al. (1966) have differentiated iconic from symbolic representation along roughly the same lines, and

Luria (1961) has described how the child's speech may alter the natural relative strengths of the stimulus elements in a complex stimulus, and thereby modify his perception. That is, the structure of the language which becomes internalized serves as the alternative to the perceived structures of the stimulus field. So while we accept and utilize this distinction we shall return to examine it critically in the context of a more general cognitive theory in the final chapter of this book.

What does the child know that makes reconstruction of the diagonal possible? We can approach this question by attempting to specify the instruction that makes such a construction possible.

4

THE EFFECTS OF INSTRUCTION[1]

... in which we construe instruction as a means of development and examine the relative effects of considering the performance on the diagonal as either a response which is learned through trial and error with reinforcement, or as the output of a verbal conceptual system which has been learned through relating the parts to the whole,

... and in which it is found that instruction directed towards developing a verbal, conceptual system was not only markedly superior to that involving responses with reinforcement, but that it appeared to result in the learning of different things.

We have already demonstrated that the child's ability to construct a diagonal pattern is a function of age, reaching an asymptote at about age five or six, and we have shown that the difficulty of the problem can be described in terms of the figure-ground properties of the diagonal in relation to the field on which it is constructed. That is, it is clear that children can construct a pattern which is dependent upon such perceptual cues as the adjacency of the relevant holes or the presence of some reference axis such as an edge. The diagonal problem is difficult primarily because it is not "given" by such perceptual cues; in this case, the pattern has to be imposed on the field by the child. The question that then arises is, what is it that the "diagonal" child knows that the "nondiagonal" child does not? A useful way of restating the question is to ask, what does the nondiagonal child have to be taught before he is able to impose that pattern on the field? We should perhaps keep in mind that these two questions may not be the same.

[1] A full account of the experiment reported in this chapter is to be found in Byrne, J. M., Acquisition of the concept of diagonality in young children. Unpublished M. A. Thesis, Dalhousie University, Halifax, Nova Scotia, 1966.

Our first attempt to teach the children to construct the diagonal was based on two related concerns. First, as suggested above, we should be permitted to make an analysis of what the child needs to know in order to deal with such a problem and, second, some theories of learning that make some predictions as to how learning takes place should be evaluated. Consider each of these in turn.

Suppose one is trying to understand what is involved in a person's being able to solve a complex problem. One can make an intuitive analysis of the problem into a set of components and then instruct the child in each of these components in turn. If learning any one or combination of these components permits the child to solve the complex problem, it can then be argued that what the child has been taught is at least a partial description of the mental operations involved in solving the problem. With reference to the diagonal, if the children are having difficulty with the diagonal because they have had no reinforced practice in integrating the responses that constitute the diagonal, then practice on that aspect should lead directly to the construction of the diagonal. On the other hand, if the construction of the diagonal has little to do with the learning of this set of responses but, rather, depends on the learning of a conceptual structure for representing the diagonal, then a rather different set of learning experiences would be relevant.

The other question on which we hope to cast some light is to what extent do learning theories predict the types of instruction that will be most effective. It is impossible to exhaust these predictions, but even a partial examination may help indicate the type of theory that is likely to account for the learning of a complex concept.

Learning theories have never contributed simply or directly to instructional theories (Gage, 1963; Bruner, 1966; Olson, 1968). Nonetheless, these theories of learning are suggestive of what should be done in order to get the child to learn a complex act. The approach taken to instruction in this first experiment is a loose derivation from two major types of theories, an associationist reinforcement position, and a cognitive structure position.

The associationist view, largely derived from the work of Thorndike (1932), Skinner (1938), and Staats (1968b), holds that the critical features in learning are contiguity, pairing S and R or a series of Rs, and following the desired response by a reinforcement. Learning is a function of this contiguity and the number of such reinforced trials. If the diagonal is construed as a response composed of a set of responses, and if learning takes place primarily through the occurrence and reinforcement of these responses, it follows that the diagonal will be learned through the reinforced practice of these responses. From this point of view, no attention is paid to the perception of the pattern, or meaning, or the structuring or organization that governs these responses.

The cognitive perspective, represented by the work of Piaget (1960), Bruner (1960), and Ausubel (1963), emphasizes the "structure" or the relationship that the child imposes upon any set of relevant components. Given any set of input information, the child constructs a model that most coherently and economically "represents" or accounts for that input. That is, he organizes the information as far as possible into a good Gestalt. To facilitate such learning, instruction in this case would emphasize the "relatedness" or structuring or patterning of the elements such that the child would come to see the relation of the component parts to the whole. This position shall be examined exhaustively in the next chapter.

An interesting compromise between these proposals has been suggested by Mandler (1962). Essentially, he argues that at the earliest stages, learning is simply a matter of forming associations, but as over-learning continues, the subject begins to see patterns in the responses, that is, they become organized into a structure. He presented some evidence that as adult Ss learned their way through a bank of switches, there was a tendency to move from simple responses to response-patterning. The proposal may or may not be true for development. That is, adults may come to see patterns in a set of discrete moves because they already possess the structures to which these simple responses may be assimilated. For example, upon repeated exposure an adult may be led to say, "It is in the shape of a Z." Children, on the other hand, may lack these structures into which the earlier responses may be recoded. The crucial question, then, is does the child build these structures from the reinforced trials or associations? That is, is it an adequate theory of the formation of structures to say they are formed from overlearned associations?

To summarize, the specific questions that this experiment was designed to examine were:

1. Can one draw any inferences about the nature of a concept, in this case the diagonal, from a description of the instructional procedures most effective in teaching it?

2. Can one evaluate the utility of associative as opposed to cognitive theories in predicting the way in which the concept of the diagonal would be most effectively learned? Means of effectiveness in this study were taken as:

    a. Efficiency of learning (time and trials to the criterion)

    b. Transfer to a new task

    c. Recall after three weeks

METHOD

Subjects

One hundred and eighteen children, aged 3 to 6 years, drawn from Halifax Ladies College, Le Marchant Street School, and St. Thomas Acquinas School, and their surrounding areas in Halifax, Nova Scotia, served as subjects for this experiment. These schools vary from lower-middle to upper-middle class, and are somewhat representative of Halifax children in general. A slight biasing of the sample may have occurred in that some volunteered three- and four-year-olds were included in the sample. Casual observation suggested that mothers volunteer only precocious children. However, as this study compared equated experimental and control groups, this slight bias, if it exists, does not jeopardize the results.

The Instruments Used

All the hypotheses tested in this experiment employed the "bulb-board," an apparatus which was invented by J. S. Bruner and has previously been described by Olson (1966). It consists of a matrix of five rows and five columns of red bulbs one-half inch apart mounted on an even gray surface. Normally the bulbs, which were individually controlled by switches at the back of the machine, were in an off position. If a bulb was part of a prearranged pattern, it lighted up when it was pressed by the child. When the child released it, it would go off. Bulbs that were not part of the prearranged pattern remained dark, even when pressed. All bulb presses were recorded on an Esterline-Angus graph recorder.

Models representing the patterns to be pressed on the bulb-board were held in a vertical position by a frame directly back of the bulb-matrix. On the dark grey surface of the model, one-half inch red spots corresponded to the pattern of the bulbs which would light up and the other bulbs were represented by one-half inch light grey spots. A picture of the bulb-board was shown in Chapter 1, Fig. 1–1. The procedure used with this equipment was as follows. One pattern was mounted above the bulb-board at a time. The child was told that the model was a picture of the bulb-board and that bright red spots on the model indicated which of the bulbs on the bulb-board would light up when pressed. The child was then asked to run his finger over the pattern on the model and finally asked if he thought he could press the bulbs that would light up. The preliminary or warm-up problems consisted of a top row, a bottom row, the left column and the middle column. The critical problem was the left-oriented diagonal ($\searrow$).

The Experimental Groups

Of the 118 *S*s tested, 28 *S*s were selected for the experiment on the basis of their performance on some preliminary trials. These were *S*s who succeeded in copying models involving either rows or columns on the bulbboard but who failed in their attempt to copy the diagonal pattern. The *S*s were assigned randomly to one of the two experimental groups with the constraint that half the *S*s in each group were boys and half were girls. The equivalence of these groups was assured both by the random assignment and the fact that all *S*s performed in the same way on the pretest, that is, they succeeded on the row and column arrays but failed on the diagonal.

Group I (Trial and Error-Reinforcement Group). Children in this group were asked to look at the model carefully, to point to the bulbs on the picture that light up, and then to press the bulbs on the bulb-board until they could press all of the ones that light up and none of the ones that did not light up. Correct presses were reinforced by the bulb lighting up. Periodically, the Experimenter, *E*, reminded the children to look back at the model to see which of the bulbs were supposed to light up; *E* also encouraged the child to continue pressing the bulbs until he could navigate the diagonal without pressing any of the bulbs that would not light up.

Group II (Structured Learning Group). Children in this group were given assistance or tutored in forming a structured concept of the diagonal. The general aim of the instruction was to relate the diagonal to a conceptual system so that the result is the acquisition of knowledge about a diagonal, not merely a set of motor responses (Scheffler, 1965). More specifically the concept of the diagonal was related to other relevant concepts such as corner, straight line, and middle.

The procedure was this: *E* drew a square with a side approximately equal to 6 inches. *E* then pointed out the opposite corners and told the child, "If we want to go from this corner to this corner, we go straight across here" (*E* demonstrates). From here, *E* tried to get the child to indicate what a diagonal was and how it could be produced on the paper. The other material used in the instruction was a model resembling those used with the bulb-board, except that all the spots were marked with grey dots. Again, by either questions or exposition, *E* pointed out the properties of the square in such a way as to have the child formulate a general verbal rule of the form, "The criss-cross starts at a corner, and goes straight across the middle to the other corner."

Variations in the instruction were employed to motivate the children. These involved such problems as, "Pretend these are stepping stones. How would you get from here to here?" (*E* indicates opposite corners), or, "How could Santa get to the chimney the shortest way?" In all cases, the teacher–child verbal exchange revolved around such words as "corner," "opposite corner," "straight across," and "shortest way." After the child had formed some such rule, he was again introduced to the bulb-board and given exactly the same instructions as the children in Group I; namely, "Run your finger over the pattern and then press the bulbs that are indicated by the pattern."

For both groups, the criterion for acquisition was five complete diagonal runs (each run on the diagonal consisted of five sequential bulbs pressed in the diagonal pattern). Training, practice, and testing were on the left oriented diagonal. Following acquisition, the children were tested on a transfer task: the opposite, right-oriented diagonal. As for previous problems, they were shown the model, asked to point out the pattern on the model, and then asked to press the bulbs that corresponded to the pattern.

Approximately three weeks later the children in both groups were given a recall test on the original left-oriented diagonal and the transfer right-oriented diagonal, again using the bulb-board.

RESULTS AND DISCUSSION

A summary of the percentage of children at each age level that succeeded on the diagonal prior to training is reported in Table 4–1. This table indicates that the percentage of children able to copy the diagonal increases from about 25% at age three to 100% at age six. These increasing percentages run parallel to those obtained with the checkerboard, described in the previous section. They suggest, however, that the bulb-board diagonal is slightly more difficult than the checkerboard diagonal. The reason for this discrepancy is primarily attributable to the fact that the

TABLE 4–1

PERCENTAGE AT EACH AGE LEVEL WHO ARE ABLE TO PRESS THE DIAGONAL BULBS PRIOR TO TRAINING (N = 118)

Age in years	Percentage able to do diagonal	Total number of subjects at that age
3	28.57	14
4	37.74	53
5	77.78	36
6	100	15

TABLE 4–2

CHARACTERISTICS OF THE TWO GROUPS TAUGHT THE DIAGONAL BY DIFFERENT METHODS

	Group 1 Trial and error	Group 2 Structured	t
N	14	14	
Age			
Mean	4–6	4–7	0.22
s.d.	5.5 months	6.3 months	
Days between training and recall			
Mean	26.21	26.64	0.16
s.d.	5.03	8.41	
Time taken in training			
Mean	50.36 minutes	24.29 minutes	4.59**
s.d.	19.29	8.96	
Trials to acquisition			
Mean	470.43	34.14	4.10**
s.d.	396.68	35.86	
Trials to transfer			
Mean	55.07	23.64	3.46**
s.d.	26.03	21.90	

** $p < .01$

checkerboard has a "memory;" that is, the checkers remain in place once they are positioned, whereas the correct bulbs go out when they are released; hence the child is even more dependent on an internal model, or schema, when working on the bulb-board. Moreover, these age norms are strikingly discrepant from those of children in East Africa, as we shall see subsequently.

Table 4–2 presents the characteristics of the two groups employed in the instruction experiment. This table indicates that the groups are well matched in regard to age, and that the interval between training and retesting was comparable for the two groups. It may be recalled that the groups are matched as to sex, and that they are matched on ability in that all Ss used in the experiment had the ability to copy the row or column patterns and were unable to copy the diagonal. The comparability of the groups makes it safe to attribute any differences found between the groups to the method of training or instruction employed.

The performance of these two experimental groups on the acquisition and transfer of the diagonal in terms of the number of presses to criterion, is also shown in Table 4–2. The criterion for acquisition was five correct runs on the diagonal pattern (one run consisted of the correct sequential pressing of the five bulbs in the diagonal pattern). The criterion employed for the transfer task was three runs of five presses each on the correct bulbs. As no attempt was made to train all Ss to criterion, but rather to test until a judgment as to transfer could be made, many Ss failed to reach the criterion. In these cases, bulb pressing was terminated after approximately one minute (50 to 60 trials).

As Table 4–2 indicates, the structured method (Group 2) was significantly superior to the trial and error with reinforcement (Group 1), both in total time to acquisition and the number of trials to acquisition. The magnitude of the difference between the groups makes it unlikely that the lack of homogeneity of variance in the trials to acquisition ($F = 122.37$; $p < .01$) makes any difference in the interpretation of these results.

This latter score, trials to acquisition, is not the best index of efficiency of learning because Group 2 had the benefit of approximately 25 minutes of instruction before going to the bulb-board; hence, if that training has any effect it is only to be expected that they require fewer trials.

A better index of learning is found in the transfer task. Table 4–2 also indicates that the structured method (Group 2) required significantly fewer trials to correctly perform the opposite diagonal. As was pointed out

TABLE 4–3

NUMBER OF ERRORS IN THE FIRST 20 TRIALS FOR THE TWO GROUPS OF SUBJECTS ON THE ACQUISITION, TRANSFER AND RECALL TASKS

	Group 1 Trial and error	Group 2 Structured	t
Acquisition			
Mean	13.57	3.14	9.93**
s.d.	2.62	2.93	
Transfer to opposite diagonal			
Mean	14.14	6.00	4.76**
s.d.	3.65	5.26	
Recall			
Mean	4.93	3.43	0.90
s.d.	4.34	4.45	
Recall of opposite diagonal			
Mean	11.57	2.93	4.08**
s.d.	6.41	4.65	

** $p < .01$

TABLE 4–4

THE NUMBER OF SUBJECTS IN THE TWO GROUPS WHO WERE ABLE TO TRANSFER AND RECALL THE DIAGONAL

	Group 1 Trial and error	Group 2 Structured	X^2
N	14	14	
Transfer			
Immediate	0	12	17.65**
Subsequently[1]	3	14	14.97**
Recall			
Original Diagonal	11	13	1.33
Opposite Diagonal	5	12	7.34**

[1] Ss were permitted to press bulbs only until it became obvious that they could or could not transfer to the new task; that is, approximately 20 trials were permitted.
** $p < .01$

above, this data is somewhat limited by the fact that many Ss failed to reach the criterion on the transfer task. This limitation necessitated two subsequent analyses. First, all Ss did make at least 20 responses and one can assess the effects of the treatments by examining the number of errors in the first 20 trials on acquisition, transfer, and recall tasks. These data are presented in Table 4–3. This table shows that the Ss in the structured group were superior on the acquisition, transfer, and recall of the opposite diagonal; there was no difference between the groups on the recall of the trained diagonal.

Second, E's qualitative judgments of the child's ability to transfer and recall are not dependent on the child's failure to reach the criterion. Children were judged to have the ability if they could view the model and directly press the bulbs indicated by the diagonal models with one or no errors. This judgment is highly dependable because the probability of the child's pressing the correct bulbs by chance is infinitesimally small, as we shall see when we analyze individual learning curves.

Employing this analysis, the number of Ss in each experimental group able to transfer and recall after being trained to criterion on the acquisition task is shown in Table 4–4. This table shows that the structured group was superior to the trial and error group on transfer, and for recall of the opposite diagonal. There was no difference between the two groups in their recall of the original diagonal. More specifically, whereas none of the 14 trial and error Ss could perform the opposite diagonal after looking at and running their finger over the model, 12 of the 14 structured Ss performed the opposite diagonal immediately. The picture changes only slightly when *S*s were permitted to press a few bulbs, approximately 20, in order to reorient to the new problem. In this case, all 14 *S*s in Group 2 succeeded, and three of the trial and error *S*s were now able to do the transfer task. The difference is still highly significant. This was in spite of the fact that both groups had mastered the original diagonal. A similar

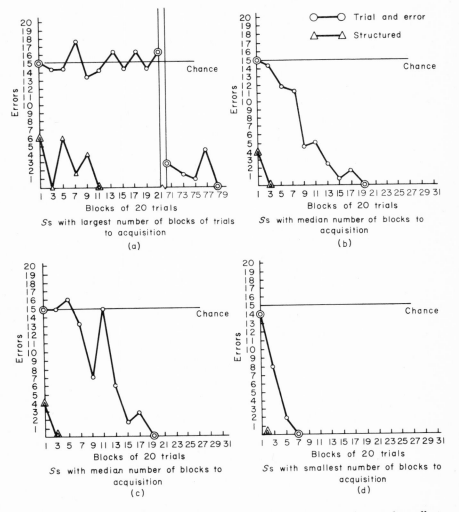

Fig. 4–1. Subjects in the two groups who have the largest, median, and smallest number of blocks of trials to acquisition.

observation was made on the recall of the opposite diagonal after a three-week period. Recall for both groups of the originally learned diagonal was high for both groups after the three-week period.

One interesting anomaly is that the number of Ss in the trial and error group showing transfer to the opposite diagonal increased over a three-week period. This may be resolved when we examine more closely what these Ss have been learning.

The two methods are radically different, not only in the efficiency in reaching the specified criterion, but also in that Ss under these two conditions were learning quite different things. Consider the analysis of the individual learning curves and response patterns under these two conditions.

The first indication comes from a comparison of the learning curves for the least successful subject in each group (Fig. 4–1a), for the two median Ss of each group (Figs. 4–1b and c), and for the most successful Ss in each group (Fig. 4–1d). These error scores are plotted on blocks of twenty trials. Note that for children in the reinforcement group, the errors, even after examining the model, begin at chance levels. That is, they do no better than if they had not seen the model at all. For the slower child in this group, approximately 500 trials (25 blocks) were required before he was pressing the diagonal bulbs at an above chance rate, and almost 1600 trials (79 blocks) were required before he was making no errors at all. For the slowest child in the structure group, the error rate is much lower: about 1 press in 5, and the errors drop off quickly. Note that for Ss in the trial and error reinforcement group the learning curves are very similar to what you would expect from a cat or a pigeon learning an operant response. The error curves for the structured group begin at such a low level and drop off so abruptly, the performance is poorly described by a learning curve. It has much more the appearance of the all-or-none insightful or meaningful learning that Gestalt psychologists insisted upon.

But the error curves themselves are hardly sufficient to support the assertion that children in these two conditions are in fact learning different things. The best evidence for this point is presented in Fig. 4–2 which shows the response protocols of the sequence of bulbs pressed in the last block of 20 trials for 3 of the 14 Ss in the trial and error reinforcement group. The response records presented here indicate that the children failed to press all the bulbs in the sequence, and yet they made few or no errors in pressing the bulbs. They thought they had succeeded even when they consistently skipped one of the bulbs. The obvious inference is that they did not see the arrangement of the bulbs as a pattern or a whole. We conclude that the children in this group had learned to make correct

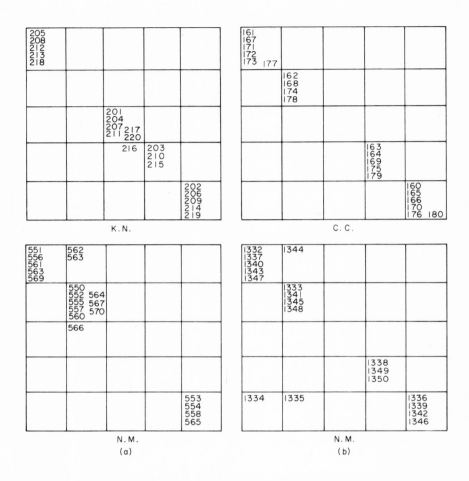

Fig. 4–2. Illustrations of nonsequential presses by three subjects in the trial and error group.

responses, but that these responses had not been integrated into a structure or a pattern corresponding to the diagonal.

This point is also illustrated by the pattern of responding of one child (Barbara S.) whose performance may be described a little more fully. Even after examining the presented model, she systematically searched each row for any bulb that would light up. When it was found, she would system-atically search the next row for the one that would light up in that row. The process was repeated row by row, over and over again, until the positions of each bulb in each row was located. Thus, the responses were being mastered independently and the learning was not being structured into the total pattern of the diagonal. This in spite of the fact that the bulb pressing was, as always, preceeded by the close scrutiny of the model which, in any case, was always left mounted above the bulb-board.

Another line of evidence from which we may draw the same conclusion is the transfer data that was mentioned earlier. If children have learned a set of simple responses then there will be little or no transfer to the opposite diagonal. If, on the other hand, they have learned the concept of the diagonal, then the opposite diagonal will be essentially no more difficult than the originally learned one. The evidence presented above in Tables 4–3 and 4–4 show that there is little or no transfer in the trial and error group. Again, we conclude that the children in this group are learning responses, not the concept of the diagonal.

CONCLUSION

These findings may now be brought to bear on the questions we raised at the beginning of this section.

First let us consider the adequacy or relevance of the learning theories for making predictions as to how learning takes place. In view of the consistent superiority of the structured group over the trial and error reinforcement group, it seems clear that when one is dealing with conceptual learning a simple application of associative, contiguity, or reinforcement theory is not adequate to the task. A cognitive theory that emphasizes the relation between the whole and its parts, or between a concept and its attributes, is much more in line with the evidence found in this study. The chief limitation with the latter theory is the difficulty of specifying without ambiguity what a component, or concept is. Moreover, the training procedure used in this experiment is difficult to describe precisely. If the latter perspective is to be more useful or more adequate than the trial and error reinforcement perspective it seeks to replace, it will need to be much more carefully specified. We shall return to this problem in the next section.

Second, this evidence is relevant to the suggestion made by Mandler (1962) that structure arises from the overlearning of simple associations. As we have seen, the children in the trial and error group tended to learn simple, unrelated responses. Even when the child was making only correct responses, he had not integrated them into the diagonal; he was still not pressing bulbs in the full sequence, and the learning failed to transfer to the opposite diagonal. Overlearning of responses led to just that: overlearning of responses, not the acquisition of a general structure corresponding to the concept of the diagonal. The evidence is not absolute on this point; 3 of the 14 children in that group were able to transfer their learning to the opposite diagonal, and after the 3-week delay, 5 of these children were able to. Hence, it is possible that some of the children were able to integrate the responses into the pattern. In any event, it is possible to conclude that the overlearning of association is not a sufficient account of the learning of structures. It would seem to be the case that adults are adding something to their knowledge of the simple associations in order to generate a structure; what they are adding, our preschool Ss are generally incapable of adding. An indication of what that other factor is is indicated by the training condition that was successful. In that case, it was the articulation of a complex structure into a set of related components; the structure was imposed upon a set of responses and thereby organized them. This is just the opposite of the associationist assumption.

Teaching the child the concept of the diagonal permitted him to impose a structure on the bulb-board, and hence to press the correct bulbs; the opposite, that the pressing of the correct bulbs leads to the development of the structure of the diagonal is not the case. This is related to a profound and currently unanswered question as to the relation between culture and cognitive development. Whorf (1956), Bruner (1966), and Vygotsky (1962) have argued that conceptual structures arise from the adult articulating the world for the child whereas Piaget and reinforcement theorists imply that it is more apt to be discovered by the child's own interaction with the world. Our evidence tends to favor the former alternative. This issue shall come up in almost all of the subsequent chapters.

Another issue raised by this experiment that must be bypassed, at least for the time being, is the psychological nature of instruction. The procedure used in Group 2 is well described as instruction, that is, active, verbal guidance, whereas that employed in Group 1 is not well described by the term instruction; it is merely arranging the contingencies of reinforcement. There is no obvious way in which instruction can be written into or added to either learning or cognitive theory. This gap has been recognized by such people as Bruner, Gage, Vygotsky, and Ausubel, but there is, in my estimation, no satisfactory theory linking the two. Hence, a completely satisfactory account of these results is dependent on the invention of such a theory.

Finally, what do we know about the diagonal as a result of our attempts to teach it to the children? First, it is best not construed as a response. There is an obvious discontinuity between a response and a concept; perhaps the diagonal is considered as a concept precisely because it cannot be learned as a specific response. Second, the child's inability to cope with the diagonal is not immutable; it is modifiable by instruction. Third, as we saw from the evidence of the transfer value of the two types of learning, conceptual learning is of a massively more generalized nature than learning a response.

Even if we have specified somewhat the type of instruction that makes the construction of the diagonal possible, the learning experiences employed have been so general that it is impossible to be sure of the specific "quantum" of information that made the construction possible. The psychological literature contains several suggestions as to what may be involved, at least one of which seems implausible in the light of the preceding evidence: namely, that the concept of the diagonal is a series of responses that are stamped in by differential reinforcement.

Three more plausible alternatives may be mentioned. The first involves the nature of the perceptual information that is "picked up" by the child: he may misperceive the stimulus because of an absence of the appropriate perceptual schemata (Bruner, 1957), or he may not have learned enough of the perceptual distinguishing features (Gibson, 1965; Maccoby and Bee, 1965). A second, and, to my mind, the most plausible alternative is that the child may not have an appropriate system or schema for thinking about or representing the diagonal as a basis for his reconstruction. The third possibility is that the child's knowledge may be adequate, but the complex motor skills involved in carrying out what the child knows or intends may be inadequate.

The next chapter reports some experimental evidence that helps us choose among these alternatives and, in so doing, explicate just what it is that happens to the content and organization of a child's knowledge in the course of cognitive growth.

5

THE CHANGE IN THE MIND OF THE CHILD

... in which the questions are posed: What does the child who
is capable of constructing a diagonal know that another child
does not? What is the nature of that knowledge? What is its
source?

... and in which beginning answers, based primarily on anecdotal
evidence, are formulated by pursuing the difference between
perceptual structures and conceptual ones, the former being
primarily unanalyzed configurations, the latter being knowledge of an event in terms of its components or attributes. The
sources of this knowledge are discussed in terms of the inventions
transmitted by the culture.

We have suggested that when the child comes to be able to construct
the diagonal it is because of the development of some conceptual structures
as opposed to perceptual ones. But what are these cognitive structures?
How may they be characterized? What does the child who can construct
the diagonal know that the other child does not? Three categories of
psychological events will serve for our first consideration of what the
child knows. First, the child may have misperceived the diagonal. Second,
the child's perception may be adequate but his representation or conceptualization may be inadequate. Third, the motor integrations necessary for a
performance may be inadequate. This chapter consists of a consideration
of each of these in turn. It is important to note, however, that while these
three categories may serve as a place to begin analysis, they may, in the
long run, be inappropriate. For example, one cannot forever simply differentiate perception and conceptualization. More seriously, such categories
may fundamentally misconstrue behavior as Staats (1968a) has argued.

PERCEPTION

The simplest and, hence, the most attractive alternative in interpreting
the breakdown in the child's constructing the diagonal is that the stimulus

or model is perceived incorrectly; it is assigned to the wrong perceptual category (Bruner, 1957). Early observations of the young children attempting to solve this problem appeared to support this alternative. When the child saw a model of the top row he moved quickly and confidently to his board and copied the model. When the diagonal was presented he also glanced quickly at the model and constructed on his board a middle row or column, or sometimes an edge, apparently with the same degree of confidence. On the bulb-board the children acted surprised when the bulbs they pressed did not go on, but even then they frequently did not bother to look back more critically at the model. On the checkerboard the child looks at the model, and then constructs something that at best bears remote resemblance to the model. However, some children hesitated, some requested a second look at the model, and some simply said, "I can't do it." It was necessary to test the hypothesis that the child's failure to construct the diagonal was due to misperception of the model.

An Experiment

Subjects. Ten children from the Peabody Terrace Nursery School were selected to test this hypothesis. All ten of these children succeeded in constructing a row or a column identical to that of the model, and failed in their attempts to copy the diagonal.

Procedure. The procedure was similar to that employed in other parts of study in that E would present the model to the child, have him run his finger over the model, and then remove the model when the child began his own construction. The modification introduced was that after the child had constructed what he thought corresponded to the model, E presented both patterns, E's and S's, side by side, and asked the child which pattern had been shown to him. The procedure was then repeated.

Results. In view of the long delay after the child viewed the original model the results are surprising. Eight of the ten Ss immediately and consistently pointed to the model that they had originally been shown. The other two also succeeded in pointing to the original model when the intervening stage, the child's attempts at construction, was removed. The probability that these children could pick the correct model by chance alone is $(1/2)^{10}$.

Discussion. Perception, as measured by recognition, is intact, yet none of these 10 Ss could construct the diagonal. We conclude that the child's failure to construct the diagonal is not due to some perceptual error Perception far outstrips performance.

The generality of this finding and the inference we have drawn from it is somewhat limited by the fact that the alternatives between which the child was choosing could be varied to produce almost any desired level of difficulty. For example, if the models differed only in one checker, it is possible that the choice would have been more difficult.

Our studies of diagonality (which, in the last section, was shown to be not simply diagonality, but a more basic problem: the development of conceptual systems for dealing with events not "given" to perception) has led directly into another thorny theoretical issue: the lag between perceiving and performing. Maccoby and Bee (1965) have suggested that this lag may be due to the number of discriminated attributes involved. They suggest that one attribute may be sufficient for recognition, whereas several may be required for construction. For example, in the diagonal problem, a checker in one corner may be sufficient for the choice in the recognition task, while it would hardly serve for constructing the diagonal. Maccoby and Bee (1965, p. 375) state, "to reproduce a figure, the subject must make use of more attributes of the model than are required for most perceptual discriminations of this same model from other figures." This hypothesis is undoubtedly true to some extent; it accounts for the studies they review and it is compatible with the findings of Herman, Lawless, and Marshall's (1957) replication of the Carmichael, Hogan, and Walter experiment in which Ss who noted all of the features carefully were able to make a more adequate reproduction. In the present study, the number of attribute hypotheses has some power, as was suggested above.

But the hypothesis that the perceptual distinguishing features account for the ability to copy a geometric form leaves some problems. First, a purely quantitative notion of the difference between perceiving and performing would run counter to one of the more plausible statements of this relation, that of Piaget and Inhelder (1956). The latter make a sharp distinction between perceptual space and representational space. Just because a child can recognize a square is no evidence that he knows "of what a square consists," or that he can draw it. They point out, "The fact that at least two years work is required in order to pass from copying the square to copying the rhombus . . . shows pretty clearly that to construct an euclidean shape, something more than a correct visual impression is required (p. 74)." The child's drawing is an index of how he represents space, just as one drawing of a stick-man represents what we know about a man, and not some printout of the perceptual world. Gombrich's (1960) discussion of representation in art makes the same point. Representation does not come simply from more looking or from more and better perceptions, but from the invention of a system for representing the world. Piaget's theory is one systematic treatise on how it is ever possible to move from perception to representation. Suffice it to say, at this point, it does not come simply from more looking at more of the features. This distinction may be more easily seen if we adopt the convention of using the term "distinguishing feature" to refer to those cues that are presumably involved in perceptual recognition or discrimination, and using the term "attribute" to refer to those cues that are involved in a conceptual system such as ordinary language or mathematics.

Second, it appears that the hypothesis is dependent on the "psychologist's fallacy," as William James and John Dewey formulated it. Maccoby and Bee attribute the end product of their own cognition to the world and to their raw sensations. Specifically, attributes are assumed to be preexistent, and it remains for the mind simply to link them up. In some context this may be true; as a general statement, it must be false. Consider the diagonal as a concept. One could argue that its attributes are corner, opposite corner, straight, line, etc., all of which are just as conceptual as the diagonal itself. The concept can't come from hooking up attributes because the attributes are not preexistent to be hooked up. Once conceptual systems are developed the situation may change, but that does not help us understand this ontogenesis. As concepts have attributes, at least some hypothesis about the nature of origin of these attributes would seem to be necessary.

Third, there remains the problem of how one makes use of an attribute in the copying of a form. Production, unlike recognition, is a sequential or segmented process as Lashley (1951) pointed out, and as Maccoby (1968) has acknowledged.

One strength of the hypothesis is that it is testable. If the lag from perception or production is to be accounted for in terms of the number of discriminated features, we can hypothesize that the learning of this larger set of features would lead to the construction of the diagonal.

Although the history of our attempts to teach children to construct the diagonal in the manner suggested by this hypothesis is long, and not uninteresting, and shall be reported in detail in the next chapter, only two points shall be mentioned here. First, it turned out to be a major problem to figure out what the "features" of the diagonal were, and second, when the children were taught them in a card sorting test, they were still unable to construct the diagonal. Of the 16 children in the first experiment to whom we attempted to teach the diagonal by card sorting on the various features presumed to underlie the concept of the diagonal, only one S reached the performance criterion. We shall, however, consider this hypothesis again, along with Maccoby's revision of it, in the next chapter.

We are left with the lag between perceiving and performing. We shall argue presently that it is to be accounted for in the child's representation, in his conceptual system, as Piaget has argued. The possibility remains that the lag is to be accounted for in the performance itself, in the motor integrations and coordinations involved in the response side of the organism. It is to this latter possibility we now turn.

PERFORMANCE

If the failure on the diagonal cannot be attributed in any simple way to perception, the next most accessible source of the child's failure is in terms of the performance itself, the complex motor integrations involved, or what may be described as a limitation in visually guided behavior. It is possible that both the perception and the conceptual representation of the diagonal are adequate, but this knowledge is not observable because of the complex motor integrations involved. For example, a child asked to mirror draw a square may do very badly even if his knowledge is adequate. In both children's printing and adult's art, some people are better draftsmen than others. In other cases, the technical skills may be adequate but the conceptions guiding them, limited. For example, merely improving the draftsmanship would never solve the problem of representing sunlit green grass with yellow paint as Constable did in his landscapes (Gombrich, 1960). We can differentiate then between knowing what to draw, including the knowledge utilized to verify, select, or reinforce the successful moves, and the mechanical drafting skills involved in bringing it off.

Both Piaget and Binet assumed and demonstrated, to a considerable extent, that the child's drawings were a good index of the way he represents, that is, thinks about, or imagines, objects. In evaluating the drawings of a square, for example, the evaluation is based less on the beauty of the figure and more on the presence of critical features such as four-sidedness and four-corneredness. The same principle holds true in the Goodenough Draw-a-Man test of mental development. We conclude, while motor performance skills may interfere with the child's drawing or representation of his conceptual knowledge, this is not necessarily the case and there is strong evidence that, for some tasks, the motor aspect may be safely ignored.

Consider the evidence. First, different types of motor performance may be used to evaluate the same internal representation. Piaget tested the concept "straight" both by drawing and by aligning a set of toothpick "telegraph poles" with little difference in the results. We have observed that the construction of the diagonal is closely related to the child's ability to arrange the checkers on a plain white card which, in turn, is closely related to being able to draw it. While these skills all appear at about the same time, some are better indices of the diagonal than others. The drawings and checker positioning on a clear paper are very difficult to evaluate while the checkerboard is completely unambiguous. It follows that since all three cases are very different, the responses themselves are of only minor relevance to our understanding of the task.

At the risk of flogging a dead horse, two other lines of evidence are relevant to the argument. On the checkerboard, it is no more difficult to put a checker in one hole than any other hole. The same is true in sequences. Children can put checkers in any row or column of holes; on the A board many "nondiagonal" children can even put them in the diagonal holes. As the motor skills in these last tasks are identical to that of the diagonal under study, it is impossible to attribute the failure on our diagonal to motor performance or motor responses.

The most important point in discounting the argument that the diagonal is a motor problem is the finding by Binet that a task of this type, specifically drawing a diamond, was a good index of intelligence, unlike, for example, coloring a picture. If the task measured only motor functioning it would be a poor measure of intelligence. Again, we infer that the task is assessing some central, cognitive process.

We have narrowed the range of possible explanations by showing it is not perceptual or an input error, neither is it motor performance at the output level. There remain the higher cognitive processes: in this case, a cognitive process that develops between the ages of 4 to 6 years. The remainder of this section is an attempt to specify the nature of these cognitive processes.

CONCEPTUALIZATION

As we have systematically eliminated the alternative explanations, it is hardly surprising to suggest that the failure and success of the child on the diagonal is determined by the nature of the conceptual systems of the child. It is the reorganization of the child's knowledge that permits the child to construct the diagonal. It now becomes the problem to specify how the prediagonal child represents or conceptualizes the diagonal, and how this is changed when he learns the diagonal. We shall state the account first as a series of assertions and subsequently examine the evidence relating to each of these assertions in turn.

1. The prediagonal child knows the diagonal as a unitary unanalyzed

configuration. He does not know it in terms of its parts, properties, attributes, or segments.

2. At the same time the prediagonal child knows the parts in isolation when they are taken out of the context of the configuration.

3. What occurs at the transition is that the child develops a system which relates these parts to the whole, the attributes to the concept. It is the system and not any specific element or mediator that accounts for the transition. The system has the following properties:

a. The system specifies as elements both the whole and the parts, as well as the relations that hold between them (sometimes called "structure").

b. The system makes possible the translation of a stable perceptual image (or at least perceptual knowledge) into a temporal sequence necessary for reproduction.

c. The system is stable and general.

d. The system is reversible.

e. The system is conceptual in nature. As such, it resembles a theory which is imposed on objects or events to represent or account for them, rather than the events themselves, or even our organized perceptions of them. (This is a weak restatement of the rationalist theory of the concept.)

The final point examines the origins of this system:

f. The system is invented by the child, or communicated by the adult and applied to the configuration; it is not given, or even inherent in the stimulus array or in the perceptual recognition.

An Experiment

The largest part of the evidence to be considered in reference to this problem is anecdotal, arising from the close observation and interrogation of nursery school children in their attempts to copy the various patterns constructed on the checkerboard.

Subjects. Employed in this part of the study were the 35 children from Peabody Terrace Nursery School, Cambridge, Mass., and 24 children from the Eleanor Nursery School, Cambridge, Mass. Of particular interest were the children who were willing to continue to try to copy the various patterns presented but who still failed to get them all correct. In other words, closest attention was paid to "transitional" subjects.

Procedures. As in the preceeding study, patterns were presented on one checkerboard by E; the child would then be asked to "look at the picture on my checkerboard," run his finger over the pattern, and then make one like it on his checkerboard. In this study, however, the procedure varied from S to S with E trying in as many ways as possible to find out what the child was doing. The features of the child's performance that were most consistently examined in this study were as follows:

1. Correcting nondiagonal patterns. E constructed various nondiagonal patterns on the checkerboard and asked the child: "Is this a criss-cross?" "Why?" "What would you have to do to make it a criss-cross?"

2. Correcting nondiagonal pictures. E constructed sets of cards with pictures of objects arranged either in a diagonal or a nondiagonal pattern (these cards, subsequently used in the Card-Sorting test, are described more fully in the next chapter). Children were asked, "Is this a criss-cross?" "Why?" They were asked to indicate either by words or by pointing where the criss-cross array would be.

3. Completion of diagonal patterns. E constructed a diagonal pattern with only one or two checkers not in place. These checkers would then be handed to S who was asked to put them in place.

4. Knowledge of parts of the diagonal. E positioned checkers, one at a time, in the holes making up the diagonal. After one checker was positioned, the child attempted to copy the model. Then the checkers were removed and E positioned the next checker in the sequence for S to copy. This was continued for all five checkers.

5. Perceptual markers for the diagonal. E constructed a model of the diagonal using contrast-colored checkers at the ends of the diagonal and observed the effect on the children's constructions.

Results. As the results from these activities are anecdoted, they shall be described in the context of the discussion of the assertions presented. Consider the evidence for each of the assertions in turn:

1. The nondiagonal child knows the diagonal as a configuration without any componential analysis. Three lines of evidence are relevant. First, the child recognizes the diagonal consistently even if he cannot reconstruct it. Of the 10 Ss who failed to reconstruct the diagonal, all 10 were capable of recognizing it. Second, with the task of sorting pictures of the card sorting test of diagonals versus nondiagonals (see Chapter 6, and details provided in the next chapter) the following relevant observations were made. Even children who could not construct the diagonal could sort diagonal from nondiagonal arrays, and mastering the sorting procedure never led to success in constructing the diagonal.

If one utilized this card-sorting method to measure the presence of the concept, one would conclude that these children had the concept of the diagonal. We would argue rather that they know or recognize a perceptual configuration. They know it to see it, but they don't know what the diagonal consists of, hence they can't reconstruct it. This is shown by the further observation that although these children could sort correctly, none of them could consistently specify the nature of the error. They could recognize it as a nondiagonal but they were unable to point out or describe the thing about the array that disqualified the array as a diagonal. For example, the array that began at the top as did the diagonal but bent abruptly downward just before it reached the second corner was excluded from the class "criss-cross" by all the children. Yet very few were able to point to the area where the error was, and none of them could point out with a finger or with words that it should continue straight on to the corner. Similarly for all the other variants of the diagonal, nondiagonal children could exclude them but they were usually unable to point out the change or correction that should be made. Not all children made exactly the same error, and, with instruction, some errors appeared to be more easily overcome. Subjectively, it appeared that when the child did begin to specify the error, or to show with his finger where the diagonal should go (on a nondiagonal card) he was coming close to being able to construct the diagonal. Again, nondiagonal children know the diagonal as a unitary configuration and can discriminate a class of diagonals from a wide array of nondiagonals but, as we have shown, they do so without any knowledge of the component parts, properties, or attributes of which it is comprised.

Third, the same phenomenon as above was observed and measured on the checkerboard. Here too, nondiagonal children could recognize and classify the diagonal array as a criss-cross and could reject all variations as noncriss-crosses, thereby demonstrating their ability to recognize or know the diagonal as a configuration. But again, although they can reject nondiagonals on any and all variants, they are unable to specify the error, and they were unable to correct the error. Of the 10 nondiagonal children considered here, approximately half could correct some simple error as the omission of a single checker, but none of them could correct even a fraction of the variations shown to them. For example, the children were shown the checkerboard set with the diagonal array, with the exception that the bottom right checker was moved over one space to the left. All of them immediately said that it was not a criss-cross. When they were asked why, or how they knew, none of them was able to say or show why, and none of them was able to correct the error, to move the checker to the correct hole.

We conclude that the child knows and recognizes the diagonal as a configuration which is not broken up into parts, segments, or attributes; furthermore, the prediagonal child is not capable of articulating it into these parts and manipulating these parts. Moreover, we suggest that additional looking is not the factor that would make the attributes or components available; it is an independent skill and it has its own relatively independent developmental history.

2. The child knows the parts in isolation. It is somewhat appealing to suggest that the child fails in the construction of the diagonal simply because he lacks a coordinate system for indexing the specific holes into which he must place the checkers. While it is likely to be the case that the four year old does not have a system of Cartesian coordinates, it is not specifically this lack that accounts for his failure to construct the diagonal. That the problem is not one of being able to give "addresses" to specific checkers can be shown empirically.

Ten nondiagonal children were presented with a model with checkers in the very holes that would constitute the diagonal; this time the checkers were shown one at a time (procedure 4). Under this condition the nondiagonal children could copy the model. Few errors occurred (errors $<5\%$); when they did, they could be corrected, and they occurred on the checker one in from the corner, the same error that occurs occasionally with the diagonal children. We conclude that the nondiagonal children know the parts in isolation; they don't know them as tied into the whole.

The point may be pressed even one step farther. For the diagonal child and the adult, the knowledge of the concept or the structure of the diagonal makes knowledge of the specific parts redundant. If this individual had a checkerboard 100 by 100 he could begin his construction and continue until the checkers ran out and still know that he was proceeding correctly, even if he could not place a checker at the hole 53 down and 53 in if it was presented singly. That is, it is the knowledge of the structure that generates the parts, not vice versa. It is as if the child has an equation for writing the diagonal and he can substitute new values into the equation indefinitely, still maintaining the integrity of his production. The analogy is even more striking when one considers that the diagonal child can draw the diagonal as well as construct it on the checkerboard.

3. What the nondiagonal child does not know that the diagonal child does know is a system that relates the parts, or components, to the whole that attributes to the concept. The two previous sections have elaborated, in detail, on the independence of the part from the whole; the reverse of all these observations is true of the child who is capable of producing the diagonal. He not only recognizes the diagonal as a configuration, he easily breaks it into components for his reconstruction (e.g., the diagonal begins at the corner). When he is shown instances of diagonals and nondiagonals, he not only discriminates them, he is able to specify the nature of the

error and to show on the cards where the array should have gone or, on the checkerboard, to relocate the checkers to the appropriate holes. These observations led to the assertion that the transition involves the establishment of a system of relationships between the whole and its components, such that the relations between them are stable and explicit.

Before examining the evidence on the properties of this system in detail, it is necessary to justify the introduction of so clumsy a construct as system, rather than the more popular and parsimonious "mediating response" or "verbal mediating response." This can be done simply by showing that there is no single or simple "mediator" involved. The nondiagonal children make the same general discriminating responses to diagonals and nondiagonals in the card sorting test as do the diagonal children; we have shown this above. Nor is verbalizing the classification as criss-cross and noncriss-cross relevant to the construction of the diagonal. In our early pilot trials we thought that the labeling may make a difference, but it quickly became apparent that if they could sort, they would readily accept the label; the sorting was apparently neither helped or hindered (except for E's convenience) by the presence of the label. What was certain was that giving the generalized label in no case led to the construction of the diagonal. As neither the knowledge of the general perceptual class of diagonal, nor the common discriminating response to diagonals, nor the general label criss-cross was different for diagonal and nondiagonal children, the postulation of a simple mediating response, verbal or otherwise, as an account of the transition had to be rejected. We are left with the more complex alternative, a system which Piaget in other related contexts has called a "grouping." We return to the evidence relating to the properties of this system.

a. The system specifies, as elements, both the whole and the parts, and the relations that hold between them. It is impossible to exhaust this proposition empirically. It says that the whole or the concept (we shall try to justify this substitution in Section e) is not just a cluster of attributes; it includes the relations that hold between these elements, the structure. Our nondiagonal children often knew the features that serve as attributes or properties of the diagonal but they failed to relate them in an appropriate way to the diagonal. For example, most of our children knew the concept of corner long before they came to the experiment; most of them also knew that of criss-cross, especially after doing the card-sorting; yet they failed to act as if they knew that the criss-cross starts at the corner.

Four specific cases illustrate this point. David P., age 3, could construct rows and columns but failed repeatedly on the diagonal. His attempted constructions of the diagonal began at the middle of the top or one over from the middle, not at the corner. He could sort diagonals and reject all nondiagonal instances, including those that failed to start at the corner. After one such attempted reconstruction, *E* asked, "Where does the criss-cross start?" The child looked at the model and moved his checker to the corner; all subsequent attempts began at the corner. Although he knew corner, and he knew criss-cross, and had looked at and pointed to the corner of the criss-cross several times, he had no system relating the part and the whole.

Talal O., age 4, could construct rows, columns, and the diagonal on the A board. She could reject all nondiagonals in the card sorting task. Her constructions of the diagonal began appropriately at the corner but tended to go down the second or third column. *E* asked, "Where does the criss-cross end up?" Talal looked back at the model, pointed to the lower right corner of the model, and said "Down here." She then returned to her checkerboard, placed the first checker in the top corner, the second in the lower opposite corner, and filled in the remainder appropriately.

Both Danya C. (whose case is described in detail later) and Melissa S. behaved in a similar way. They failed to relate the corner to the criss-cross until *E* specified, "See the criss-cross starts at the corner." From then on their productions, in fact, began at the corner.

We conclude that even if the attributes or properties were known, and the whole was known, the child would have had no system relating them. Note too that the relations involved are specific, not just associations; for example, "the diagonal begins at the corner" not "the corner begins at the diagonal." When the child possesses such a system, he has some conceptual equivalent of the lexical entry, "the diagonal is a straight line joining two nonadjacent vertices of a rectilineal or polyhedral figure."

b. The system makes possible the translation of a stable perceptual image into a temporal sequence for reproduction. The necessity for such a translation was first pointed out by Lashley (1951) who stated that while memory traces are largely static and persist simultaneously, reproductive memory is transformed into a temporal succession, perhaps by some other level of the coordinating system that scans the first. Miller, Galanter, and Pribram (1960) attack the same problem. Granting that the organism has some internal representation or knowledge of the world, these authors state, "What we must provide . . . is some way to map the cognitive representation into the appropriate *pattern* of activity (p. 13)." This leads them to postulate a temporal plan as a basis for guiding behavior. More recently, Bruner (1966) in describing the nature of symbolic representation has made the provocative suggestion, "But once the task becomes complex enough and involves a serial task such as reproduction, then language is necessary as an aid to reconstruction (p. 52)."

If this is an aspect of what is involved in the transition from being unable to construct the diagonal to being able to construct it, it should follow that removing this sequential aspect of the task would remove the differences between diagonal and nondiagonal children.

An Experiment

Subjects. Serving as Ss for this part of the study were 14 children from Peabody Terrace Nursery School, 9 of whom could not construct the diagonal.

Procedure. A block wheel, 24 inches in diameter, with a white rod attached to it was constructed and mounted on a central axel so that it could be easily rotated. A protractor mounted on the back of the equipment permitted E to read the exact position of the rod. A large black cloth was draped all around the equipment to mask out some of the reference points that a child may otherwise use in remembering the position of the rod. E set the rod in any one of three positions, horizontal, vertical, or diagonal (45°), asked the child to note carefully where the line was, gave the wheel a spin, and asked the child to return the rod to the starting position.

Results and Discussion. The task was somewhat poor in that the problem was not sufficiently interesting to keep our young subjects trying hard enough to remember the original position (chocolate candies helped somewhat). The reported "forgets" occurred approximately equally for all three problems. The mean number of degree displacement for two attempted repositionings of each of the three positions for 9 nondiagonal children and 5 diagonal children were as follows:

	N	Horizontal	Vertical	Diagonal
Nondiagonal	9	3.6	4.5	9.0
Diagonal	5	3.0	2.9	7.8

Almost 40% of the diagonal repositionings were reversed, but we have not considered that reversal relevant to this problem.

Although the procedure and equipment were too crude for any fine grain analysis, it is clear that there was no marked difference in the ability of the diagonal and nondiagonal children to reposition the rod in the diagonal orientation. For both groups the mean error was greater for the diagonal than for either the vertical or horizontal.

We attempted to make the procedure more like the diagonal by having children reposition a green stick over the checker board in the diagonal position. There appeared to be no difference between the groups but the difficulties of scoring this procedure were so great that it was abandoned. Some children took greater care than others in seeing that the stick was placed appropriately, but the carelessness was not specifically a characteristic of the nondiagonal children.

In retrospect it may have been more appropriate to have the children attempt their repositionings within a square frame rather than without reference axes, as in the present study.

Since the nondiagonal children can deal with the nonsequential task, but not the sequential construction of the diagonal, we conclude that the transition is dependent on a system that permits the translation from the static perceptual image into the temporal sequence necessary for reproduction. The diagonal child looks at the static model presented to him, translates it into sequential properties, for example, "the diagonal begins at the corner," and proceeds with his reproduction. The role of language in this translation is ambiguous, but may be necessary as Bruner (1966) suggests.

This account ignores the question of why it is that the child can build the top row sequentially after looking at the static model, since this also implies such a translation. At this point we can only suggest that if the plan is suggested by the perceptual environment, such as the edge or some other reference axis, the child does not require a complete internal plan to regulate his production.

c. The system is stable and general. It is stable at any point in time in that the diagonal child, unlike the nondiagonal child, can attend to any part of the configuration without destroying it or the relation of the part to the configuration such as is necessary in correcting a nondiagonal array of checkers. The system is stable over time in that once acquired it is not lost or interfered with by intervening activity. In the preceeding chapter on instruction we presented evidence that all of the 14 subjects who were taught the diagonal retained it when retested three weeks later. By saying the system is general, we mean that once acquired, it transfers to the opposite diagonal, to diagonals on a larger board, and to production in other media such as pencil drawing of the diagonal, all of which appear to hold for the diagonal children.

d. The system is reversible. The diagonal child, unlike the nondiagonal child, can shift from attending to the whole to attending to a part, and back again. Moreover, he can make these reverses without destroying the integrity of either the part or the whole. This is clearly

shown by the fact that the child can construct the diagonal after looking
at the static model and that he can correct the errors in the nondiagonal
arrays. One nondiagonal child (Cindy D.) particularly illustrates this
point. She was shown a diagonal with only one checker, the center one,
missing from the array. She said this was not a criss-cross, but when she
was given the additional checker she was unable to position it correctly.
Apparently, when she considered that specific checker, she was not at the
same time considering the diagonal as a whole, for she would position the
checker near either side of the gap but not in the middle. When E moved
the checker board back 3 feet, she saw the array as a diagonal and she
was not able to see where the checker should go. She was unable to achieve
the reversibility from the part to the whole which was necessary for this
correction. When it was produced manually by E she was able to correct it.
Almost identical observations were made on Talal O.'s attempted corrections. For the nondiagonal child this reversibility can be produced only
through manual operations; for the diagonal child the reversibility can be
produced internally or conceptually. As Piaget (1960) would say, the
system is in equilibrium.

e. The system is conceptual in nature.[1] It is clearly differentiable
from the earlier perceptual knowledge by the performance it leads to. The
only direct evidence that the system is conceptual or representational in
nature, however, is that the discrete parts that make up the whole become
less relevant than the attributes that make up the concept. The point I
have in mind is parallel to that raised earlier. A "part" has more to do
with the immediately perceived event, while an "attribute," being less tied
to the immediately perceived event, has more to do with the elements of a
theoretical or conceptual system.

Another way of saying this may be that a part is specific to the medium in
which you are working, while an attribute is not. We have already argued
(Section 2, p. 65) that the knowledge of the concept or structure makes the
knowledge of the specific parts redundant. Moreover, we gave some
evidence (Section 3c, p. 69) that for the child who has learned the diagonal,
the learning was general and could be applied to other media, such as
drawing, which involved none of the same parts, but do involve the same
attributes or properties.

The conceptual status of the child's knowledge that permits the reconstruction of the diagonal is also shown by the fact that while the perceptual
configuration of the diagonal appear to remain relatively stable over time,
the conceptual representation of the configuration may shift radically.

[1] For a more adequate theoretical account of the distinction between perception
and conception, see Piaget (1960, pp. 53–86).

The nondiagonal child may have represented it as middle or top row (we would guess from their constructions). The diagonal child may represent it in several different ways such as "starts at the corner and bisects the area" or "a straight line joining two nonadjacent corners." It could even be shown that the diagonal could be conceptualized (that is, assigned a set of properties in an infinite number of ways depending on the geometrical system in which it was imbedded.) Since there is no one geometry, as Felix Klein showed at the end of the last century, there is not one single set of properties of an object; rather the properties of an object that are considered as attributes of the corresponding concept are determined by the conceptual system used for representing that object. Not all ways of representing the diagonal, even if consistent with some geometrical system, would necessarily lead to the appropriate construction on the checkerboard, however.

It may now be possible to understand the translation from a stable perceptual image into the temporal sequence for reproduction that was discussed earlier. If the point we have been stating is true, that is, if the knowledge that permits the reconstruction of the diagonal is conceptual in nature and if the properties involved are given by the conceptual system and applied to the perceptual configuration, we would be led to suggest that reproduction is not a simple translation into a temporal sequence but a complete transformation of the perceptual image into available conceptual categories. It is these conceptual categories that are then temporally ordered for such productions as constructing diagonals and drawing pictures. Since words are so closely related to these conceptual categories, language is at least implicated.

f. Where does the system come from? I argued that it does not come from looking at the models or from better perceptions; the card sorting test in not a promising approach to developing the system that would permit reproduction. Where then? Although this is a problem that shall come up again, it may be suggested that it comes from either a creative or productive intellect, an invention such as that of Euclid, Klein, or Newton, or else from the suggestions of an informed adult, that is, from the culture. These two alternatives are not completely independent. Some of the knowledge (or intuition) that would make the invention possible would be necessary to even understand someone elses inventions. About the first of these alternatives, our work says least. Piaget has already shown the high degree of inventiveness involved in children's play. A spoon at the table, as well as being a utensil, becomes a man, then a car, then an airplane, then a dog, etc. Many of our children, particularly those over 5 years, even if they apparently have never seen a diagonal, and certainly have never seen anything like our checkerboard, look at the model, (perhaps) invent some adequate way of representing it to themselves, and reconstruct it. It is impossible to know exactly how they went about it, so this evidence is of limited value.

We take our lead rather from Gombrich's discussion of the problem of representation in art that was mentioned earlier. Recall Gombrich's example of Masaccio who loved to paint folded drapery "true to natural life." Before Masaccio, no one did, after Masaccio, many artists did. Gombrich then asks, "What difficulty could there have been in this simple portrayal which prevented artists before Masaccio from looking at the fall of drapery for themselves (1960, p. 12)."

Gombrich shows quite convincingly that the methods of representing nature, as well as the ways of viewing nature, are invented, not discovered. The way that nature is represented depends on the development of a "vocabulary of forms." What you can say in art depends on the limitations of your vocabulary. Art evolves by progressive development of a vocabulary of forms—a vocabulary not acquired inductively by simply looking intensely at nature, but by learning this developed vocabulary largely through looking at pictures. If it is invented, it is, of course, not a unique solution, alternative ways of representing an event are possible, as any admirer of artists with such different vocabularies as, say, Rembrandt and Picasso, or Constable and Monet.

The same invented, conceptual status of knowledge in the natural sciences was also described earlier by reference to the work of Cassirer (1923, 1957) and Kuhn (1962). Just as such theories specify what events shall be accorded the status of facts, so the concept specifies those characteristics or properties that shall be considered as attributes. This highlights the severe limitations of a theory of concept formation that is based on the assumption that the world comes in attributes and that concepts are formed by linking these attributes together or the basis of contiguity. The conceptual system determines the attributes as much as it does the concept.

In spite of the fact that it is three quarters of a century since modern science abandoned a "copy theory" of physical reality and recognized the invented, conceptual quality of scientific concepts, psychologists are tempted to believe that concepts arise inductively from simply correlating attributes that exist in the real world. If that were the case, it would seem to follow that there would be only one conceptual system for, say, geometry or matter, when, in fact, an infinite number are possible, depending, as Klein (Cassirer, 1957) showed, on which aspect one postulates as invariant.

After having flown so high it is difficult to return to the diagonal. To move from the recognition of a perceptual configuration to the conception of the diagonal (and we have argued that it is the conceptual system that permits the construction of the diagonal) requires more than merely looking at the diagonal, or even at the features that may permit discrimination of diagonals from nondiagonals. Rather it depends on some adult showing the child or telling the child that the diagonal can be represented thus, and so. The evidence that bears on this point is that for our subjects to come to be able to construct the diagonal, or to know of what a diagonal consists, it was necessary for E to provide the articulation, the segmentation, or the attributes to the child, as well as how the attributes relate to the concept; then the child could construct the diagonal.

There are two lines to this evidence. First, the training that was effective in the preceding chapter consisted of telling the child "of what the diagonal consists." "See, the criss-cross starts in the corner." "It goes straight across the middle." "It ends in the other corner." This kind of training produced 100% success in the first training experiment ($N = 14$), and about 75% success in the experiment to be described in the next chapter. Alternative methods not involving language were markedly inferior, whether they involved the reinforcement of a series of responses constituting the diagonal, or the sorting of diagonal from nondiagonal cards.

Just as effective as telling the child, was asking the child, "Where does the criss-cross start?" One case history is representative of this development. Danya C. was unable to construct the diagonal on either the A or B Board, or on the white square of paper; her constructions resembled a middle row or a middle column. In spite of this limitation, she could recognize a middle row and all variations from it and correct these variations; she could recognize a criss-cross and discriminate it from noncriss-crosses, but she could not correct the errors. She was given the card sorting test and she quickly mastered it; although she made three errors on the first ten cards, she eliminated these errors subsequently. However, she could not point out where the criss-cross should go; her finger followed the pattern on the card. Following this she was still unable to construct the diagonal even on the Diagonal Board. E then told her, "A criss-cross starts at the corner." She then constructed a diagonal without error on the Diagonal Board. She was next given a plain white square and some checkers and asked to make a criss-cross. Danya said, "It starts at the corner." Shen then put a checker at the corner but built along the top row (she looked somewhat puzzled).

E then returned to the Diagonal Board and asked Danya to make a criss-cross. She did so correctly, while saying out loud, "A criss-cross starts at this corner, and at this corner, (pointing to the appropriate opposite corner)." She was again given the white paper square, and asked to make a criss-cross. She put the first two checkers at the opposite corners and then filled in the space to make a reasonable approximation to the diagonal. Finally, she was given the Square Board. She placed the first two checkers appropriately, paused, added two checkers incorrectly, and said, "I can't do it."

Why did she not see, by more looking, that the criss-cross started at the corner? In card sorting she had already rejected those pictures of diagonals that failed to start in the corner. It appears that looking is not the way we build up a conceptual representation of the diagonal, or other events, for that matter; it comes rather from inventing or being taught a way of representing these events. We may tentatively conclude that our subjects see the diagonal as a perceptual unity and, on that basis, discriminate it from nondiagonals, but they lack the conceptual system for representing the diagonal in terms of the properties or attributes necessary for its reconstruction. And, finally, failing to invent it for themselves, the only access children have to it is to be shown or told.

Note too, that it is not simply a matter of telling or showing; there were facts about the diagonal that, although we told the child, never came to influence her behavior. Obviously any input by E must be matched by some existing structure in S, or no statement could ever be assimilated. This matter of readiness will also come up subsequently.

The second line of evidence concerning the origins of this conceptual system comes from observations of four nondiagonal children who consistently failed to begin their construction at a corner. If E substituted a black checker for the end of the diagonal, or even for both ends (Procedure 5), the child, often for the first time, made his construction start and end at the corners. That is, if E provided the segmentation or the articulation, the child was from then on able to make at least that part of the diagonal correctly. Again, the transmitted quality of the properties is apparent.

In summary, we have been arguing that the conceptual systems that permit the seeing of the configuration in terms of a concept and attributes is invented and communicated to the child as a way of viewing or representing that configuration. In other words, even simple geometrical concepts are invented and then imposed on the world as ways of representing that world; they do not arise simply from looking at the world. Two important limitations of this argument have been mentioned. First, it is not simply a problem of telling or communicating; a child of two or three years is not much influenced by that telling. The child appears to be unable to "hold" systems of this type until four or five years of age. The recalcitrance of the problem of the diagonal strongly suggests a large maturational component in the development of this system.

Second, what about all the children who did manage to construct the diagonal the first time they even saw such a piece of equipment? Since their ability to construct the diagonal could have come from any one of a hundred sources, we have not even studied them. It seems unlikely, however, that they all had a dictionary entry for diagonal. We can only suggest that perhaps once they have some system for dealing with elementary geometrical concepts, they use it or elaborate it for the purpose of constructing the diagonal.

If our analysis of what it means to know the diagonal in such a way as to be able to construct it is adequate, it should have some bearing on the way in which the concept is taught. The experiments on instruction of the diagonal are described in the following section.

6

INSTRUCTION REVISITED: PERCEPTUAL, MOTOR AND LINGUISTIC FACTORS IN COGNITIVE DEVELOPMENT

... in which we examine the effects of three training programs patterned on the basis of our preceeding analysis of conceptual development,

... and in which we find that while that analysis is substantially correct, we are left with the problem of being unable to specify the relation between instruction and development and the role language plays in those two processes,

... and in which we call into question the general assumption about the role of verbal mediation or symbolic representation or internalized speech as a basis for thought,

... and in which we examine in a tentative manner the effects of a Montessori form of instruction on conceptual development.

PART I[1]

PERCEPTUAL AND VERBAL TRAINING AND THE ACQUISITION OF DIAGONALITY

If our analysis of the developmental changes that occur in the mind of the child are approximately correct, we should now be in a position to specify more precisely what happens due to the impact of instruction.

[1] The results in Part I of this study have been published elsewhere: Olson, D. R. From perceiving to performing the diagonal. In D. R. Olson, and S. Paglioso, (Eds.), From perceiving to performing: an aspect of cognitive growth. Special Issue: *Ontario Journal of Educational Research*, 1968, **10**, No. 3, 155–236.

The analysis should in fact specify the specific components of the instructional process. It should be noted that at this point we are treating instruction as simply the reciprocal of development; In Part II we shall examine the psychological nature of instruction more critically.

Recall that in our first attempt at instruction we were able to show the inadequacy of considering the act of constructing the diagonal as a response and the importance of teaching structure, that is, the relation between parts and the whole, or as we described it, between a concept and its attributes. We were unable at that point to give any more satisfactory account of either instruction or structure (as at that exploratory state it appeared unwise and unnecessary to control out procedures any more carefully).

This preceding analysis permits us to state more precisely, in hypothesis form, what is most critically involved in this instruction. The description of the changes that occur in the mental structure of the child that must be reflected in this instruction is that the child must learn to see the original diagonal configuration in a new way, in terms of a set of components or properties related in a specific way to the pattern as a whole. We have emphasized how this articulation of the configuration into a set of conceptual part-whole relations is prompted primarily by the culture through the distinctions coded in the language. It is this articulation that must be provided by the instruction. Language is assumed to be both the primary means for teaching the child how to articulate the diagonal and the means by which the child can represent to himself, that is, think about, the conceptual structure of the diagonal. From this point of view, it is the instruction, the systematic influence of the culture, that is the normal means of intellectual development.

Because the form of the instruction employed in this experiment derived largely from our account of how conceptual intelligence grows, this experiment will also permit us to cross-validate our analysis. If the children learn under conditions we have specified, namely, in which children's conceptions are articulated by language, then that evidence would tend to cross-validate the analysis provided in the preceding chapter.

Specifically, the questions under consideration are:

1. Does teaching the child to represent the diagonal in terms of a set of conceptual components permit him to construct the diagonal?

2. Is language the critical factor involved in this conceptualization?

3. Is this conceptual representation equivalent to the perception of attributes?

The revised conjectures about what is involved when the child learns to construct the diagonal permit us to establish more relevant control conditions. These come by means of Gibson's (1965) hypothesis of distinguishing features as the basis of perception and Maccoby and Bee's (1965, p. 375) hypothesis that was cited earlier: "To reproduce a figure, the subject must make use of more attributes of the model than are required for most perceptual discriminations of the same model from other figures." The most important control, therefore, involves training children to discriminate the diagonal from various nondiagonals on the basis of the set of critical features.

The hypothesis arising from the analysis in the preceding chapter was that the factor which permitted representation of the diagonal in terms of a set of components was the use of language. To oversimplify, discrimination plus linguistic coding equals conceptual representation. Hence, discriminated features alone would not produce the ability to construct the diagonal while features articulated by the language and related by the language to the diagonal as a whole would.

METHOD

Subjects

Two groups of Ss were used for testing these hypotheses. The first case involved 16 Ss drawn from the 35 children from Peabody Terrace Nursery School, Cambridge, Mass., who had served in earlier parts of the experiment described in the previous chapter. In the second case, 40 Ss were drawn from 132 children aged 3-1 to 6-1 years attending middle class and upper middleclass nursery schools and kindergartens in Cambridge and Newton.[2] All Ss employed in these experiments were children who succeeded on the warm-up constructions of the top row and middle column, but failed in the criteria construction, that of copying the diagonal. For convenience these children were described as nondiagonal children. The percentage of children at each level who could be classed as nondiagonal is indicated in Table 6-1. Because of their repeated use in earlier parts of the experiment, the data obtained from the first groups of children was considered as pilot. It should be recalled from the previous chapter that it was these nondiagonal children who were able to recognize the diagonal.

[2] We are grateful to the staff and students of Peabody Terrace Nursery School, Shady Hill School, and Wellington Public School, Newton, Mass. for their cooperation.

TABLE 6–1

PERCENTAGE OF CHILDREN AT EACH AGE LEVEL WHO WERE ABLE TO COPY THE DIAGONAL PRIOR TO TRAINING

	Sample			
	1		2	
Age	N	% Succeeding	N	% Succeeding
2	7	0.0%	–	–
3	18	16.5%	29	31.04%
4	5	40.0%	65	61.5%
5	3	66.7%	35	91.4%
6	–	–	3	100.0%

Materials

The checkerboard used in testing the child's ability to copy the diagonal and other patterns has been described earlier (see Fig. 3–1).

A card sorting test was designed to instruct children on the distinguishing features or attributes of the diagonal.

Two sets of five-inch square cards, with ten cards per set, were used in this task. In each set one half of the cards had diagonal patterns, while the other half had patterns that failed to qualify as diagonal for any one of several reasons, such as: (1) failure to start at a corner, (2) failure to go straight across the middle but followed rather the contour of the card, (3) failure to end at the opposite corner, (4) failure to go in a straight line but descended by steps, and (5) failure to terminate at the corners but ran parallel to a true diagonal.

Patterns in the first set of cards were made up of dots arranged to make either a diagonal or a nondiagonal pattern. Although all of the dots on any one card were identical, they varied in size, color and number from card to card. For example, one diagonal pattern was made up of four evenly spaced ¼-inch purple dots. Patterns in the second set were made up of pictures of small objects such as butterflies, flowers, turtles, fish, bottles, trees, and ice cream cones. Again, the drawings were identical on one card but changed in object, size, and number from card to card. Four of these cards are shown in Fig. 6–1. Children were shown one card at a time and were asked, "Is this a criss-cross?" They were then requested to put the card in the box on the left if it was, and in the right if it was not. Each set of cards began with a diagonal array, and for the first card,

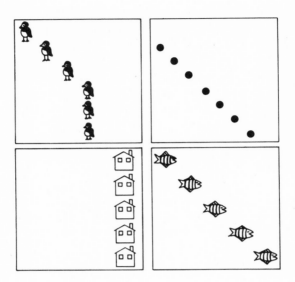

Fig. 6–1. Four sample cards from card sorting test.

E, instead of asking, said, "This is a criss-cross." *E* recorded the number of errors in each block of ten cards. A correction procedure was employed; if a nondiagonal card was called a criss-cross or put into the criss-cross box, *E* simply retrieved the card, showed it to the child and said, "No, this is not a criss-cross."

The measure of a child's knowing a perceptual attribute was that he could discriminate a pattern possessing that attribute from one not possessing it, or possessing some variant of it. If, for example, the child rejected patterns failing to start at a top corner and accepted those that did, it could be inferred that the child knew that perceptual attribute.

Procedures

The experimental work reported here was conducted primarily in the Mobile Laboratory of the Harvard Center for Cognitive Studies. Children were taken from their classes one at a time and permitted to play with the checkerboard for a short period of time prior to beginning the experiment. The general testing procedures were the same as those described earlier (Chapter 3).

Phase 1. Sixteen nondiagonal children were employed in this part of the study. Training consisted of giving the child one block of ten cards and asking him to sort the diagonals from the nondiagonals with a correction procedure. Following this, he was again shown the model of the diagonal on E's checkerboard and asked to construct one identical to it on his own board. If the child's construction was still inadequate, he was given the second block of cards, that involving pictures of objects to sort. This was again followed by retesting on the checkerboard. This procedure was repeated for four to six blocks of trials, or until the child succeeded in his construction. The data was examined to answer two questions. First, could children who were unable to copy or construct the diagonal recognize or discriminate diagonals from nondiagonals in the card sorting test? To answer this, the sorting errors were recorded.

The second question, based on the assumption that perception of the critical attributes leads to construction of the diagonal, examined whether training on these perceptual attributes led to an improvement in the child's ability to construct the diagonal.

Phase 2. The major part of this experiment considerably broadened the basis of training on the diagonal by adding a verbal articulation group as well as removing some of the limitations of the first part of the Phase 1 training.

For this part of the experiment, 40 nondiagonal Ss were drawn from four nursery schools in Cambridge and Newton. As before, to qualify for the experiment, children had to succeed on the row and column problems and fail on the diagonal. Following this qualifying test, Ss were randomly assigned to one of four treatment groups.

Group A was the retested control group. During the time that Ss in other groups were sorting diagonals from nondiagonals, control Ss worked on an irrelevant card sorting test. Following each ten-card sort they were retested on the diagonal problem.

Group B was the primary experimental group in that the Ss were trained and tested in a way identical to that described in Phase 1 above; that is, following each block of trials on the card sorting test, Ss were retested on the diagonal problem.

Group C was treated in a manner identical with Group B except that for each card that was classed as a nondiagonal, E asked S for the reason why it was not a diagonal or "Where does the criss-cross go?" If he was unable to answer, E provided the answer, for example, "Because a diagonal is supposed to start at the corner."

Group D did not use the card sorting test but simply used one card with a row of dots making up a diagonal (from Set 1), and one blank card. The training was primarily verbal and the same general questions that had been asked in Group 3 were asked and answered using only these two cards. These questions included, "Where does the criss-cross start?" "Where does it end?" "Where does it go?" At the time intervals corresponding to that in the other groups, Ss were retested on the diagonal problem.

The four groups then may be described as: (a) the retested control, (b) card sorting on the discriminated attributes of the diagonal, (c) card sorting plus verbal or conceptual articulation of these attributes or properties, and (d) verbal or conceptual articulation alone. The first two of these groups are necessary for testing Maccoby and Bee's discriminated attribute hypothesis; the latter two are employed to examine the role of verbal articulation of the properties of the diagonal pattern in producing the conceptual representation that makes possible its reconstruction. This latter is an alternative account of the lag between perceiving and performing.

RESULTS

Phase 1

The card sorting test of sorting diagonals from nondiagonals was mastered with very few errors by the children who were unable to construct the diagonal. Of the errors which occurred, a single correction was sufficient to remove the error completely. For instance, some children at first classed the card with the sloped array that ran just parallel to the diagonal as a "criss-cross" but E's correction was sufficient to eliminate the error. Another error made by a few subjects was to reject the criss-cross composed of only four elements all relatively far apart. Again, the simple statement by E was sufficient to eliminate the error. The shift in the patterns from dots to small objects, such as kittens, led to a few amusing errors on the part of some of the children. The following dialogue with Kristen S., age three, was not atypical:

E: (Pointing to the diagonal array of kittens): Is that a criss-cross?
S: No, it's a cat.

For the 16 nondiagonal children the mean number of errors in each block of ten trials is presented in Table 6–2. This table shows that the mean number of errors per block is always less than one out of ten sorts; that is, the sorting approaches errorless performance. These results compliment those reported in the last Chapter in which Ss who were unable to construct the diagonal were able to choose the original model of the diagonal over their attempted reconstruction. We now see that these

TABLE 6–2

MEAN ERRORS IN EACH BLOCK OF TEN TRIALS ON CARD SORTING TEST

	Block of trials			
	1	2	3	4
Mean errors (Max. = 10)	.77	.23	.15	.00

nondiagonal children are also able to choose the diagonal from among a relatively wide array of diagonals and nondiagonals.

The effect of overlearning the attributes of the diagonal by means of the card sorting test of the ability to construct the diagonal is shown in Table 6–3. Only the first four blocks of the training task were included in the analysis, as some *S*s were reluctant to continue beyond four blocks of trials. This table shows clearly that the training on the discriminated attributes in the card sorting test failed to lead to successful performance on the copying task. Only one of the 16 *S*s so trained learned to construct the diagonal. This slight change in performance from pretest to posttest is reflected in the nonsignificant results of the McNamar Test for the significance of changes ($X^2 = 1$, n.s.)

The ineffectiveness of the training procedure may be exaggerated by the fact that the *S*s used in this experiment were employed in several other parts of this series of experiments. Those who were close to learning the diagonal had already succeeded and hence were excluded from the training experiment; those who remained may have been particularly

TABLE 6–3

NUMBER OF SUBJECTS LEARNING TO CONSTRUCT THE DIAGONAL AFTER VARYING
DEGREES OF OVERLEARNING THE CARD SORTING TEST

	Before training	Block of training trials				After training	Gain due to training
		1	2	3	4		
Number pass	0	0	1	0[1]	0	1	$X^2 = 1$
Fail	16	16	15	15	15	15	n.s.

[1] The sixteenth subject was dropped from the training following his success.

TABLE 6–4

THE NUMBER OF SUBJECTS LEARNING TO CONSTRUCT THE DIAGONAL FROM EXPOSURE
TO FOUR TYPES OF TRAINING

$N = 40$	A Control		B Card sort		C Card sort and Verbal		D Verbal	
	Pre	Post	Pre	Post	Pre	Post	Pre	Post
Pass	0	3	0	3	0	6	0	6
Fail	10	7	10	7	10	4	10	4
X^2	1.33		1.33		4.17**		4.17**	

** $p < .05$

resistant to instruction. The fact remains, however, that the training on the perceptual attributes failed to lead Ss to correct performance.

Phase 2

The effects of the four types of training on the development of the ability to construct the diagonal is shown in Table 6–4. The primary group for testing the number of attributes hypothesis is Group 2, which succeeds at exactly the same rate as the retested Control. This result is parallel to that in the first part of this experiment. The verbal treatments (C and D) appear equal to each other, and both appear superior to the nonverbal treatment (B) and the control. If we again examine the change from pretest to posttest by means of the McNamar test for significance of changes, we can assess the effects of these training conditions. The resulting X^2 for each of these comparisons is also presented in Table 6–4. The retested control (A) and the card sorting group (B) perform not significantly different from what could be expected under the null hypothesis. Both verbal training groups (C and D) showed a significant improvement in their performance. If Group B is compared with Group C, the difference, although marked, fails to reach a satisfactory level of significance ($X^2 = 1.84$, $df = 1$, $p < .20$). If the nonverbal groups (A and B) are combined and compared with the verbal groups (C and D), the X^2 test of independence approaches significance ($X^2 = 3.64$, $df = 1$, $.05 < p < .10$). These levels of significance oblige us to consider as tentative the differences between the groups.

Discussions and Conclusions

We now have two lines of evidence that children who are unable to construct the diagonal are able to succeed in perceptually recognizing the diagonal. In the previous chapter we found that nondiagonal children could select the originally exposed diagonal model over their own attempted reconstruction; in this study we find that they could card-sort a wide variety of diagonals from nondiagonals. We may conclude that these results illustrate the lag between perceiving and performing. Hence, our instruction experiments may be considered from two points of view: (1) how to account for the effect of instruction on intellectual development, and (2) how to account for the lag between perceiving and performing.

As to the latter, recall that the criterion for assuming knowledge of the discriminated attribute was that the child could sort a card manifesting that attribute from one not manifesting it. Hence, in the card-sorting training conditions we may conclude that the child perceived those relevant attributes, yet neither group so trained (*S*s in Phase 1 and those in Group B, Phase 2) made any noticeable improvements in their attempted reconstruction of the diagonal. It follows that the Maccoby and Bee hypothesis does not, at least in this study, account for the lag between perceiving and performing.

Maccoby (1968) has subsequently revised her original hypothesis somewhat to suggest that younger children perceive the whole shape rather than select details—whole shape is adequate for recognition but not for copying a simple geometric form. She cites a study by Goodson that shows that the training best suited to help children learn to copy a square, a circle, a triangle, and a diamond involved the breakdown of the stimulus figure into components by means of visual illustrations and language, a result very similar to that of the present experiment. She leaves open the question as to whether the training was perceptual, conceptual, or both.

In this present experiment the gap between perceiving and performing tended to be closed only for Groups C and D. These are the training conditions based on our account of the nature and conditions for conceptual development, specifically the learning of a conceptual system that articulates and relates the parts to the whole. Once the child has a means for representing the diagonal in terms of its components, he can reconstruct the diagonal. The primary means for accomplishing this representation, the factor common to training conditions C and D, was the use of language to articulate and at the same time represent the critical knowledge of the diagonal. Thus, the statements "Where does the criss-cross start?" or "The criss-cross starts in the corner," were critical to their learning. It was only when such perceptual properties were coded in that language that they began to influence performance.

In discussing Maccoby's results and the results of the present experiment, Arnheim (1968) suggested

> . . . that the incapacity exists because perception is not primarily the apprehension of shapes or colors. Rather, to perceive is mainly to receive the expressive or dynamic *effect* of shapes and colors . . . when an average person looks . . . at a human face he sees its tenseness or plumpness or slyness or its harmony rather than the shapes and colors producing that effect . . . The difference, then, is not primarily between the perception and representation, but between perception of effect and perception of form, the latter being needed for representation (p. 206).

He went on to suggest that the use of verbal definitions had their effect by drawing attention to the form features themselves, a point made also by Christensen (1969).

Arnheim's distinction is similar to that described by Polanyi (1968) as the difference between "tacit inference" and "explicit inference." In the former, the child sees the pattern but fails to recognize how each of the checkers or features contributes to the overall effect; in the latter, he sees how these features produce the effect of the whole. Moreover, in this study, it is clear that the culture, that is, the language of instruction, was the primary factor in this articulation.

Hence, we conclude that it is the conceptual articulation of the diagonal that at the same time describes the development of conceptual systems and accounts for the lag between perceiving and performing.[3] We would suggest that what is required in both cases is not more and better perceptions but, rather, the development of a system for representing or conceptualizing the criterion problem in terms of a set of attributes.

Our account in terms of perception-conceptualization-performance while somewhat vague, particularly in terms of the role of language in both instruction and representation, is suggestive of the views of Cassirer (1946) who saw interposed between man's receptor and effector systems a symbolic system; this system is responsible for language and culture which constitute man's unique adaptive mechanisms.

If the account we have provided is approximately correct, it puts a

---

[3] To do so we have largely ignored Arnheim's important suggestion. It shall come up again in the conclusion when we reexamine the relation between perception and conceptualization.

primary emphasis upon the role of language in intellectual development. We shall further examine this centrality in the next experiment in Part II.

The emphasis placed upon the effects of language in articulating the perceptual knowledge necessary for the copying of forms has some implications. Processes that are conventionally labeled as perceptual in education and clinical settings, such as the copying of patterns on the Bender-Gestalt, may, in fact, be more adequately considered as representational or conceptual. This alternative is more tenable in the light of the evidence that learning to represent the diagonal verbally, even with few exemplars (Group D) led to success in copying the form, whereas perceptual training in the card sorting test (Group B) did not. The hypothesis arising from this view is that at least some types of perceptual handicap can be overcome by verbal training in which one is simply taught a vocabulary adequate to represent such visual patterns. The assumption is that, given a certain minimum level of motor skills, one's ability to copy a pattern is more a function of his vocabulary for representing forms than of his correct perceptual image. It is this strong position that is examined in the next training experiment and is found to be at least partially invalid.

PART II

PERCEPTUAL-MOTOR AND VERBAL TRAINING IN THE ACQUISITION OF DIAGONALITY

On the basis of the experiment reported in Part I we inferred that the conceptual articulation of the diagonal such that the child could reconstruct it was provided not by perceptual discrimination training but, rather, by linguistically representing or symbolically coding the diagonal in terms of its parts, attributes, or components. In Chapter 4 we showed that the diagonal should not be constructed as a simple response or response chain but rather in terms of a structure articulated by the language of instruction. In both cases our children came to be able to construct the diagonal by means of verbal instruction. If we acknowledge that some general experience underlies the ability to profit from instruction, it becomes critical to specify how a child's sensory-motor experience is related to verbal instruction to produce a concept. This is, in fact, the critical problem for which we need a theory of instruction. No such theory is available.

We sought to clarify this relation through another experiment. As we suggested earlier, our conjecture was that for the child's knowledge to become conceptual, it had to be verbally coded. The word, as Vygotsky (1962, p. 153) suggested, becomes the means both of instruction and the means for the representation of knowledge; "the word is a microcosm of human consciousness."

First, consider some of the attempts to specify the relationship between what is learned by experience and what is learned by instruction. Children do learn from experience but it is not clear that what is learned is the same thing as what is learned symbolically via verbal instruction. Up to this point we have argued that it is not, and we have drawn support from our data and from the views of Cassirer (1946). The psychological theories of Vygotsky (1962) and Bruner *et al.* (1966) are worth mentioning in this regard.

Vygotsky argued from the Marxist view of man that the society and its institutions as reflected in the language and culture were the primary formative influences on human cognition. He argued that logical thought and systematic, hierarchically organized conceptual systems developed because of, and through, the learning of "scientific concepts" which were the formal subject matter of the schools. The highest form of thought, verbal thought, was internalized speech which proceeded on the basis of the pure meanings of words. Hence, systematic organized thought was verbally regulated.

In several recent experiments within this tradition, Luria (1961) presented complex visual stimuli consisting of a red circle on a grey ground and a green circle on a yellow ground to children aged 3 to 5 years. The children learned to press one balloon with one hand for one stimulus complex, and another for the second stimulus complex. When the ground colors were then interchanged the child kept responding to the figure of the stimuli, apparently not even noticing the changed grounds. The problem then became how does one come to attend to and respond to the ground of the figure-ground complex? Luria found that a verbal command could be used to alter the effects of the stimulus cues and thereby get children to respond to the ground of the complex stimulus; this was particularly true if the verbal instructions were meaningful. From this he concluded that language altered the natural strength of the stimuli, and as the child comes to generate his own language he can modify the stimuli he responds to; this gives his behavior a planned or volitional character.

Bruner *et al.* (1966) have suggested that while development may lead to an end state of "symbolic representation" which is similar to that described by Vygotsky, en route two preparatory stages are passed through in which experience is coded first "enactively" and later "iconically." For example, the child first learns a substrate of knowledge via his motor activity which underlies his visual and spatial, or iconic, knowledge. Both of these may subsequently provide the basis for his verbally coded or symbolic knowledge. It is not clear from the account how the earlier forms of knowledge are translated into or even relevant to the symbolic knowledge that develops.

There are alternatives to this point of view. The set of classical learning theories we designate as behaviorism all specify how one learns from experience but, as they tend to ignore language (particular language in instruction), they are not directly helpful. As Premack and Schwartz (1966, p. 298) say: "Organisms without language can be trained, but those with language can be instructed. We see instruction as presently resisting completely all attempts at stimulus responses explication."

More directly relevant is the general educational theory of Dewey, and the developmental theory of Piaget. Dewey's (1916) conception of the relation between intelligence and experience remains one of the most cogent. His activity and experience based school curricula proceeded in light of the premise that intelligence elaborates on the basis of problem-solving situations that arise in the course of pursuing socially-relevant goals. It is never made clear, however, just how this practical experience was translated into conceptual intelligence. Was it the ensuing verbal discussion that did this, or the practical experience itself? How is language implicated? These questions require a level of specificity to which Dewey never addressed himself.

As we indicated earlier, Piaget (1960) emphasized even more the role of sensory-motor experience in the development of intellectual schemas. Both schemas and the operations that come to organize them develop from sensory-motor experience and the internalization of that activity. In his account, neither language nor instruction are specifically implicated. Learning that appears through instruction is to be feared because it may lead the child to "recite the little family lecture," not what he really thinks or believes. When instruction is used, as in Sinclair-DeZwart (1967) it is of a strikingly nondirective nature.

What one learns through experience and what one learns through language in instruction, and how they are related, remains unknown. This question is undoubtedly related to that of the relation between language, perception, and thought. Earlier reviews of this literature

(McNeill, in press; Olson, 1970a) concluded that language affected memory primarily by directing attention.

We are left with the general question of the relation between sensory-motor experience and verbal instruction in the development of conceptual thought. The specific hypothesis underlying this experiment, parallel to that tested in Part I, was that perceptual and sensory motor experience with a square and a diagonal would be inefficient for learning the concept of the diagonal, while experience articulated verbally would be a sufficient condition for this learning. The assumption was made that verbal articulation of experience would change the coding of the experience to the level of symbolic representation, and that experience coded symbolically would permit the construction of the diagonal. It turns out we had misconstrued the problem; perhaps for good reason.

Two different training and retesting phases employing the same group of subjects were involved in this study. These phases shall be reported separately.

Phase 1

METHOD

Subjects and Procedures

All the children in two Toronto Nursery Schools[4] were tested to determine their ability to reproduce the set of patterns on the square (5 × 5) checkerboard. The warmup patterns consisted of the top row, middle column, and bottom row. The critical pretest problems were the left-oriented diagonal and the right-oriented diagonal. Subjects actually used in this training experiment were those who:

  1. were able to place three or fewer checkers correctly in the diagonal pattern,
  2. could succeed in the warm-up problems,
  3. understood English, and
  4. were cooperative.

According to these criteria eleven children were selected from each school, six of whom were put into the Experimental Group and five into

    [4] We are grateful to the teachers and students of the YMHA Nursery School, Toronto, and the Sacred Heart Nursery School, Toronto, for their cooperation.

TABLE 6–5

AGE, SEX, PRACTICE-PROBLEM SCORES, AND PRETEST AND POSTTEST SCORES ON THE DIAGONAL FOR THE CHILDREN ASSIGNED TO THE EXPERIMENTAL AND CONTROL GROUPS

Group		Experimental	Control
N		12	10
Sex	*M*	7	3
	F	5	7
Age	School 1	3–8	3–4
	School 2	4–0	3–10
	Mean	3–10	3–7
Practice problems[1]	School 1	35%[2]	70%
	School 2	80%	73%
	Mean	58%	72%
Pretest scores on diagonal	School 1	17%	24%
	School 2	13%	16%
	Mean	15%	20%
% of *S*s succeeding[3] on the diagonal			
	Pretest	0%	0%
	Posttest	25%	20%

[1] Top row, middle column, next to bottom row.

[2] Average percentage of the five checkers correctly placed.

[3] Succeeding implies 4 or 5 checkers, that is, 80% or 100% correctly placed.

the Control. In the first school they were assigned randomly to groups with the restriction that the average age of the two groups be approximately the same. The ages, sex, practice-problem scores, and pretest scores on the diagonal for children in the two schools assigned to the two experimental groups is shown in Table 6–5.

While the *S*s for this experiment were selected so as to be matched on their pretest performance on the diagonal, this table shows that the groups are not well matched either as to sex or to scores on the warm-up problems (in the first school). This latter difference may bias the experiment against the hypothesis being investigated. However, if the training effects are as profound as we anticipate, any subsequent superiority of the experimental group would be an even more convincing test of the hypothesis.

Experimental Training Group

Subjects were trained in pairs. A square was constructed on the floor using four cardboard strips each 30 inches long and 2 inches wide. A toy was placed at each of the four corners: a duck, bear, rabbit, and a cow. Ss were asked to identify the objects. E pointed out that this was called a "square." Ss were requested to "walk around the square three times." The corners were then pointed out, counted, and the children questioned about them. The diagonal or criss-cross was then taught using a cardboard strip 40 inches by 2 inches placed along the diagonal. It was stressed that the diagonal went from corner to opposite corner. The strip was removed and each child rolled a ball on each diagonal.

Children were then taught to draw a diagonal as follows: A 15-inch square outline form with animal pictures at each corner was placed over the blackboard. Square, corner, and diagonal were again named and indicated. Each S was asked to draw each diagonal twice. Ss were given as much assistance as needed to help them execute a diagonal in this procedure, and in the other drawing sessions as well.

Next, an 8-inch square with an inside border of sandpaper was presented to the children who felt around the square while the properties of the square were again being taught. A strip of sandpaper was then inserted along the diagonal and children ran their hands over it while the E again gave a description of the diagonal. The sandpaper diagonal was removed and a sheet of paper was inserted behind the square; the children were requested to draw a diagonal, one on each side of the paper.

Finally, a plain sheet of paper, 8 inches square, was given to the children, who were asked to draw a criss-cross and then to cut along the line they had drawn.

Ss were rewarded by having a gold star glued to the back of their hands. The procedure was repeated on the two following days. On the fourth day, the posttest was given.

Control Training Group

The materials were set up as in the experimental group, but with no diagonal strips. No concepts were explicitly taught, neither square nor diagonal. First, Ss identified objects at the corners, and rolled the ball anywhere within the square after walking around it three times. Second, the square was placed over the blackboard but children drew anything they chose. Third, the sandpaper square was felt, but the diagonal was not inserted. In the two remaining tasks, children drew what they chose and cut the paper accordingly. The time spent with both groups was equivalent and the reward was the same. This procedure was repeated on the two following days. On the fourth day the posttest was given.

Posttest

The posttest, like the pretest, consisted of a set of pattern-copying tasks including the three warmup problems: top horizontal, middle vertical, and bottom horizontal, followed by the left-oriented diagonal and the right-oriented diagonal. If the children failed in their attempted reconstruction, they were given a second trial. *E* recorded the children's construction on a score sheet by placing a number in the square that indicated both the position and the order in which the child placed the checkers in the particular positions. These performances were then scored in terms of percentage of checkers correctly placed (with the limitation that two or more checkers must be placed on pattern consecutively, and that the child put a maximum of seven checkers on the board). Performances of either 80% or 100% were considered as indicating the ability to construct the diagonal. Reversals were noted, but not considered incorrect.

Results and Discussion

There was no difference between the two training programs in their effects on the children's ability to copy the diagonal. Only three of the twelve *S*s in the experimental group, and two of the ten in the control group were able to construct the diagonal after training (See Table 6–5; see also Table 6–6, column 4).

The remarkable ineffectiveness of our training program led us to re-examine the effects of training on the diagonal. *S*s gave the appearance of knowing the diagonal verbally, that is, of knowing the concept of the diagonal so that they could give fluent descriptions of the fact that "a diagonal goes in a straight line from a corner to the opposite corner" and they could draw a good approximation of a diagonal on a sheet of paper; yet they were unable to copy the diagonal on the checkerboard. Why? Perhaps the training was too mechanical and the children did not clearly understand how what they were saying and doing was related to constructing the diagonal. Why did the learning of a conceptual or verbal means of representing the event not lead to transfer?

While one can never prove the null hypothesis,[5] the failure of the child's knowledge to transfer to the construction of the diagonal led us to reconsider the role of language in this conceptualization and to emphasize the perceptual experience that is presumably articulated by that language.

[5] Failure to get significant results does not prove that the hypothesis is false; the results may have occurred for any one of several reasons, including that, because of poor methodology, the hypothesis was not appropriately tested.

These two factors were not differentiated in the earlier, more successful training procedure described in Chapter 4, and Part 1 of this chapter. It appears that we have made an error in instruction that occurs frequently in the school, that is, we assumed that children mean the same thing by their words as we do by ours. As Piaget argued, merely knowing the verbal equivalent or description of an event is perhaps not a sufficient condition for knowing that event; it may be partly "empty verbalization." Even that is not very convincing; the children appeared to know the verbal concepts, they could define the diagonal, and they could draw the diagonal on paper.

We had assumed that it is the codification of the child's knowledge into language that was responsible for the conceptual learning that made the construction of the diagonal possible. Is that assumption necessary?

Let us summarize and reassess the assumption about the role of language in representation or conceptualization:

1. Children under 4 or 5 years fail to copy a diagonal on our checkerboard upon exposure to it.

2. By 5 or 6 years, they can copy such a pattern.

3. The development is not biological or maturational, as it does not occur for Kenyan children until much later; we shall see this in the next chapter.

4. The factors apparently responsible for its later appearance in Kenya appear to consist both of general experience resulting from exploratory spatial activity and of the articulation of experience by language, especially in the schools.

5. Our prior instructional attempts in teaching the diagonal had been successful if they involved the articulation of the diagonal in terms of its components or parts.

6. The means by which this articulation occurred was primarily verbal.

7. Hence, we had hypothesized from our instructional experiments that it was the coding of the event in the language that was responsible for the child's being able to conceptualize it.

8. Conceptualizing it in terms of its components is the basis for reconstructing the patterns.

9. But here in this last experiment we have children who appear able to code the diagonal in words, yet they cannot construct it!

The answer to this enigma came very slowly. Eventually, several lines of evidence that we have been systematically ignoring became focused on point 7, above. Because we found that language had served as an important instructional means, must we infer that the resulting knowledge was verbal? The assumption is prevalent in the literature, both in the notion of "symbolic representation" (Bruner *et al.*, 1966) and in Vygotsky (1962) who said:

> School instruction induces the generalizing kind of perception and thus plays a decisive role in making the child conscious of his own mental processes. To become conscious of a mental operation means to transfer it from the plane of action to that of language (p. 92 and p. 88).

It is our assumption, made explicit in Vygotsky's hypothesis of the "higher plane of verbal thought," that now appears suspect.

Consider the alternative hypothesis. Words are not the means of representing reality or the form of the knowledge critical to the construction of the diagonal, but rather one means of directing the child to the critical aspects of the diagonal or to their interrelations. Instead of being a verbal representation of reality, thought is a perceptual or motor schematic representation of reality similar to that developed in nonlinguistic situations; words are rather a means to modify these schemata. (Ideally, we would still need a theory to specify this relation.) To paraphrase this point, language is one means of schema modification, perhaps a limited means, not the end product of conceptual development. The result of development is not, from this view, internalized speech or symbolic representation.

We have encountered (and ignored) considerable evidence compatible with this view. First, recall that a red checker served to articulate or point up the fact that the diagonal began at a corner just as well as the question or statement, "The criss-cross begins in the corner." Second, the children in our culture who know how to construct the diagonal at five years of age are unable to give a verbal account of their action. Third, as we shall see presently, the geometrically impoverished perceptual world of two bush communities in East Africa, as well as the limited spatial or geographical exploration by some of these children, are both related to the difficulty they have in reconstructing the diagonal. Fourth, as we shall see presently, children learn from an educational toy that provides for no verbal specification. Fifth, children gain, often significantly, from repeated test trials on the diagonal. The results obtained from the pretest of the present study combined with those from the pretest of the first educational toy study (Chapter 9) are presented in Fig. 6–2 which shows that the second trial on the diagonal is frequently better than the first trial, even if the event is not coded verbally. Whether a gain occurs,

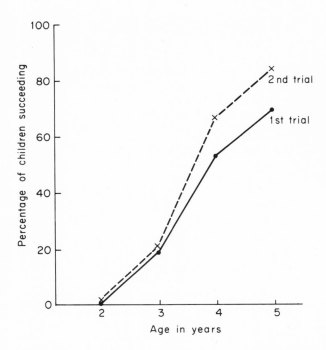

Fig. 6–2. Percentage of children succeeding on each of the first two trials on the diagonal.

however, is highly dependent upon the age of the child. A test of the independence of the gain/no gain on the second trial from the age of the subject was found to be significant $(X = 8.86, df = 1, p < .01)$.[6] A similar pattern of gains from Trial 1 to Trial 2 will be reported in the East African data (Chapter 7, Fig. 7–3, Ss ≠ 132, p. 000) in which a Logoli child placed only two checkers correctly on the first trial, three on the next, and all five after the third reexamination of the model. Note, however, that this is not true for all of the subjects; more looking at the model does not help the younger children. Sixth, consider some further data collected in the present experiment.

[6] The number of subjects falling into the categories gain/no gain was tabulated for the four age levels separately, producing a 4 × 2 contingency table. Although there were 49 Ss who failed the first attempt on the diagonal, and therefore had an opportunity to show a gain, two of the cells had zero entires. The resulting $(X^2 = 13.12, df = 3, p < .01)$ is therefore suspect. For this reason, the two youngest ages and the two oldest ages were collapsed, yielding a 2 × 2 contingency table and the X^2 value reported above (Seigel, 1956).

Phase II

In view of the fact that only 25% of the experimental group, and 20% of the control group were able to copy the diagonal after the first training sessions, training was continued. Recall that experimental Ss could recite verbally what a diagonal was in terms of its properties such as corners and straight lines, while the Control Ss had acquired no such knowledge.

METHOD

Subjects

Ss from both groups in Phase 1 who had thus far in the experiment not succeeded in copying the diagonal were combined and exposed to two new forms of training in succession. Twelve Ss were given Training A; 14 Ss (including 9 who failed to benefit from Training A) were given Training B.

Procedures

Training A. This training component consisted of the following segments:

1. Ss drew a vertical line on the middle of an 8 -inch square piece of paper.
2. They then put checkers into a continuous row along that line.
3. They next put only five checkers along this line (thus leaving spaces between them). Help was given by way of an example if it was necessary for the child to learn to leave the spaces between the checkers.
4. The checkerboard was then taken and turned upside down and S was asked to trace a middle vertical line on the back of the board.
5. They then made the line with only five checkers, thus leaving spaces between them. Ss were then posttested on the diagonal, as in the pretest.

Training B. This treatment took the same form as Training A, except that it was done exclusively on the diagonal. Thus, Ss drew a diagonal line (with help of E if necessary) on a square sheet of paper, put a continuous row of checkers along the line, put only five checkers along the line (thus leaving spaces), traced the diagonal line with a finger on the back of the checkerboard, put checkers along that imaginary line, and then were posttested on the diagonal.

These training sessions lasted from 5 to 7 minutes and each child went through a training session only once. Note that only children failing to learn to construct the diagonal in an earlier phase of the experiment were given this subsequent training phase. These sessions were designed to train the children to go from performances involving continuous production (such as line drawing) to performances involving discrete productions (such as placing checkers in a line with spaces between them). In that way the training was made more specifically appropriate to the actual construction of the diagonal. This training is in contrast to that of verbal conceptualization of the diagonal that was carried out in Phase I of the experiment.

Retest. Finally, all *S*s were retested on the diagonal on the 5 × 5 and the 7 × 7 checkerboard[7] one week after the training sessions and posttests. Scores used in this analysis, as in the previous part of the experiment, were the percentage of checkers correctly placed in the best of the child's two attempts at copying the diagonal. Scores of 80% or over (71% or over on 7 × 7 board) were considered successful in copying the diagonal.

RESULTS AND DISCUSSION

The results of these training sessions for Phase I, as well as the two training programs of Phase II, are presented in Table 6–6. As we noted in Phase I of this study, there were no differences between the children in the experimental group who had been trained on the diagonal, and those in the control group. (Column 4 of Table 6–6 shows that in the experimental group, 25% of the children could construct the diagonal, as compared to 20% of the control group.) Moreover, there were an equivalent number of subjects, five, in each group that showed a gain from any part of the training up to the end of Training A. It is therefore legitimate to ignore these Phase I groupings while examining the effects of Training A and Training B.

Training A, i.e. training from a continuous line to a set of discrete checkers representing that line on the middle vertical, led only one out of the 12 trained (8%) to success on the diagonal. However, for the *S*s who

---

[7] This checkerboard had the same figure-ground properties as the original 5 ×5 checkerboard, except that the former was larger, having seven rows and seven columns and a 7-checker diagonal.

still were unable to copy the diagonal after Training A, who were trained by Training B from a continuous line to a set of discrete checkers along that line on the diagonal, seven of the 14 (50%) were now able to copy the diagonal. If these differences are tested using a test for the significance of the difference between two correlated proportions, the resulting ($z = 2.24$) is significant ($p < .05$).[8] However, because of the small N, this value may be an overestimate. Alternatively, of the 12 pairs of scores, six show a greater score for B than for A, one shows a lower score, and five show no change. The Sign Test for related samples (Seigel, 1956) yields a $p = <.06$. Hence, we may tentatively conclude that there is a difference between A and B.

Whereas our training in verbally conceptualizing the diagonal in the earlier part of this study had failed to lead to the construction of the diagonal, as did the additional training on representing a line with a set of discrete checkers (Training A), Training B on the diagonal did have a significant impact. That is, this brief training directly relevant to the construction of the diagonal led to success in copying the model even for those *S*s who had not had the previous verbal training on conceptualizing the diagonal. We conclude that it is not the coding of the diagonal symbolically, i.e., with words, that is critical to the reconstruction of the diagonal, but rather it is only the coding or articulation of the diagonal in terms of its components that is critical; language is one means of doing this. We shall argue in a later section that language is a means of instruction, not the means of thought or representation; the knowledge of the diagonal (suitable for its construction on the checkerboard) may be built up by more than one means.

The retest, conducted one week later, yielded an interesting interaction between the first training sessions on the conceptualization of the diagonal, and these later training sessions. Recall that the experimental group received training in conceptualizing the diagonal while the control group did not, and neither of these led to success on the diagonal. In the final stage of this experiment, training specifically in the construction of the diagonal led to success for children regardless of their earlier training. The retest after one week permits us to ask if that latter training was more permanent for those *S*s who previously learned to verbally conceptualize the diagonal.

---

[8] For this analysis, two *S*s were dropped from the Training B group to make the Ns equal; the three *S*s in each group who did not take both treatments were exactly matched on their pretest scores to meet the requirements of this analysis. The proportions tested ($p_1 = .08$ and $p_2 = .50$) were not altered by this procedure.

TABLE 6–6

CHILDRENS' PERFORMANCE ON THE DIAGONAL AS A FUNCTION OF TRAINING PHASES
I AND II

Exp. group	Subject	Pretest	Phase I	Phase II Training A	Phase II Training B	Retest
	A[1]	60	60	–	100	71
	B	0	0	–	0	71
	C	0	0	–	100	0
	D	0	0	–	100	71
	E	0	0	–	40	
Experi-mental	F	40	100	*[2]	*	100
	L	0	0	0	0	0
	M	0	100	*	*	80
	N	0	40	0	40	40
	O	0	0	0	0	0
	P	40	40	60	100	100
	Q	40	100	*	*	100
% Ss succeeding		0%	3/12 = 25%			7/11 = 64%
	G	60	100	*	*	29
	H	0	80	*	*	0
	I	60	60	100	*	0
	J	0	0	0	–	0
Control	K	0	0	0	–	0
	R	0	40	40	0	0
	S	40	0	40	100	100
	T	0	0	0	100	100
	U	0	0	0	0	0
	W	40	0	60	100	40
% Ss Succeeding		0%	2/10 = 20%	1/12 = 8%	7/14 = 50%	2/8 = 25%[4]
Significance of Differences		Matched	$t = .173$ n.s.	$z = 2.24$[3] $p < .05$		$X^2 = 2.77$ $p < .10$

[1] Ss A to K were from School 1; L to W were from School 2.

[2] Ss represented by asterisks were omitted from this training session because they had already succeeded on the diagonal.

[3] See p. 99 for discussion of this procedure.

[4] Ss J and K were excluded from the Experimental vs. Control comparisons because they (1) had not received Training B, and (2) had not succeeded in an earlier phase of the experiment.

Of the Ss from the experimental group, seven out of eleven, 64%, could copy the diagonal one week after cessation of training, while of the control group, only two out of eight, 25%,[9] could still copy the diagonal; the difference approaches significance ($X^2 = 2.77$; $.10 < p < .05$). From this we infer that the earlier training in conceptualizing the diagonal was not irrelevant; it made the learning in the second session more permanent.

With this observation we come back to the relative effectiveness of the first two training sessions (Chapters 4 and 6, Part I). Those training sessions had both conceptualizing the diagonal, and training relevant to the specific construction of the diagonal on the checkerboard; hence, they were both successful and permanent. Our earlier error was to attribute the effectiveness of the training to "conceptual or symbolic representation" per se.

One other observation bears some attention. Ss in this experiment benefitted from instruction, but not uniformly. One may assume that something about the child's previous knowledge and/or ability determined whether or not he would profit from instruction. There is strong evidence that such is the case. All of the children admitted to the experiment were unable to construct the diagonal; however, among these children there was some variation in that approximately one-third placed two or three checkers correctly (partial diagonal), and two-thirds scored zero or one checkers correct in the pretest. The question now is, does score on the pretest account for the ability to profit from instruction? Clearly, yes; all of the children who were partially correct on the pretest learned to construct the diagonal ($8/8 = 100\%$); only a third of those who scores zero or one on the pretest benefitted from the instruction ($5/14 = 36\%$). The difference is significant ($X^2 = 8.70$; $p < .01$). This finding parallels an earlier one in that the children who showed some gain in their second attempt to copy the diagonal were almost exclusively the older subjects.

While conceptual development is produced by experience as formalized in instruction, it also depends on some underlying readiness to profit from that instruction. In this case, that readiness is not any obvious bit of background knowledge; our instruction was built to make minimal assumptions about background knowledge. The lot thus seems to fall on capacity or ability which may be more maturationally determined. In this case, for example, those who failed to benefit from instructions not only performed more poorly on the pretest, but also tended to be younger. That limiting factor may be something as basic as a limited "apprehension span" but it has not been assessed in this study.

---

[9] Two Ss from this group had to be dropped from the analysis as they (1) had not received Training B, and (2) had not succeeded in an earlier phase of the experiment.

SUMMARY AND CONCLUSION

In this chapter we have considered the results of two further instruction experiments on the child's acquisition of diagonality. The results are best considered together as they are somewhat contradictory. In the first experiment, we found that a perceptual training condition involving the sorting of a wide variety of diagonals from nondiagonals was markedly inferior to one involving the conceptual and linguistic articulation of the diagonal in terms of its properties or components. From this we concluded that it was not the recognition or discrimination of a diagonal that accounted for its production, but rather the development of a system for representing or conceptualizing the criterion problem in terms of its set of attributes. Finally, it was inferred that language was the primary means for this representation.

In the second study, originally intended to be a simple replication of the first, in which *Ss* were trained to conceptualize the diagonal in terms of a set of components and to linguistically represent this knowledge, we found little or no improvement in ability to copy the diagonal.

When instruction was resumed along different lines, namely, showing the children how a continuous diagonal line could be composed of a set of spaced, discrete objects (checkers) in the context of the checkerboard on which they were to make their productions, performance improved significantly.

The effectiveness of this specific training relative to the ineffectiveness of the earlier training in terms of the linguistic or conceptual representation of the diagonal, together with several other dissonant lines of evidence, led us to reconsider some of the limitations of these studies, as well as our assumptions and our interpretations of some of our earlier results.

First, the limitations. We have had obvious difficulty in arriving at a training procedure that was both psychologically comprehensible (theoretically derived), and effective. Frequently, the more successful the technique the more difficult it was to specify. Part of this was due, as in Phase 2, to the fact that the training sessions were added because the theoretically derived training failed to produce the expected results.

A more basic reason for this difficulty may reside in training studies generally, in that they involve what may be called "two-paradigm" experiments. The basic paradigm used to account for learning by the child may be described in terms of such variables as form of the response, number of trials, organization of the responses, generalization, transfer, and so on. The second paradigm presumably involves the production and comprehension of sentences with a communicative intent. In an instruction experiment one tries to jump from the communicative intent of the instructor all the way to the performance by the child. At worst, too much uncontrolled activity occurs between these two points to make an account possible. At best, we may require a combination of those two paradigms or a new paradigm in the form of a theory of instruction. While our training treatments in this experiment were considerably more precise and explicit than in the earlier chapters, it is still difficult to specify what went on, particularly in psychological terms. The language of psychology may have an adequate vocabulary for discussing learning, but it has an obvious lacuna of the vocabulary for even discussing instruction. The solution of simply calling each step of the training a "stimulus" is to beg the question. Maccoby (1968) has also expressed an uneasiness with instruction experiments of the form described in the early part of this chapter.

There is another basic problem with using an instructional approach to the study of intellectual development. It is that the methodology biases the account in a major but generally undetected way. This bias, clearly shown in the work of Vygotsky, Luria, and to some extent, Bruner, as we have seen, appears to be based on the following inference:

1. Instruction is the basis of cognitive development.
2. Language is the basis of instruction.
3. Therefore, language is the basis of cognitive development.

However, if instruction was not used as the experimental means of studying cognitive development, as in Piaget's experiments for example, language would not be considered the basis of cognition. This insight is important to our reconceptualization of the evidence we have examined in the present study.

Some of the observations from the present study that could be reassembled to make a more coherent, if tentative, picture of what was going on in the instruction interaction follows.

As we predicted, children did not learn to construct the diagonal from more looking at the diagonal (although older children did improve somewhat through simple retesting), nor from sorting diagonals from nondiagonals, nor from sensory-motor or spatial exploration of a square and a diagonal (it was even difficult to phrase the question of the relationship between sensory-motor experience and conceptual learning, especially in a way that implied different forms of instruction). And, as we predicted, children did learn to construct the diagonal from learning to differentiate diagonal from nondiagonal in terms of a set of attributes that were articulated by language.

But contrary to our predictions, they did not learn to construct the diagonal from learning to conceptualize the diagonal in terms of a set of linguistic coded components. On the other hand they did learn to construct the diagonal by learning to transform a continuous line drawn along the diagonal into a discrete set of checkers along the diagonal in the context of the checkerboard. Finally, children who could draw the diagonal on paper after instruction could not construct it on the checkerboard, thereby implicating the medium (i.e., the checkerboard) in which they were working.

To deal with these findings and others we found it necessary to drop the assumption that language was the basis of conceptual thought or symbolic representation. Conceptual development, at least as assessed by the diagonal, can occur without language, and the learning of a language to define the diagonal does not guarantee that the child will be able to construct it.

Language is then cast into a less central role. It may be considered as a means of instruction, of directing the child's attention to critical features and their relationships. The resulting concepts are nonlinguistic and identical in form, if not in content, to those formed from nonlinguistic experience. What is critical to the development of the concept is perceiving the diagonal in terms of a set of components of features that differentiate it from other concepts or productions with which it is in danger of being confused. This conclusion comes closer to Arnheim's (1968) suggestion that the reconstruction of a pattern requires the perception of form, i.e., the features that contribute to that particular effect, rather than the perception of the effect itself.

While instruction may produce conceptual development, there are additional problems of specifying who will benefit from instruction. In these studies we found that for Ss who could not copy the diagonal, the score on the pretest of the diagonal predicted their ability to profit from instruction. We have then implicated another component in the process of conceptual development, usually called "readiness" which, although it merits further specification, is beyond the scope of this study.

Finally, even if we have managed to successfully instruct children in the concept of diagonal, there remains a clumsiness in the psychological description of the training involved. There is a curious lacuna in the language of psychology for describing precisely what is going on, a lucana that can be filled, in my estimation, only by the development of a theory of instruction.

Addendum

A MONTESSORI APPROACH TO THE ACQUISITION OF DIAGONALITY[10]

In the preceeding section it became clear that it was necessary to differentiate the means of instruction, which may be verbal, from the resulting cognition or knowledge itself, which is presumably nonverbal. But if language is just a means of instruction it should be possible to arrive at the underlying cognitions or knowledge by completely nonverbal means. Specifically, it should be possible to arrange a nonverbal form of instruction that results in the child's being able to reconstruct the diagonal. Such a form of instruction is the basis of the Montessori (1914) method of early education. As a general psychological model this approach to learning has been called modeling or observational learning (Bandura, 1969; Aronfreed, 1969).

It should be obvious from the early chapters of this book that nonverbal instruction appeared to be unrelated to conceptual development. It is easy to imagine that nonverbal instruction is useful to "sensory-motor" development, but it is less easy to see it relevant to conceptual development, particularly if it is assumed, as we did in the earlier chapters of this book, that language is the sine qua non of conceptual development. Once we grant that language is a means of providing information, not the information or knowledge itself, the possibility of a nonverbal means is no longer anomalous.

The severity of the anomaly is reflected in the way that I originally came upon and treated the first observations to be reported in this section. In the course of recruiting children for our own verbal-instruction experiment (Part I), I took the checkerboard to a Montessori school in Cambridge. When I told the teacher how young children usually had difficulty in reconstructing the diagonal, the Montessori teacher, in disbelief, took the board, some checkers, and a very young child, aged about 3. He constructed the diagonal in the child's presence in a rather elaborate way which I shall describe presently, and to my amazement, the child going through the same exaggerated motions copied the diagonal without error. At the time, that observation so violated my intuitions as to what was involved in this development that I simply ignored (or repressed) it. I dismissed it as a case of elaborate motor learning that could tell me noth-

---

[10] This section was written considerably later than the earlier parts of this chapter. The experimental work was done after all of the other studies reported in the book were completed. It is included here because it deals with the problem of instruction.

ing about cognitive or conceptual learning. It is only recently, 3 years after making that observation, that I realize that the phenomenon could be genuine, and that the effect must be accounted for by any theory of cognitive development. This section reports the form of that Montessori instruction and a modest effort to replicate it with 6 other children. Because of the small sample and variability in the training method, the results presented here are not definitive. They are presented only to show that such an effect is possible, and to show how such observations may be incorporated into a theory of cognitive development.

Method

Subjects. All the children involved in this part of the experiment were shown the completed diagonal pattern, ran their fingers over it, and then had failed in their attempted reconstructions. As in other training experiments, these *S*s could be classed as nondiagonal. They ranged in age from 3–2 to 4–9 years.

Montessori Training. When I first observed the training I had no adequate conception of what was going on; hence, I could not easily describe the method. It appeared to involve the teacher's first engaging the child's attention with the "to-be-placed" checker and then wandering it about the checkerboard while nodding his head negatively when the checker moved away from the appropriate hole and positively when the checker approached the appropriate hole. After about 5 seconds of this activity, the teacher finally "zeroed-in" on the correct hole and deposited the checker. He then picked up the next checker and proceeded in the same manner until the pattern was complete. At no time did the teacher say anything to the child, and at no time did the child do anything except watch. When the demonstration was complete, the teacher gave the board and the pile of checkers to the child who then attempted to make the same pattern.

The same procedure, borrowed from the Montessori teacher was utilized by *E* with the other 6 children in the study. These latter 6 children were trained 3 years after the first one. Instruction for each child lasted from 1 to 5 minutes. Following instruction, the child went to a second *E* who gave the posttest which consisted of the two diagonals and the X-pattern.

Results

Of the 7 children so instructed, 4 succeeded on both of the diagonals of the posttest. This record of achievement is similar to that obtained in other instruction experiments.

The way in which the successful *S*s carried out their performance was striking. Children not only put the checkers in the correct holes, but they preserved the accompanying moving around of each checker along with the appropriate nodding of the head. The performance of 3 who failed is also interesting. They were all children who had done relatively poorly on the pretest of the diagonal (0 or 1 of the 5 checkers placed appropriately). The difficulty in the training seemed to be in getting the children to attend closely. They seemed unwilling or unable to watch the entire demonstration carefully. Hence, they tended to pick up some superficial aspect of the demonstration and exaggerate it. One child, for example, wandered the checker around the board making very exaggerated head shakes but still ended up in putting the checker in the wrong hole. The impression of the difficulty being attributable to a failure to attend was so great that *E* was reluctant to stop; he felt that if the child would only look, he couldn't help get it correct.

Discussion

Although this experiment warrants careful replication, the results are sufficiently impressive to warrant the conclusion that nonverbal instruction of a Montessori type can lead to the ability to construct the diagonal. As we have previously provided evidence that it is the development of conceptual knowledge that permits this reconstruction (Chapter 5), it may be inferred that this training had resulted in the development of conceptual knowledge of the diagonal. Conceptual knowledge is, therefore, not necessarily verbal knowledge.

What the children learned in this experiment is quite different from what they learned in the first training experiment (Chapter 4) under trial and error with reinforcement. In that case learning was extremely slow, temporary, and failed to transfer; in this case the learning was rapid and it transferred to the opposite diagonal. It is clearly a more effective means of instruction than simple operant conditioning. Why is it so effective?

As was pointed out above, at the time the observation was made I had no adequate way to describe the method. All the sliding around of the checker and the accompanying head shaking, I took to be mere stylization which had no instructive value. To anticipate the final chapter of this book, I would now describe the process as not just showing the child the finished pattern, not just "modeling" the correct process of putting the checkers in the correct holes, but of showing the child, in the context of each checker-placing decision, what the alternative moves were and how to choose between these alternatives. But lacking a theory, I could not adequately observe and record an objective fact![11]

If my tentative conclusion as to what is involved in learning from the Montessori method is true, it may permit a somewhat more enlightened form of experimentation on these methods. The central feature of the method, I have suggested, is that the teacher anticipates the alternatives between which the child must choose in his attempted reproduction. The teacher then shows to the child, by modeling, what these alternatives are and how the child is to choose between them. The child equipped with this new information can reconstruct the diagonal.

However, these alternatives and the choice between them could be indicated by means of language or by other means. The point is that at some level the information obtained from watching a good demonstration, hearing a comprehensible sentence, and from the feedback from one's own performance are equivalent. There is no point in doing further experiments just to show that on the whole the Montessori method is better or poorer than a verbal method or any other method; the results simply reflect which group managed to get more of the information of relevance to the posttest into their program in the interval. Rather it is important to find answers to such questions as, "What information is critical?" and "What are the alternative means of treating the child so that he apprehends that information?" Is any particular method more appropriate to some particular unit of information? Do different methods make different assumptions about the child, i.e., have different prerequisites for learning?

Moreover, if this position stands up to critical argument and further experimentation, it provides an account of why a Montessori method works and, for that matter, why a verbal method works. Equipped with such an account, it is no longer legitimate to attribute to the methodology per se the intellectual effects it produces. There is therefore, no reason to dogmatically embrace a methodology whether it is of a Montessori performance type or of a verbal skills type.

[11] This is intended as a blow to the empiricist tradition that assumes that the observations or facts are neutral and directly apprehended, while theories are built out of relating these facts. In this case just the opposite occurred.

7

PERSONAL AND CULTURAL EXPERIENCE IN CONCEPTUAL DEVELOPMENT: THE ACQUISITION OF THE DIAGONAL IN EAST AFRICA

> . . . in which we examine the effects of a primitive African culture, both in terms of the general experience and the ordinary language of the culture as well as in terms of the formal schooling experienced by some of the children, and in terms of the child's acquisition of diagonality.
>
> . . . and in which we conclude that the experience of the children, especially as codified in the formal schooling, are strong determinants of intellectual growth, particularly the differentiation of spatial knowledge. We do not suggest, however, that the structure of intellect of nonwestern children is thereby primitive, but rather that development occurs to meet the requirements of the physical and cultural environment.

In the preceeding chapters we have documented how the child's conceptualization of an event is influenced by the way in which the culture, particularly as formalized in instruction, articulates the event. Thus, the question, "Where does the criss-cross start?" articulates or draws to the child's attention the fact that it begins in the corner. We have also shown that this articulation is not provided exclusively by the language; for example, if a red checker is in the corner of the diagonal, the child may suddenly notice that this is where the diagonal starts, a fact that had previously gone unnoticed.

We now turn to the more general question of how the child's experience in our ecology and our western culture, plus his human nervous system interact to produce such conceptual knowledge as we have considered here. This problem may best be studied by contrasting an aspect of development in our culture with the same development in another culture in which it is likely to proceed quite differently. The Logoli and Kipsigis tribes of Kenya are ideal for this purpose. The appearance of their environment is radically different from ours, as are the demands placed upon the children. Before we examine specifically what effect this may have on the acquisition of diagonality, consider the problem of language, culture, and intelligence more generally.

The extent to which one's world view, or Weltanschaung, is influenced by one's culture, as coded in the language, is shown in Snell's (1960) account of the Greek's discovery of "mind." Homer had no one word to describe the mind or soul,[1] but rather a whole set of words, used in different contexts that more or less covered the same domain. For example, in providing a reason for Telemachus' going to seek Ulysses, his father, Homer could not say, "He decided or he thought and acted thus and so," because there was no concept of mind as the agent of decision. Rather he says that the goddess of wisdom, Athena, came and told him to do thus and so. Somewhat later, the Pre-Socratics invented the general concept of mind, perhaps to distinguish it from another concept they invented about the same time, body. This permitted them to talk of being of the same mind, of being in conflict, of reflecting, and of making decisions. Snell says:

> Homer is unable to say "half-willing, half unwilling." Instead he says, "He was willing, but his *thymos* was not." This does not reflect a contradiction within one and the same organ, but the contention between a man and one of his organs; we should compare our saying, "my hand desired to reach out, but I withdrew it." Two different things or substances engage in quarrel with one another. As a result, there is in Homer no genuine reflection, no dialogue of the soul with itself (p. 19).

Again,

> It is easy for us to say that Clacus pulled himself together, that he recovered his self-control; but Homer says and thinks, nothing of the sort; . . . If Homer . . . wants to explain the source of an increase in strength, he has no course but to say that the responsibility lies with a God (p. 20).

The discovery of mind was perhaps the original psychological break-

---

[1] Nor did they for that matter have any general term corresponding to our word "body".

through. It is possible, however, that we are misled by our own concept of mind when we say "I made up my mind," as Ryle (1953) has pointed out; and we are clearly deluded when we say, as one young child did recently, "I didn't want to, but my mind made me do it."

There are contemporary primitive societies that apparently get along without the concept of mind. Thus, Greenfield and Bruner (1966) report that Wolof bush children in Senegal do not distinguish between their own thoughts or beliefs about things and the objective statements themselves. They could answer the question, "Why is such and such true?" but not the question, "Why do you think such and such is true?" They find the latter question puzzling in the same way that Homer would have found puzzling the question, "Did Telemachus decide to go and seek his father?"

The language is the most direct means of examining the Weltanschaung common to a culture. The language is closely tied to the referents or objects and events in the environment, and it reflects the needs and interests of the language community. There are, understandably, more words for snow among the Eskimos and more words for language among the linguists. Similarly, because of the regularity of fiscal inflation, there is a word for devaluation in our culture, but no word for valuate upward. Anthropological linguists have provided many interesting examples of this. In our culture, the color spectrum is divided along three dimensions: hue, saturation, and brightness. For other cultures it is broken up in quite a different way; for example, the Hanunoo divides the spectrum along only the two dimensions: brightness (black to white), and wet-dry (red to green) (Conklin, 1955). Grammatical categories similarly are culturally determined; in our language, unlike that of the Hopi, nouns are sharply differentiated from verbs. The effects of this were noted by Whorf:

> We are compelled in many cases to read into nature fictitious-acting entities simply because our sentence patterns require our verbs, when not imperative, to have substantives before them. We are obliged to say 'it flashed' or 'a light flashed', setting up an actor IT, or A LIGHT, to perform what we call an action, FLASH. But the flashing and the light are the same; there is no thing which does something, and no doing. Hopi says only *rehpi* (1956, pp. 262–263).

Different cultures, therefore, as reflected in their language, draw conceptual and linguistic distinctions in radically different ways.

But there are very different inferences that may be drawn from these observations. For example, Levy-Brule (1922) observed and took as indicative of the structural organization of primitive man's mentality a parallel fact. He noted that the primitive man uses different words for walking, depending on the direction, upon the sex of the walker, and upon whether he was going into or out of a house. He concluded that they had no abstract concept of walking, and that their thinking was therefore more concrete. However, this conclusion overlooks one critical factor. Language evolves to serve the distinctions that the culture takes as critical. As Roger Brown (1958) pointed out, an event comes to be described, not objectively, but at the level of social utility, that is, in a manner most compatible with the frequency and general use in the culture. We could add, in a manner that most clearly differentiated an event from the culturally significant alternatives. Hence, one culture may be expected to draw some distinctions and omit others in a way that is quite different from another culture.

A radical alternative to this point of view is that language changes from culture to culture, but cognition remains the same. Cole, Gay, Glick and Sharp (1969) found that while the linguistic biases of the Kpelle of Liberia did not influence their ability to solve the transposition problem, it did predict children's ability to give a verbal account of their choice. From this they infer that it is only in the accounting or communicating of the products of thought that language differences become primary. They did however, find that the ability to solve the problem was significantly influenced by schooling.

In spite of the substantial differences in the ways in which peoples describe the world, it is still a controversial question as to whether these differences affect the perception of the people involved. Certainly, accounts of the history of ideas, including Snell's, imply that it does. Moreover, as we stated earlier (Chapter 2), Gombrich (1960) has taken and defended the point that we see the world differently as a result of looking at artists' portrayals of the world, and that artists in different periods have viewed the world differently.

One of the more radical views of this relationship was stated by Whorf (1956, p. 213), "We dissect nature along lines laid down by our native languages." Brown and Lenneberg (1954) found that linguistic codability of a color patch was related to the ease with which that color patch could be selected from a set of alternatives. The authors conclude that the codability has its affect primarily through its effect on memory, not necessarily on the ease of perception itself. However, Segall, Campbell, and Herskovits (1966) have found that some nonwestern subjects were affected differently by some visual illusions, including the Muller-Lyer, than were their western subjects. They attribute these effects to the radical differences between the nonwestern visual environments and our own uniquely "carpentered world;" this ecology in turn specifies which perceptual cues are useful or valid.

It has also been suggested that language has a pronounced influence not only via the semantic categories, but through its structure. For example, Sapir (1921) argued that language was an instrument that may be used to reorder and to reflect upon our experience. Greenfield and Bruner (1966) have provided evidence for this alternative. After reviewing several experiments on language and perception they conclude that "Members of different cultures differ in the inferences they draw from perceptual cues, not in the cues they are able to distinguish (p. 90)." They hypothesize rather that language influences thought by providing a hierarchically organized lexicon that serves to organize the child's experience. In a card sorting classification test they found that children who could generate a general class word such as color, could shift to other class words such as shape or function as a basis of classification. Moreover, the production of the general class word was dependent on the culture, French versus Wolof in general, and on schooling in particular. They conclude that the differential advantage of a language on thought was determined not simply by the number of words in use but rather by the hierarchical structure of the lexicon.

We would agree, but that thesis may be misleading in two ways. First, it suggests that the hierarchical structures cannot develop without the language suggesting them to the child. While we do not know that this is false, it obscures the fact that there are at least three other equally plausible alternative accounts of the origins of hierarchically or logically organized thought.[2]

Second, one may question the generality of the effect of not having a hierarchically organized lexicon. Does it affect all thinking, or only that relative to the experimental task? There is some evidence that it is the latter; children from unschooled populations have sufficiently logically ordered conceptual systems to succeed with Piaget's conservation task if the task is administered in a medium that is familiar and of significance to the child being tested. Thus, Price-Williams (1961) in a study of conservation with Tiv children in Nigeria, found that all the Tiv children achieved conservation of both continuous and discontinuous quantity by age eight. Moreover, in a study of classification ability of these Tiv children utilizing

---

[2] The three alternative accounts of the development of logically organized thought that appear most plausible to me are: an increase in apprehension span (Pascual-Leone, 1967; McLaughlin, 1963), the internalization of actions (Piaget, 1954), and the development of spatial representation (Desoto, London and Handel, 1965; Olson and Baker, 1969; Huttenlocher, 1967). These positions have been reviewed elsewhere (Olson, 1970a).

indigenous materials, familiar plants, and animals, Price-Williams (1962) found little difference between the literate and illiterate (unschooled) children in the area. Both groups of children were required to classify first plants and then animals on the basis of such abstract qualities as edibility or domesticity, and to switch the basis of their groupings. He found that both literates and illiterates could succeed on these tasks at about the same rate, doing very well on grouping plants in terms of edibility, and quite poorly on grouping animals in terms of domesticity.

There are three criticisms one may make of these findings however. First, he has proven the "null hypothesis," an illegitimate statistical inference. Second, the plant groupings in terms of edibility are the primary evidence of an "abstract attitude," yet for this problem there is no developmental shifts, the $6\frac{1}{2}$ year olds doing as well or better than the 11 year olds on a task in which other developmental research would lead us to expect a step-wise shift at around age eight. Hence, one questions the validity of the item. Third, in dealing with the animal classification, task groupings are given primarily on "perceptible" properties such as color or size, as Greenfield and Bruner (1966) found to be characteristic of the perceptions of younger children.

The predominance of concrete or perceptibly-based groupings was not inviolable. Thus, Price-Williams found that "It is only with probing of the individual that the interrogator receives an abstract classification such as domesticity (1962, p. 58)." When children did give some indication of the grouping of domesticity, it was very rare for the child to use the appropriate linguistic classification *ilev:* "The distinction was acted out by curcuitious descriptions of animals that one found in the compound, . . . which did not attack one, and the like (p. 59)."

Thus, to this reviewer, although the evidence is somewhat ambiguous with regard to the presence of operational thought, it does lead us to conclude that children perform better on problems indigenous to their culture than on problems irrelevant or marginal to their culture.

This permits us to formulate a hypothesis compatible with the results of both of these lines of study. Intellectual development is not a matter of a simple and pervasive "abstract attitude" or "linguistic representation" but, rather, a matter of developing or differentiating those conceptual structures relevant to the demands of the culture. Thus, it seems most reasonable to hypothesize that "primitive" people do not simply lack logically organized conceptual systems just because they lack this one; in the same way the Greeks did not lack all logically ordered hierarchical systems just because they lacked a superordinate concept of mind. Rather, they have such systems as have evolved to serve the particular requirements of their culture. And, as we cited from Brown earlier, people do use words, invent them if necessary, to serve the purpose of differentiating some events from others with which they are in danger of being confused. Hence, we may infer that the primitive culture determines which elaborated conceptual structures will develop. The ones that are developed are coded in the language for the purpose of communication among adults and transmission to the young. But the lack of some such structure says more about the requirements of the culture than it does about the structure of the primitive mind. At what age these logical operations first develop in any culture remains an interesting question.

Schooling may be construed as a way of formalizing the culture; as such it plays a critical role in the elaboration or articulation of the child's conceptual world. Bruner *et al.* (1966) have suggested that this may be the case because schooling usually requires that the child learn and think about objects and relations in their absence. To deal with these same objects manipulatively and visually may occur at the level of "iconic representation," and not foster the growth of conceptual or "symbolic representation." He argues that

> . . . in order for the child to use language as an instrument of thought, he must first bring the world of experience under control of principles of organization that are in some degree isomorphic with the structural principles of syntax. Without special training in the symbolic *representation of experience*, the child grows to adulthood still depending in large measure on the enactive and ikonic modes of representing and organizing the world, no matter what language he speaks (1966, p. 47).

We shall review some of the evidence that schooling has a dramatic effect on intellectual development when we consider the results of the present experiment.

But even if it is at the level of the conceptual and linguistic categories that the culture has such an impact, does that exempt perception, one's basic mode of constructing reality, from the effects of language?

Two lines of recent evidence suggest how the latter may be possible. Sperling (1960) showed that the information that gets into the short term visual icon is much greater than that which ends up being encoded into long term memory. If a rectangular array of letters is tachistoscopically presented, an adult subject can report about 4 of them. But if a signal, in this case a high, medium, or low tone, is presented indicating any particular row of letters, that row can be reported. That is, the reporting may be restricted to 4 letters, but they may be any 4 from the visual icon.

This phenomenon fits well within the theory that perception is selective (Neisser, 1967). It is then a small step to argue that language is a strong determinant of which of the perceptual features are selected from the icon. That is, the language or the culture may determine which cues an adult attends to. Thus, if an adult indicates color while the child is looking at the object, this will determine that one of the limited number of features apprehended from the object is the color. This has been clearly shown[3] in a modification of an experiment originally suggested by Daehler *et al.* (1969) in which three colored lights fixed in three different positions were flashed on in some order. Children were asked to recall its order either in terms of the color of the lights or the position of the lights. If, while viewing, the child had verbally coded the color, his recall was high for color but low for position; if he verbally coded the position, his recall was high for position but low for color. Clearly, language determines what was coded in memory. That coding becomes even more critical when an event has dozens of optional codings, or dozens of aspects that may be attended. All aspects cannot be noted and language may be used by the adult or the teacher to indicate what should be coded and what may, for the purposes of that culture at least, be safely ignored. Note, however, in this case it is the language of the adult that influences a child's perception, not the child's own language, as has been implied by theories of language and thought (cf. Olson, 1970b).

Thus, in examining the effects of the culture on intellectual development, pertaining to the diagonal, we will focus on three aspects: the extent to which spatial and geometrical discriminations are required by the culture for such purposes as measuring, building, assembling, and fitting; the extent to which these required discriminations are coded in the language; and the extent to which these distinctions are built into the formal curriculum of the school.

EXPERIMENTAL DESIGN

This study examined the effects of two related East African cultures on the development of the ability to construct the diagonal. To this end the diagonal and related problems were administered to 143 children of the Logoli and Kipsigis Tribes in Kenya. The data was collected by Drs. Robert and Ruth Munroe, an anthropologist and a child psychologist respectively,

---

[3] Gail Crawford, Verbal coding in a visual stimulus recall task. Paper prepared for course Ed. 3200, Ontario Institute for Studies in Education, Toronto, 1969. This is actually a rediscovery of an effect described by Külpe (1904) at the turn of the century.

of Pitzer College under the auspices of the Child Development Research Unit, University College, Nairobi, the director of which is Professor John W. M. Whiting of Harvard University. The Munroes were assisted in this work in each case by a University College undergraduate who was a native speaker of the language.

The Logoli[4] are Bantu speaking people living north of Lake Victoria while the Kipsigis, speakers of a Kalenjin language, live on the highlands east of Lake Victoria. As the communities are less than one hundred miles apart, they are quite similar, consisting of generally fertile, well-watered areas, about 5000 feet above sea level, with rolling hills dotted by clearings and thatched roof houses. Both are subsistence economies based upon farming and animal husbandry.

Both tribes have had a limited exposure to western culture since colonization in the late ninteenth century. A majority of the men of both tribes have worked for wages at some time in their lives, and each community has a store from which such items as matches, tea, and sugar are purchased with East African coins. All the children studied would have seen such shops, and all could identify a shilling. Finally, the communities under study had schools which were attended by less than half of the children. The school program will be mentioned presently.

In spite of this influence, many basic indigenous patterns exist, such as some patterns of religious beliefs and the criterion of wealth; for the Logoli this criterion is land ownership, for the Kipsigis it is primarily ownership of cattle.

The most relevant feature, from our point of view, of both of these tribes in the nonrectilinear nature of their visual world. Houses are primarily round rather than rectangular, manufactured objects are rare relative to the West, and, especially for the Kipsigis, the land is largely unsurveyed. While there are numerous important differences between these tribes, they are both sufficiently similar to each other and sufficiently different from our reference group that, for some purposes, they will be combined.

Subjects

Subjects in the study were 143 Kenyan children, 97 Logoli and 46 Kipsigis, aged from 5 to 13 years, 61 of whom had never gone to school; the others had gone to school for 1 to 4 years. About one-half of the subjects at each age and grade level were girls.

---

[4] This description comes primarily from the descriptions of these cultures provided by Munroe and Munroe, 1967, 1968; Munroe, Munroe, and Daniels, 1969; Peristiany, 1939; Wagner, 1949; Manners, 1967.

Method

As in the previous studies reported herein, children were shown a pattern constructed on the Experimenter's checkerboard and were asked to copy the same pattern on their checkerboard. The same six tasks were used: the top row, the middle column, one row below the middle row, the right-oriented diagonal (/), the left-oriented diagonal (\), and the X pattern. As these tasks are an ordinal series, they were given in the order of increasing difficulty, with two trials per problem. Unlike the other studies, if the results on the first two trials were ambiguous, a third, and occasionally fourth trial was given. The testing stopped if the child failed repeatedly on any problem, it being assumed that if he couldn't solve the simpler task he would not solve the more complex ones. For this reason, 26 of the 143 Ss never attempted the diagonal problem. Scores were assigned on a simple pass-fail basis; a child making at least one completely correct copy in the two trials was called successful on that problem. Comparisons between groups were then made in terms of the percentage of children succeeding on each task. A multiple linear regression analysis was used to determine which factors significantly influenced the children's performance on the criterion task, the diagonal.

The problems were administered to the Logoli in Dr. Munroe's house, and to the Kipsigis in the houses and yards of the children, by the native-speaking assistants to Dr. Munroe. The instructions, as spoken in Luragoli, with their English translations were as follows:

Yiki nikibaho kicho. "This is your board."

(Place board standing in front of child.)

(The following instructions were repeated for each pattern. Each of 6 patterns was repeated twice. The child could not see the construction of the pattern, and the pattern was concealed while the child made his construction. Before presenting the next pattern, all the checkers were removed from the child's board.)

Olola pipcha yange? "Do you see my picture?"

Ulalomba ipicha kukibaho kicho ifanana niyange. "You will make a picture on your board which looks like mine."

Vititsa ku ekedete nukiri kutanga lilomba kicho. "Pass your finger over it before you start making yours."

Kalunu lomba ku ipicha ifanana niyange. "Now make a picture (on it) which looks like mine."

Equivalent instructions were presented in Kipsigis to the Kipsigis.

TABLE 7–1

CORRELATION MATRIX OF AFRICAN CHILDREN'S CHARACTERISTICS AND THEIR
PERFORMANCE ON TWO DIAGONAL PROBLEMS
$(N = 143)$

	Left-oriented diagonal	Right-oriented diagonal	Age	Years of schooling	Male	Female	Logoli	Kipsigis
	1	2	3	4	5	6	7	8
1		.73	.33	.37	.10	−.10	.19	−.19
2		—	.27	.40	.20	−.20	.20	−.20
3		—	—	.46	.07	−.07	−.10	.10
4		—	—	—	.03	−.03	.33	−.33
5		—	—	—	—	−1.00	−.12	.12
6		—	—	—	—	—	.12	−.12
7		—	—	—	—	—	—	−1.00

If $r \geq .195$, $p < .05$
If $r \geq .254$, $p < .01$

RESULTS AND DISCUSSION

The first phase of analysis yielded a correlation matrix showing the relation between the two criterion variables (the left-oriented diagonal and the right-oriented diagonal) and the factors of age, years of schooling, sex, and tribe. These correlations are presented in Table 7–1. This table shows that age, schooling, sex, and tribe are significantly related to success on one or both of the diagonals. Performance on the two diagonals is correlated .73.

More important are the results from the multiple linear regression analyses. This analysis is necessary because the predictor variables are themselves correlated. This procedure permits us to assess whether there is some unique variance accounted for by the variable after we have extracted all the effects due to all the other variables, that is, after the intercorrelation is taken into account.[5]

The performance on the right-oriented diagonal (Y_1) and the left-oriented diagonal (Y_2) is predicted by the following regression equations:

$$Y_1 = .355 + .067 \text{ age**} + .065 \text{ school*} + .103 \text{ sex} + .175 \text{ tribe*}$$

$$Y_2 = -.236 + .035 \text{ age} + .094 \text{ school**} + .195 \text{ sex**} + .151 \text{ tribe}$$

$$*p < .05; ** p < .01$$

[5] This analysis also permits us to claim that the differences reported in the graphs in the remainder of this chapter are statistically significant.

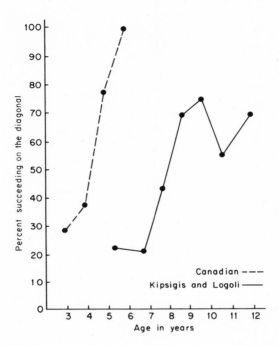

Fig. 7–1. Percentage of Kenyan and Canadian children succeeding in attempts to copy the diagonal.

Thus age, schooling, and tribe make significant independent contributions towards accounting for the performance of the children on the first diagonal; years of schooling and sex make significant independent contributions towards accounting for the children's performance on the second diagonal.

Consider now the relevance of these results to the problem of intellectual development. The most dramatic finding is the obvious difficulty that the African children have in copying the diagonal (Fig. 7–1). For them, the number of children succeeding reaches 50% only at age 9, and even by age 12 or 13, only 70% of the children are successful. On the other hand, 100% of the children in our culture succeed by age 6 (See Chapter 6). The moderate increasing success that the African children do have with increasing age cannot, from the graph, be attributed to either age or years of schooling. There is obviously something about the culture that makes it possible for American and Canadian children to look at the diagonal, code, and reproduce it, that is lacking to the Logoli and Kipsigis; moreover, there must be something that accounts for the gains that do occur there.

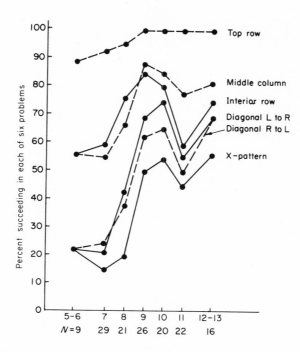

Fig. 7–2. Percentage of Kenyan children succeeding in each problem from ages 5 to 13.

Note, first, that it does not appear to be something about the strangeness of the medium or the checker-placing ability. This is indicated by the percentage of children succeeding on each problem over the age levels tested, as shown in Fig. 7–2. Virtually all the children succeeded on the first problem, and all the problems order for difficulty in the same way that they do for Canadian *S*s. Moreover, an examination of their errors, like those of younger Canadian and American children, shows that their productions were not random. The children had simply failed to note or code, at least as it influenced their constructions, some aspect of the pattern that we consider critical. Thus, several children in copying the vertical column through the middle, constructed a horizontal row through the middle. On a second try they may do the same thing, apparently judging that their performance was as close to the criteria as they could make it. As with our Canadian and American children, they had most difficulty with the diagonal. Typical errors in the African children's attempts to copy the diagonal are shown in Fig. 7–3.

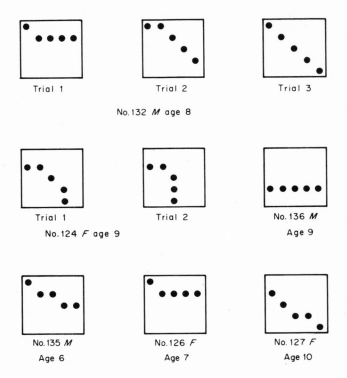

Fig. 7-3. Typical errors made in the reconstruction of the diagonal by Logoli and Kipsigis children.

An account of the specific types of errors that occur may be possible, but in the absence of any more elaborate conjecture we may at least note that the children's productions are influenced by the model that the children have just looked at and run their fingers over; they seem unable to respond to all the critical features of the diagonal.

We shall now consider in detail each of the factors that may account for the development: age, schooling, experience in the culture, spatial experience, sex, and the ordinary language.

Age

The effect of increasing age in accounting for the acquisition of diagonality is somewhat ambiguous. As the regression equations showed on the first diagonal, age was a significant factor. That is, it accounted for some

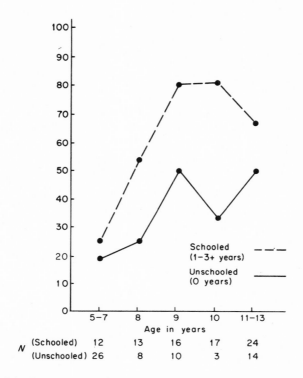

Fig. 7–4. Schooled versus unschooled children's performance on the diagonal at each age level.

variance after the effects of schooling were removed; on the second diagonal, it did not. The effects of age on the performance of the first diagonal with schooling removed are shown in Fig. 7–4. While the effect is statistically significant, it is not marked; the performance of even the oldest children is less than 50%. Increasing age is clearly not a sufficient account; if it were, there would be no difference between the schooled and unschooled, or between the African and the American samples. From this we infer that while age, and the general experience it implies, is a significant factor in this development, it is a relatively minor one. (The theory that intelligence grows regardless of the substance or content on which it feeds would seem to suffer a set back in the light of this evidence.)

Schooling

The effects of years of schooling on the ability to copy the diagonal for Logoli and Kipsigis boys and girls is shown in Fig. 7–5 and 7–6. These

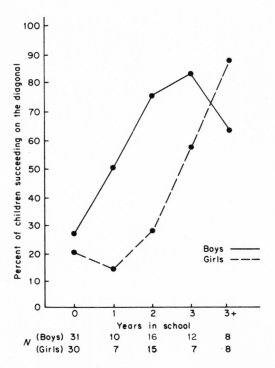

Fig. 7–5. Percentage of Logoli and Kipsigis boys and girls succeeding in copying the second diagonal as a function of years in school.

figures show that schooling is strongly related to success on diagonal ($r = .37$, $p < .01$); it is, in fact, the major factor. The marked sex difference will be commented on later. Note, however, that the number of children with one year of schooling is small compared to those with no schooling, and that may account somewhat for the sudden jumps that occur at that point in Fig. 7–6.

The fact that the curves never reach 100% is puzzling since they do reach that in our Canadian and American subjects.[6]

The regression equations reported above showed that the effects of schooling when separated from the effects of age were highly significant for

[6] In view of the fact that scores appear to drop off for boys after 3 years schooling, it is tempting to conclude that no boy with any sense would stay in school past the third grade anyway, a conclusion that passed for wisdom in some circles a few decades ago. However, John Whiting (personal communication) has pointed out that both of these tribes put a high value on education. It is not known if the children do also.

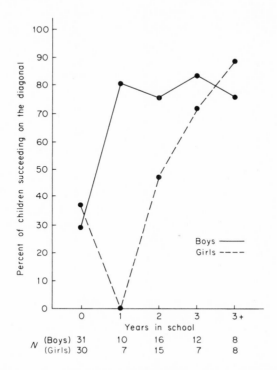

Fig. 7–6. Percentage of Logoli and Kipsigis boys and girls succeeding in copying the first diagonal as a function of years in school.

both the first and second diagonal. As Fig. 7–4 showed, the gains that do occur with age are primarily attributable to schooling.

Schooling, however, is too complex a process to have much explanatory value. Are its effects general or specific to the curriculum? An examination of the primary curriculum shows that it is remarkably western in length (9½ months) and orientation, and includes two 30-minute periods per day of reading and writing of the mother tongue, approximately one period per day of English, mathematics, physical education and games, as well as some arts and crafts, religion, science, and social studies. The mathematics involves more attention to number than to geometry. The teacher's guide (Francis, 1965) suggests that some attempt be made to have children in the first standard sort square, circle, and triangle shapes, and to have children fold papers into such shapes as baskets and windmills. The difficulty of following these latter instructions, coupled with the general unpreparedness of the teachers, made it somewhat unlikely that students actually succeeded at these enterprises. Probably more important are such school activities as drawing, and copying and discriminating words, letters, and visual forms. It is reasonable to infer that in learning to differentiate forms that he would normally treat as equivalent, the child's conceptual systems are markedly developed. That this development proceeds relatively slowly is indicated by the fact that most Logoli children cannot read after two years of schooling (Munroe, personal communication).

The results obtained in this experiment correspond to those obtained by several other investigators, in that years of schooling were found to be highly related to the ability of Wolof children in Senegal to conserve (Greenfield, 1966), of Wolof children to use hierarchical classifications (Greenfield, Reich and Olver, 1966), of South African children to solve a spatial-geometrical problem of the Raven's Matrices (Schmidt, 1960), of South African children learning to sort pictures of objects by function rather than color (Evans, in press), and of the Kpelle's ability to solve the transposition problem (Cole, Gay, Glick and Sharp, 1969).

General Experience

Note now the less formal aspects of the physical and cultural environment, and how they affect development. Although a good proportion of the Logoli houses and at least some of the Kipsigis are now rectangular, their preponderance of round thatched houses marks a sharp contrast to our own "carpentered world." The general nonrectangular quality of their physical environment, relative to ours, would tend to make an elaborate system for designating the slight differences, such as those involved in the diagonal, irrelevant. More critical is the fact that the children of these tribes do not play with building blocks and drawing games that occupy such a large proportion of our children's time. The Munroes have noted that the Logoli do indulge in the same types of creative fantasy that Piaget described as characterizing young children, and they do play rule games, some of which are so subtle that some observers have failed to note that there was any activity going on at all. The general point remains that the objects and events in their environments are not conducive to the development of elaborated or articulated conceptual systems for representing space.

Language of the Culture

The extent to which these distinctions are coded in the language is indicative of their importance in the culture, that is, their use in differentiating objects. In this light, it is remarkable that there are no words, at least in the judgement of our informant, in Luragoli, the language of the Logoli, for any of the following: square, triangle, circle (round), diagonal, rectangle, or straight line jointing the opposite corners. There is a word *inungi*, meaning straight, which also corresponds to the words for pole and road. This word has the same root as *muringi*, which means pious or righteous (upright). The other relevant word is *kona*, meaning corner, and it is obviously borrowed indirectly from English through Swahili. In other words, the language of the culture provides for very few of the distinctions critical to the construction of the diagonal, and one of the few that is available, *kona*, has been borrowed from English!

Tribe

There is a significant positive correlation between being Logoli (as opposed to Kipsigis) and the performance on the second diagonal; the correlation on the first diagonal is almost significant. (See Table 7–1). While some of the superiority is undoubtedly due to the fact that the Logoli have had more schooling (Table 7–1 shows that there is a significant positive correlation between being Logoli and the number of years of schooling), the tribe makes a significant, independent contribution towards accounting for the performances on the first diagonal. Both greater anthropological knowledge and further research may be necessary to clarify this difference. It does, however, indicate that greater attention should have been focussed on how they differ from each other, and not only how they both differ from our own culture. Racial differences in these studies have not been implicated; we have neither empirical evidence nor theoretical basis for such an implication. If such differences do have an effect, they are clearly minor factors relative to the substantial effects of schooling.

Other factors

There is some evidence, moreover, that general motor and spatial experience is instrumental in the child's being able to construct the diagonal. The Munroes noticed the large sex difference in Logoli children's ability to copy the diagonal (See Fig. 7–5 and 7–6). They sought an account of this marked superiority of the boys in terms of a culturally defined sex role. Female Bantu children are generally expected to stay nearby to assist adults in their work, such the care of siblings. Spot checks by the Munroes confirmed that this was the case for girls more often than for boys. Since they are expected to assist in these tasks, girls are less free to wander about exploring the countryside. Thus, again by spot check, the Munroes found that in free time boys were found to be further from home than were their matched girls. The differences were significant.

Most interesting was the fact that when the sample children were tested on another spatial task, the copying of block designs, the children who had been more distant from home in the above observation period were significantly more proficient at the task than those who had been less distant. They go on to say:

> Probably the most persuasive evidence here in support of the hypothesis comes from the fact that only two girls had been further from home on the average than their matched boys, and these two were among the three girls who were better at block building than their male counterparts (1968, p. 5).

It seems, then, that we must attribute at least some of their competence to general experience in looking and finding their way around, rather than to specific instruction. The reasons for the boys' greater experience is probably a function both of the cultural expectancies, as the Munroes suggest, and of the greater activity and exploratory levels of males that De Vore (1965) has found to be characteristic of various primate groups, and that D'Andrade (1966) has found to be most common in various human cultures. The male superiority is just the opposite of what is usually found on school-related tasks, but is typical of the male superiority on various spatial ability measures. (Maccoby, 1966; Garai and Scheinfeld, 1968). It is noteworthy that such marked sex differences appear in a culture so different from our own. This evidence is the first known to this author, and has shown that at least part of this superiority may be attributed to patterns of experience. Even in this case, however, it must be remembered that these experiential differences have less effect than schooling.

One other finding may deserve comment. Fig. 7–5 and 7–6 suggest that boys improved radically in the first year of schooling but little thereafter; girls showed no improvement the first year, yet gradually reached the same level as the boys. In line with our earlier reasoning, it may be tentatively suggested that the environmental exploration engaged in by the boys constitutes a readiness for instruction such that they capitalize quickly on the modest amount of training provided. For the girls, who tend to lack that early experience, the first year of instruction merely provides the beginning of readiness for the subsequent years of instruction. The quality of this instruction plus the lack of usefulness of this knowledge in the culture as a whole would conspire to keep this learning at a rather low level.

CONCLUSION

In this study, we have examined the effects of the physical and cultural environment on the development of a conceptual system for dealing with the diagonal. First, the general experiences of the children in the physical world appear to have an effect on this development in that Logoli children who did a large amount of exploring and finding their way around in geographical space, in this case mostly the boys, were better able to code and copy the diagonal than children with less experience. Second, the language of the culture is highly related to the conceptual distinctions the children are capable of making. Corresponding to the Logoli difficulty with the diagonal is the fact that their language has a striking lacuna or impoverishment of geometric or spatially-related terms; one of the few they do have has been adapted from the English. This is a clear confirmation of the hypothesis outlined in the first part of this chapter; the language of the culture acts as an informal curriculum to the child which indicates to him what aspects of experience should be attended to and what may, for the purposes of that culture at least, be safely ignored. But the formal aspects of the culture, particularly schooling, play a clearly dominant role in the development of these conceptual structures. While schooling is the dominant factor in East Africa, vis-a-vis the diagonal, it is not in North America where most of the children are able to copy the diagonal before the formal schooling begins. They have, however, discriminated, described, defined with language, and drawn with pencils relatively fine and elaborated visual forms. Moreover, as we found in our instructional experiments, this development was not a simple matter of growing older or of more observation but, rather depended upon the culture's way of breaking up or representing these forms. The role of the culture, therefore, seems inescapable in the development of at least this form of conceptual knowledge. But from this fact we may make either of two divergent inferences.

The first and the more generalized one is that these Kenyan children do so poorly on these tasks because their general cognitive development has not been elaborated under the systematic influence of language to yield a higher level of operational thought, or symbolic representation. From this point of view, the system as a whole is concrete, undifferentiated, and unsuited for the intellectual types of tasks that are the stock and trade of the formal school. This position resembles that of Cassirer (1923); Levy-Bruhl (1922); and Greenfield and Bruner (1966).

The second type of inference is that the elaboration of a child's conceptual system that permits him to deal with the types of problems studied here is not indicative of his general level of intellectual development. The notion of general level of development, from this point of view, may be inappropriate. It may be the case that the articulation of a conceptual system to deal with the diagonal is somewhat specific to these kinds of tasks (or the medium in which one is working). Hence, a child may be unable to cope with the diagonal but he may do quite well on some other tasks like class inclusion in apportioning foods, planning routes to a goal, and so on.

There is some anthropological evidence, based on both the Logoli and the Kipsigis, for this alternative. For example, Munroe, Munroe, and Daniels (1969) state that for the Kipsigis, for whom the ownership of cattle is so critical, the men of the community could probably give the life history of every cow in the community. Larry Baldwin (personal communication) reports that for the Luo, a nearby tribe, kinship relations and terminology are so well differentiated that adults who are strangers can arrive at a common ancestor after only a few questions, much like the 20-question game strategy employed by older American children.

Although the research reported here began with the first of these assumptions, namely that one such task as this is representative of a broad range of intellectual performance, the second alternative appears more reasonable. That is not to say that the diagonal is not representative of anything at all but, rather, that it is not symptomatic of intelligence in general. Historically, these alternatives have been described as answers to the question "Is intelligence a unitary factor?" This question has continued to intrigue psychologists. If it is a unitary, we would expect that all the answers given to all types of problems would have a similar deep structure; that is, could be characterized in the same way. This is in fact the inference that has been drawn from the relatively poor performance on intelligence tests made by children of nontechnological, primitive cultures. It has long been granted that these intelligence tests may be inappropriate to the culture, requiring a rough, sometimes impossible translation, familiarity with two-dimensional representation of three-dimensional space, and so on. For this reason, test items like those used in this study, as well as those like Greenfield and Bruner's could be considered as more valuable.

However, even with these kinds of tasks it now becomes clear that children's knowledge is markedly restricted. Whether their poor performance on their conservation task and the diagonal task is symptomatic of a general conceptual lack, or specific to tasks not relevant to the requirements of their culture, is impossible to decide from these experiments. The evidence for the specificity of the retardation that we have considered from Price-Williams (1961, 1962), is complimented by the inference drawn by Levi-Strauss (1967) from a study of the intellectual structure underlying kinship, religion, mythology, and art:

> . . . the kind of logic in mythical thought is as rigorous as that of modern science, and that the difference lies, not in the quality of the intellectual process, but in the nature of the things to which it is applied . . . we may be able to show that the same

logical processes operate in myth as in science, and that man
has always been thinking equally well; the improvement lies, not
in an alleged progress of man's mind, but in the discovery of
new areas to which it may apply its unchanged and unchanging
powers (p. 227).

This conclusion seems most plausible in view of the variety of results we
have considered. Experience is absolutely essential to the development of
intellectual structures, particularly experiences systematically provided by
a parent or in a formal classroom, but this development is not a completely
general abstract attitude running through all thinking. Thus, children who
have elaborate conceptual structures for sorting foods, seeds, kinfolk, and
mythology, may lack the conceptual distinctions critical to the performance
of other intellectual tasks such as the construction of the diagonal. Development is the process of elaborating within the limits of his capacity, those
conceptual systems evolved by the culture. Thus, we conclude that the
demands imposed on the child by both the physical and cultural environments in terms of the differentiation and organization of objects and events
determine the structure and elaboration of the child's relevant conceptual
systems. The language evolves to correspond to those distinctions and
groupings that are critical to the culture. That is, the language develops to
the extent that it is useful to differentiate an event from those alternative
events with which the culture does not want it to be confused. That
evolution appears to be specific to a conceptual domain. As we saw earlier,
the presence of a superordinate term for mind did not imply the presence or
absence of such organization in other conceptual or semantic systems.
Language is a formative factor in intelligence to the extent that it is used
for the purposes of instruction—in directing the child's attention to those
ecologically valid cues that the culture has selected for attention. As such
this process is not dissimilar from that described by Gombrich regarding the
evolution and transmission of forms in art. But we shall return to a
consideration of the more specific question of the role of language in
instruction, and the more general question of the role of the culture in
intellectual development, in the concluding chapter.

8

LOOKING, SEEING AND KNOWING—EYE MOVEMENT STUDIES

> . . . in which we find that 4-year-old children see and know less than 6-year-old children because they carry out a less extensive visual search . . . and in which we find that younger children carry out a less extensive visual search because they have less of an idea of what to look for. When they know what to look for, their visuals earch appears to be indistinguishable from that of older children.

If what one looks at or focuses upon is a good indication of what one sees, it should be possible to detect differences in the way a pattern is viewed by children for different purposes at different developmental levels. In the course of examining the problem of how children perceive and reconstruct the diagonal, two studies on visual search were carried out. Because of methodological difficulties involving the collection and analysis of the data, and because of an inadequate conception of what variables to control, these studies must be considered as exploratory and the results considered as tentative.

In an interesting study that inspired the present investigation, Vurpillot (1968) presented four- to nine-year-old children with pairs of pictures of houses. Each house had six windows which varied in their appearance, one window of one house having, for example, a flower pot, while the corresponding window of the other house has curtains. The children were asked to judge if the houses were the same or different. Young children compared the corresponding pairs of windows in a fragmentary and unsystematic way, judging the houses to be different if they hit upon a difference, and judging them to be the same if they hit on a similarity. Older children compared all pairs of windows before judging the houses as the same, but they compared them only until they found a single difference before judging them to be different.

If the type of pattern of search that Vurpillot has described could be detected in younger and older children's viewing of the diagonal it may account for the poor performance of the former in their attempts at reproduction. That is, the younger children may conduct a less adequate visual search and hence see fewer of the features of the model; their attempted reconstructions are therefore inadequate. It would moreover, provide evidence in line with Maccoby and Bee's (1965) hypothesis that was discussed in Chapter 6, namely that younger children perceive fewer attributes of the model.

As we have argued in earlier chapters, it is possible that the perception of such figural patterns as the diagonal does not depend on the detection of a set of discrete attributes in the same way that the perception of a house does in Vurpillot's study. For this reason we have examined the eye-movements of young children in viewing two types of stimuli, pictures of houses somewhat similar to those of Vurpillot, and pictures of geometric patterns, including the diagonal.

It is possible moreover that the fragmentary character of young children's visual search that Vurpillot reported is due to their limited expectancies as to how the alternatives may differ. Once they become aware of the critical features, even young children may make a more complete sequential search.

The questions for which evidence was sought were the following:

1. How do young children go about recognizing a familiar stimulus such as a house or a diagonal?

2. Is the pattern of visual search different for stimuli possessing a specific feature list, such as a house, than for stimuli apparently not possessing such a feature list, such as the diagonal?

3. Does the visual search depend on the use to be made of the resulting information for such purposes as recognition, as opposed to reconstruction?

4. Do children who know how to reconstruct the diagonal view the the diagonal differently from those who do not?

5. Is the visual search a function of the alternatives among which a child must choose in a recognition task?

METHOD

Subjects

Fifty-seven[1] children, aged 4-4 to 7-3 years, drawn from a nursery and a public school in Newton, Mass.,[2] were presented with the pattern stimuli

[1] This number does not include 5 children for whom the film record was so poor that no analysis of it could be made.

[2] We are indebted to the staff and students of Underwood School and the Lutheran Church Nursery School, Newton, Mass. for their cooperation.

including the diagonal. These subjects were assigned randomly to two groups, a third group being added near the end of the experiment. Group 1, the recognition group, consisted of 26 children: 14 boys and 12 girls, aged 4–4 to 7–3 years, with a median age of 6–1. For purposes of analysis the 12 4- and 5-year olds, median age of 5–6, were divided from the 13 6- and 7-year olds, median age of 6–8. Group 2, the reconstruction group, consisted of 27 children: 12 boys and 15 girls, aged 4–6 to 7–1, with a median age of 6–2. For this group, as well, the 10 4- and 5-year olds, median age of 5–3, were divided from the 17 6- and 7-year olds, median age of 6–6, for purposes of analysis. Group 3, added near the end of the experiment, consisted of 4 children, 3 girls and 1 boy, aged 6–6 to 7–3, with a median age of 6–11.

A subset of 13 of these children, 7 boys and 6 girls, aged 4–4 to 7–3, with a median age of 4–11, were subsequently presented with the pictures of houses. For purposes of analysis the 8 younger *S*s, median age 4–7 years, were divided from the 5 older *S*s, median age 6–5 years.

Materials

All the stimuli consisted of pictures and patterns attached to the front of a black cardboard sheet 11 × 12 inches through which a 1¼-inch camera hole had been cut ½-inch below center. These black cardboard sheets (slides) bore highly contrastive pictures of 3 kinds:

1. A targeting stimulus composed of a white cross radiating out from the camera hole,
2. Five geometric patterns composed of white dots 1¼-inch in diameter set inside a 9-inch square white border. The patterns formed by the dots were similar to those employed in other parts of these studies: a top row, a left edge, a row next to the bottom row, a left-oriented diagonal, and an X pattern. The positions in the 5 × 5 matrix not occupied by the white dots were occupied by grey dots of the same size, except that the camera hole replaced the dot immediately beneath the center dot.

The materials that *S* was to reconstruct or recognize after viewing these stimuli were presented on the optical table to the right of *S*. These materials consisted of one or two of the checkerboards used in previous studies which had been painted black and furnished with white checkers to correspond to the visually presented stimuli. When not in use this equipment was kept covered by grey cardboard.

3. Five houses approximately 6½ inches × 9 inches of identical form, orientation, and coloring. The houses consisted of a basic "my house," and four variations: one was missing the door, another was missing the chimney,

Fig. 8–1. "My house."

in another the window above the door had an altered shape, the last had two living room windows rather than the expected three. In all cases the camera hole resembled a round window under a central gable (see Fig. 8–1).

Apparatus

The General Electric television camera, equipped with a Makro-Kilar 1:28/90 lens, was used for observing the eye from the distance of 10 inches. The resulting image was displayed on a 7 inch × 5 inch Miratel monitor.

A 35mm Bell and Howell movie camera type A–7, equipped with a Bell and Howell size 6 filter lens, EFL 1 inch T2.2 (f/2), with an aperture set at f/8, was used to film the picture off the monitor from a distance of 8½ inches. By means of a Low Ripple Battery eliminator and charger from Electronic Instruments, the power of the motor which ran the camera was reduced to 12 volts, resulting in a filming speed of 7.25 frames per second. Films were Kodak Plus X Pan, ASA 125. The beam of light illuminating the stimulus was provided by a General Electric Mardi-Gras Movie Light.

An optical table supported and aligned the chin rest; the stimulus holder and the movable arm supported the TV camera. The stimulus holder was black and U-shaped with grooves in the vertical sides into which two stimulus cards, one behind the other, could be inserted from the top. Also on the optical table to S's right were the checkerboards used in S's recognition and reconstruction of the visual stimuli. This apparatus was kept covered when not in use by means of a grey cardboard.

Procedure

The method used for recording eye movements was developed by Dr. Norman H. Mackworth (1968). A 35mm motion picture records the corneal reflection of the stimulus; the area of the stimulus that is reflected on the center of the pupil is the area that the S is fixating at that moment. The usual method involving the direct filming of the eye requires that the position of S's head be fixed. To permit the equipment to be used on younger Ss whose head position cannot readily be fixed, Dr. Mackworth added a television camera and a monitor. The television camera is continuously "live" and the focus is altered by E until a clear picture results on the monitor. At this point the critical stimulus is presented and the eye movements are filmed from the monitor.

Each child was seated on a chair which was adjusted until his chin rested comfortably on the chin rest at a distance of 10 inches from the frontally-presented stimulus. The stimulus holder had two stimuli, one immediately behind the other; the front one bore the focusing stimulus, the cross, which could be lifted vertically to expose the critical stimulus. A floodlight behind S brightly illuminated the stimulus, while leaving the remainder of the room and S's face in relative darkness. This had the effect of making the white portion of the stimulus clearly reflected from the unlit cornea of the S's left eye.

Immediately behind the camera holes of the stimulus cards was the lens of the TV camera. This camera was continuously focused by $E2$ by means of viewing an adjacent monitor. The eye movements were filmed by $E3$ with a 35mm movie camera from a second monitor behind S; $E3$ also recorded the performance of S on the concurrent tasks and the film footages used for each subject and each stimulus. The test was preceded by a short training period during which children were familiarized with the constraints imposed by the camera and the requirements of the tasks. These requirements varied between groups as follows:

Group 1 (Recognition). It was explained to the child that we were going to show him some pictures of some white checkers in a black checkerboard. He was to look carefully at the picture and then choose, from the patterns at his right, the one that looked the same as the one he had seen above.

Group 2 (Reconstruction). Again it was explained to the child that we were going to show him some pictures. However, these Ss, after viewing the picture, were to attempt to make a pattern on the checkerboard to their right that was just like the one they had seen above.

Group 3 (Recognition-Alternatives First). As for Group 1, Ss were to tell which of the two patterns set to their right was like the picture that was exposed to them above. However, in this case they were shown the alternatives between which they must choose before they were shown the stimulus pattern.

For all three groups, the first three geometric patterns were used as stimuli for the practice session, which continued until the children could carry out the required tasks. Eye movements were filmed only for the two trials on each diagonal and X pattern. Stimuli were presented in the same order for all Ss.

Following the completion of this series, 13 of the children were selected to view the houses. For this section of the experiment Ss were told that behind the targeting stimulus (the cross) there was a picture of a house that they were to pretend was their house. They were to look at it very carefully because they would then have to choose the picture of their house from some pictures of other houses that were almost the same as their house. In order to facilitate the child's comprehension of these instructions an analogous game was played in which S was to recognize his ball from a set of balls that varied in color, size, shape, and the presence or absence of dots. A correction procedure was used in this practice task only. When S mastered this task he was shown the houses stimuli. On the presentation of the first stimuli, E emphasized, "Pretend that this is your house. Look at it carefully so you remember it." Following subsequent stimuli, E asked, "Is this your house? Is this house the same as the first one I showed you?" If S said "No, it's not my house," or "It's not the same as my house," E followed by asking, "How do you know? How is it different from your house?" If S said "Yes," the next stimulus was presented, with the admonition, "Look

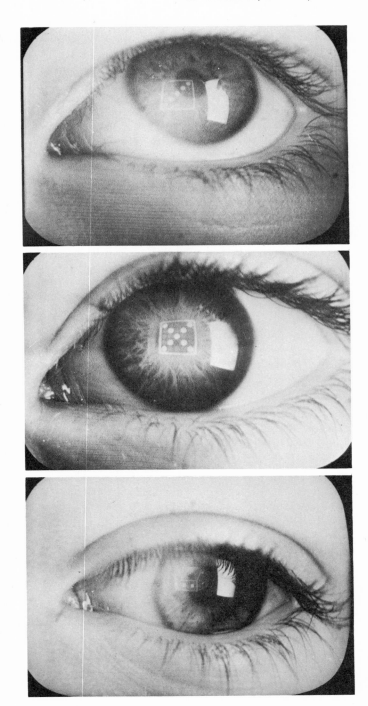

carefully now." *S*s went through the series of five pictures twice in the same order. The following day-four of the more cooperative younger *S*s were recalled in order to examine the effects on their eye movements with *E*'s indicating to them the features they had overlooked in their earlier search of the stimuli.

Scoring

The film recorded the reflection of the viewed stimulus in *S*s left eye. The part of the stimulus reflected from the center of the pupil indicated the fixation point on the stimulus. Two frames of the film record are shown in Fig. 8–2. Displacements of the reflected stimulus from frame to frame indicated the shifts in fixation point and duration of each fixation.

While judges could agree on the location of the fixation on the basis of examining the film (they agreed 87% of the time in assigning the fixation point to a position on a 5×5 scoring grid) the quality of the data was reduced by the occasional head movements and camera focusing errors which rendered about 5% of the film unanalyzible. In judging the position of the focus in the houses stimuli, judges agreed on 92% of their judgements.

RESULTS

Recognition of Houses

In the 5 older *S*s 65% of the judgements were correct; for the 8 younger *S*s only 19% of the judgements were correct (Mann-Whitney: $U_{8,5} = 1$; $p < .01$). That indicates that, especially for the younger children, houses resembling the original model in all but one feature were judged to be the same. The second time through the set of pictures, the older children's performance jumped to 85% correct, the younger to 33% correct (Mann-Whitney: $U_{8,5} = 4$; $p < .01$). Again the youngest children tend not to notice the single altered feature when the search is on the basis of memory. This corresponds to Vurpillot's (1968) finding that both younger and older children do well in recognizing things to be similar, but younger children do less well in judging them to be different—presumably because of the less adequate visual search.

Fig. 8–2. Sample frames from the eye-movement film record showing the child looking at the top corner and at the center of the geometric patterns, and at the door of the house.

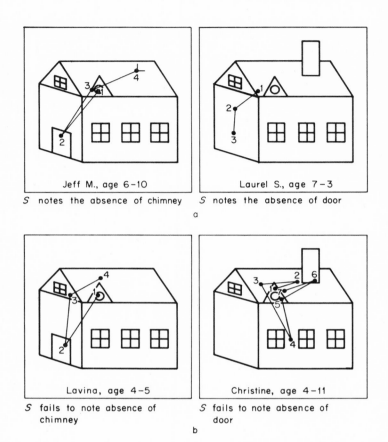

Fig. 8–3. A short visual search may be the result of either (a) the S's knowing what to look for or (b) his not knowing what to look for.

This performance is reflected in the fact that in the original viewing of the model, 4 of the 5 older Ss focused upon all four of the features that were critical, whereas only 1 of the 8 younger children examined the model sufficiently to hit on these features. The actual mean number of features fixated by the older children in the two viewings of the base stimulus "my house" was 3.6 out of the four; for younger children it was only 2.58 (Mann-Whitney: $U_{8,5} = 5.5$; $p < .02$).

However, for neither group of Ss was the set of features a good indication of the features S would remember to look for in the remaining pictures. Thus, although 10 of the children focused on the chimney while looking at the model, only 3 of them thought to look at that position of the card when the chimney was absent. Those 3, incidentally, all recognized that card as being different from the original model. This pattern of forgetting is also shown by the fact that, for the younger *S*s, less than 1 in 4 of the features that had been changed or omitted was subsequently detected, although almost 3 of the 4 had been focused upon in the original viewing of the model. The biggest problem therefore appears to be in knowing what to look for.

Of greater interest was the pattern of search. Although the degree of search on a picture varied from a low of 3 to a high of 34 fixations, that variance was not systematic. Some children looked at a stimulus briefly because they immediately knew what to look for as shown in Fig. 8–3a; others searched briefly because they did not know what to look for as in Fig. 8–3b. (The reader may have to refer back to Fig. 8–1 to interpret these figures.) The longest searches were conducted by older *S*s who appeared to know something was wrong but were unable to isolate it at first. (See Fig. 8–4.) These long searches occurred primarily on the fourth and fifth cards.

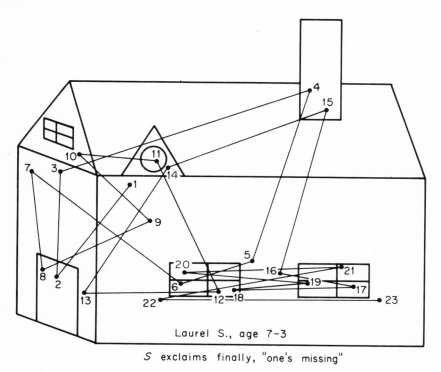

Laurel S., age 7–3

S exclaims finally, "one's missing"

Fig. 8–4. An intensive visual search in the area of an anomaly prior to its detection.

Fixation time, the length of time spent looking at a single feature of the picture, varied from .14 seconds (1 frame) to 5.4 seconds (39 frames). The recordings were not, however, sufficiently precise to detect minor changes of fixation in the order of $\frac{1}{2}°$ of visual angle that have been measured in other studies (Mackworth and Bruner, 1969). On the average, fixation time was greater for younger Ss (0.81 seconds) than for older Ss (0.69 seconds) a difference that approached significance (Mann-Whitney: $U_{8,5} = 8; p < .10$). While there appeared to be some consistency within Ss, the variability was more striking. All Ss had an occasional long fixation. These long fixations frequently occurred in the detection of an anomaly in the picture. For example, on one picture, Outi (aged 4–6)

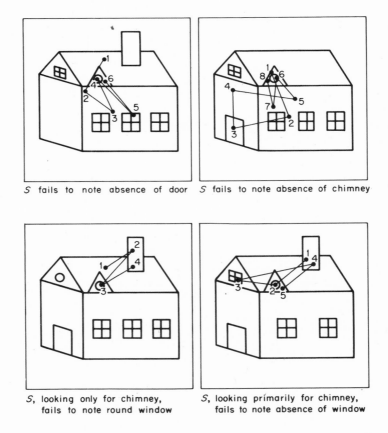

S fails to note absence of door S fails to note absence of chimney

S, looking only for chimney, S, looking primarily for chimney,
fails to note round window   fails to note absence of window

Fig. 8–5. Visual search patterns of Chris, aged 4–4, before and after learning that the chimney is a critical feature.

had an average fixation of two frames per fixation; yet on the fourth fixation, upon hitting the anomalous round window, the fixation lengthened to 38 frames (5.25 seconds). Similarly Jiff (6–10) and Donna (6–3) had long fixations upon first detecting the reduced number of windows. On some occasions it was the fixation immediately following the critical one that was noticeably longer. A third interesting pattern is also shown in Fig. 8–4 in which Laurel (7–3) took nine consecutive fixations and 49 frames (6.75 seconds), scanning back and forth across the two windows immediately before announcing that "One is missing." A similar finding is reported by Mackworth and Bruner (1969) who found that fixation times were longer when comprehension as opposed to inspection alone was required.

How the child is using that long time period is uncertain; it may be used for more viewing, or for remembering and comparing in terms of the original model. Kahneman, Beatty, and Pollack (1967) have provided evidence that when an adult is involved in a demanding mental task, he is functionally blind; that may be the case here—the eyes do not move, not because he is continuing to pick up information but because he is processing the information he has available.

When the children knew what to look for, the search pattern of even the younger Ss dramatically changed. Chris (4–4) had a fragmentary search pattern somewhat typical of the younger group: a general search followed by a judgement of "the same" even when the chimney was absent, as shown in Fig. 8–5a and b. After he had concluded his search, E pointed to that part of the roof and said, "Look here." Thereupon, S immediately exclaimed "Oh, it has no chimney." Fig. 8–5c and d show that his search pattern from

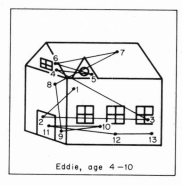
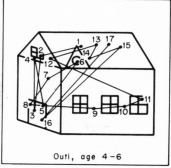

Eddie, age 4 –10   Outi, age 4 – 6

Fig. 8–6. The elaborated visual search patterns of two young children after they knew what to look for.

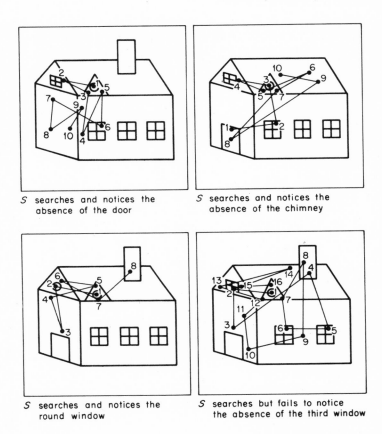

Fig. 8–7. The visual search pattern of an untutored but older child, Chuck, aged 6–8.

that point on reflects his new knowledge; he now searched the pattern only to see if it had a chimney. If it did he said it was his house, if it did not, he said it was not his house. In another case, Karen (4–4), after noticing the absence of the door on the second stimulus, went through the remainder of the series looking only for the door. By correcting a child on each of the trials and pointing out the critical feature, even the 4 four-year olds with whom this was attempted have been able to search sequentially for all 4 features as illustrated in Fig. 8–6. This elaborated visual search contrasts sharply with that of the young *S*s who were not informed (See Fig. 8–3b).

Under this form of tutoring the younger children's search came to resemble that of the untutored older children, a typical case of the latter being shown in Fig. 8–7.

In general, it appears that young children do pick up less visual information than older children because of a less adequate visual search. Part or all
of this limitation is due to not knowing what to look for; when they do
know what to look for their search resembles that of older *S*s. However,
these characteristics may apply primarily to stimuli with a highly specific
feature list, such as the houses stimuli.

Recognition of the Geometric Patterns

Recall that *S*s in this problem were to view the diagonal model while
their eye-movements were filmed. Following this, a cardboard screen was
lifted, revealing two alternatives: the diagonal, and an array like a diagonal
except that the lower right checker was moved one space to the left. On the
first trial, for the older *S*s (6 and 7 years old, $N = 13$) 85% of the judge-

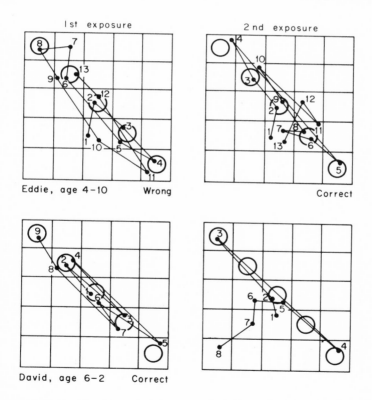

Fig. 8–8. Patterns of visual search on first and second exposure to the diagonal for a
younger and an older child in the recognition group.

TABLE 8–1

DEGREE OF VISUAL SEARCH OF TWO GEOMETRIC PATTERNS AS A FUNCTION OF THE AGE
LEVEL OF THE VIEWERS AND OF THE SUBSEQUENT USE TO BE MADE OF THE INFORMATION

| | N | Fixations | | Differences |
		Mean	s.d.	t
Recognition of diagonal				
Younger	12	10.17	3.33	2.90**
Older	13	6.69	2.40	—
Combined	25	8.36	3.36	—
Recognition of cross				
Younger	12	10.33	3.62	1.71
Older	13	8.07	2.70	—
Combined	25	9.16	3.36	—
Construction of diagonal				
Younger	10	11.50	3.32	2.25*
Older	17	8.00	3.97	—
Combined	27	9.30	4.12	—
Construction of cross				
Younger	10	12.90	4.01	2.06*
Older	17	8.88	5.02	—
Combined	27	10.37	5.10	—

** $p < .01$
* $p < .05$

ments were correct; for the younger Ss (4 and 5 years old, $N = 12$) 33% of
the judgements were correct ($X^2 = 6.84; p < .01$).

What accounts for these differences? Some typical patterns of visual
search for the two groups are shown in Fig. 8–8. Statistical comparisons for
the groups on the four tasks are shown in Table 8–1. Does how carefully
older Ss looked at the pattern account for this difference in performance?
On the contrary, Table 8–1 shows that the older children looked at the
diagonal pattern significantly less than the younger children. It is possible
that the younger Ss scanned so unsystematically that they never fixated
upon the critical checker. This possibility was examined by counting the
number of Ss in each age group that actually fixated the critical checker,
that is, the checker that would differentiate the two alternative patterns.
(Ss at this time did not know that that checker would turn out to be
critical.) However, for both groups the fixation on that checker was very
low, 3 out of 12 of the younger Ss, and 2 out of 13 of the older Ss. Neither
age group tended to fixate on that part of the pattern; yet the older ones
who tended not to look got it right anyway, while the younger ones did not.

Those few who did look at the critical checker appeared to do no better than those who did not—only 1 of the 5 who looked at it got the recognition task correct.

Even the younger children are able to conduct an appropriate visual search when they know what to look for, however. This is indicated by the fact that when they are given a second look at the stimulus card, after they have seen the alternatives between which they must choose, younger children do look at the critical checker. The number of Ss looking at the critical checker for the younger group increases from 25% to 64%; for the older from 15% to 54%. For the two age groups combined this value is significant ($X^2 = 5.78; p < .02$). And all the children use the information so selected; 100% of the children in both groups select the correct alternatives after the second viewing.

This same pattern is shown in the modified recognition group. Recall

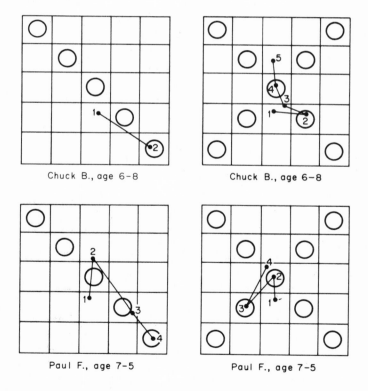

Chuck B., age 6–8   Chuck B., age 6–8

Paul F., age 7–5   Paul F., age 7–5

Fig. 8-9. Pattern of visual search of the diagonal and X pattern when children saw the alternatives before they were exposed to the model.

TABLE 8–2

EXTENSIVENESS AND ACCURACY OF VISUAL SEARCH AS A FUNCTION OF THE SUBSEQUENT
PERFORMANCE IN A RECOGNITION AND A CONSTRUCTION TASK

		Fixations			Accuracy		
	N	Mean	s.d.	t	Mean	s.d.	t
Recognition of diagonal							
Successful	15	6.93	2.67	2.92**	2.80	.98	2.31**
Unsuccessful	10	10.50	3.17		3.70	.78	
Construction of cross							
Successful	12	11.25	5.28	.78	5.0	1.73	2.35*
Unsuccessful	15	9.67	4.82		3.46	1.64	

** $p < .01$
* $p < .05$

that Ss in this group were shown the alternatives that they would subsequently have to choose between before being exposed to the stimulus pattern. Under this condition the visual search was radically abbreviated, requiring an average of only 2.75 fixations, less than half that taken by their age peers in the first condition. Moreover, all Ss viewed the critical checker. The visual search pattern for two Ss under this condition is shown in Fig. 8–9. In view of the fact that there were only 4 Ss in this condition, this finding must be considered tentative. It is, however, compatible with the "second look" data presented above.

If one ignores the age differential and compares Ss who succeeded in recognizing the diagonal with those who failed, one again finds that the degree of search is unrelated to success in the subsequent performance. The tendency is just the opposite, the 10 children who got it wrong had significantly more fixations than the 15 who got it right. This is shown in Table 8–2.

The data for the recognition of the X are less helpful. Recall that the alternatives for the X pattern were the X and a +. With only one exception, all the children succeeded in their recognition of the X pattern. Since all Ss recognized the X pattern, it is impossible to examine how visual search is related to recognition. However, on the first visual search of the X pattern prior to viewing the alternatives, some differences between younger and older Ss appeared that were parallel to those found in the recognition of the diagonal. Table 8–1 shows that the younger Ss took somewhat more fixations on the X than the older Ss, a difference which approaches significance. The greater search of the younger Ss is also reflected in the fact

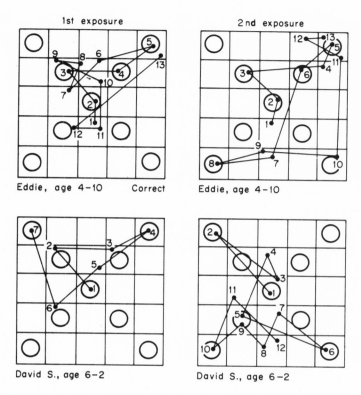

Fig. 8–10. Patterns of visual search on first and second exposure to the X pattern for a younger and an older child in the recognition group.

that they focused on slightly more of the 9 critical checkers than did the older ones (3.75/9 compared to 4.09/9). This greater visual search was, however, unrelated to the ability to recognize the X pattern; essentially all *S*s succeeding in that recognition.

The visual search tended to be more elaborate for the X pattern than for the diagonal. However, as shown in Table 8–1, for the younger children there was no noticeable change while for the older ones, there was an apparent adjustment for the complexity of the pattern, the X being searched more than the diagonal. However, these differences are not statistically significant.

Typical patterns of visual search on the X pattern are shown in Fig. 8–10. Contrary to expectations there is little or no systematic outlining of the figures by the series of visual fixations.

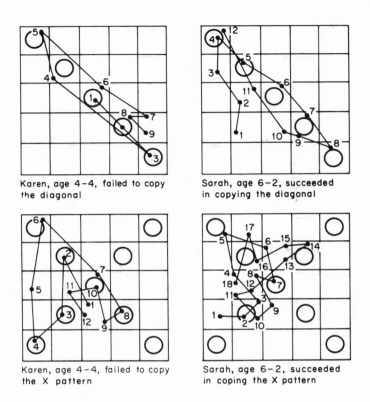

Karen, age 4–4, failed to copy   Sarah, age 6–2, succeeded
the diagonal   in copying the diagonal

Karen, age 4–4, failed to copy   Sarah, age 6–2, succeeded
the X pattern   in coping the X pattern

Fig. 8–11. Visual search of the diagonal and X pattern by a younger and an older child in the reconstruction group.

Construction of the Geometric Patterns

The visual search patterns for two Ss in the reconstruction condition are shown in Fig. 8–11. For the construction of the diagonal, only 4 of the 25 Ss at either age level failed to correctly copy the diagonal; hence it is hazardous to compare those who succeeded with those who failed. Some consistencies were noted however. Again the younger Ss search the pattern significantly more than do the older Ss. Similarly they focus upon a slightly larger number of the critical checkers (3.9/5) than the older Ss (3.4/5).

This degree of search before constructing a geometric pattern has two interesting contrasts. First, as can be seen from Table 8–1, the visual search of a pattern is somewhat greater when the task is reconstruction than when it is recognition. For the diagonal, these contrasts are 9.30 fixations compared to 8.36 ($t = .90$, n.s.); for the X pattern, they are 10.37 fixations compared to 9.16 ($t = .98$, n.s.). For the problems combined this difference approaches significance ($t = 1.82; .10 > p > .05$).

Second, the relation between the extent of the visual search and success in the construction of the patterns may be reversed from what it was in the recognition of the patterns. Recall that the successful *S*s looked less than the unsuccessful in the recognition task. For the reconstruction task for those who were successful ($N = 23$) there is a tendency to examine the model more (9.43 fixations), as compared to the small group who failed ($N = 4$), who made an average of 8.5 fixations. This slight tendency is worth noting only because it suggests a pattern which becomes quite clear in *S*s' attempted reconstructions of the X pattern.

The construction of the X must be considered as a complex problem for even 6- or 7-year-old children. Only approximately 50% of these children succeeded on it. Of the *S*s in the older group ($N = 17$), aged 6 and 7 years, 47% succeeded in copying the X pattern. Of the *S*s in the younger group ($N = 10$), aged 4 and 5 years, 40% succeeded. The substantial number of *S*s who passed and failed makes it possible to compare the visual search patterns of those who succeeded in their reconstructions with those who failed.

First, however, compare again the age differences in visual search. As for previous comparisons, Table 8–1 shows that the younger *S*s look at the model significantly more than do the older *S*s. The greater search of the younger children is paralleled by the fact that they fixated on a somewhat larger number of the checkers on the pattern. The younger fixated 4.84/9 checkers, the older 3.7/9.

Most important, however, is the comparison of the visual search of those who succeeded in the reconstruction of the X with that of those who did not. Table 8–2 shows that the 12 *S*s who succeeded in their reconstruction searched the pattern somewhat more than those who failed, though not significantly. However, when one considers the accuracy of the visual search in terms of the number of critical checkers, the *S*s who were successful in the reconstruction of the X pattern viewed significantly more of the checkers in the pattern than did those who were unsuccessful. That is, *S*s successful in their reconstructions of the X looked at the model more, at least more carefully, than those who were not. This is just the opposite of the findings in the relation of visual search to the recognition task.

Finally, as may be expected on the basis of a naive view of complexity, on the first exposure *S*s looked more at the X pattern than they did at the diagonal. Of the 47 *S*s who viewed both, 31 of them took more fixations on the X pattern ($X^2 = 4.78; p < .05$). As the order of presentation of these problems was not counterbalanced, this latter finding may not be dependable.

Recognition and Visual Search

One of the most consistent findings in all phases of the recognition problems was the extent to which the visual search is a function of the alternatives between which the viewer either knows or expects he must choose. In recognizing instances of "my house," as long as Ss assumed that general criteria such as the general shape and color of the house would permit their choice, the search was brief and general; this was true more for the younger than the older Ss. However, when they saw the information value of some critical features, the search became precise and consistent. This was clearly shown by the younger Ss who, having found out that the chimney was a critical feature, went through the remaining alternative pictures looking only for the chimney. Older children appeared to differ from younger children, not so much in their ability to carry out a visual search but rather in their initial assumptions of what to look for; the older Ss searched as if they assumed that any feature may be critical for selecting the model from the alternatives, while the younger searched as if they thought the alternatives from which they would subsequently differentiate "my house" would be radically different, involving such things as barns and castles. It is not unreasonable to expect that if these radically different alternatives had been employed, the younger would have done as well as the older.

The effects of the alternatives between which Ss must choose in the recognition problems is even more clearly seen in the geometric patterns. First, in the earlier "recognition" experiments (Chapter 5), Ss were able to recognize the diagonal even if they could not reconstruct it, yet in this study almost half of the Ss failed to recognize the diagonal by choosing it from the nondiagonal. Some of the difference may be due to the fact that the pattern was viewed from very close, thus requiring more visual search to see the whole configuration, but even more critical is the fact that the alternative to the diagonal was like the diagonal except for one checker. Once they was the context of alternatives, all Ss could recognize the diagonal as in the earlier studies.

Second, the X which could be construed as a more complex pattern in that it is more difficult to reconstruct, was recognized with almost no error. This relative ease can also be traced to the fact that the alternative differed in such a general feature as orientation, the X pattern having an oblique orientation, the alternative +, having an vertical orientation. This feature could be detected anywhere in the visual field, hence visual search would be quite irrelevant to it. Had the alternative been more subtly different, the performance of the recognition task could be expected to change to resemble that of the diagonal.

Third (for the recognition group on the diagonal), on the second exposure to the model, approximately three times as many Ss look at the critical part of the model as did on the first exposure before they saw the alternatives between which they were to choose. That is, their looking was a function of their knowledge of the alternatives between which they were to choose, not the stimulus per se. Similarly, in the modified recognition group, in which discriminable alternatives were presented first, the search was focused on the critical checker, the remainder of the pattern being virtually ignored. The primary variable in this account of visual search (what the viewer thought he was looking for; that is, his inference as to what the alternatives were likely to be) was therefore largely uncontroled. Yet, it is reasonable to conclude that the visual search is a function of what the S knows to be the alternatives between which he must choose, or if he does not know the alternatives, what he expects or hypothesizes to be the most likely set of alternatives. Visual search, then, follows the pattern that Garner (1966) finds to be characteristic of perception in general; specifically, that the perception of an event is a function of the perceived or inferred set of alternatives. The alternatives being entertained by the viewer account for another observation that would otherwise be anomalous. Once the children knew that the presence or absence of the chimney provided information for their judgements, they looked for the chimney even when it was absent (See Fig. 8–6). One is hard pressed to describe this behavior—it is not a response to a stimulus in the conventional sense because the stimulus is absent. It also strains conventional usage to describe it as "notices" since there is no stimulus to notice. These observations are comprehensible in terms of the hypothesis that the viewer has expectations of the alternatives, and even the nonoccurance of an event may provide information to choose between those alternatives. This property of perception has previously been described by Sokolov (1969), as the missing stimulus effect.

An implication of this point is that the term "recognize" may be somewhat of a misconstrual of the actual process involved. The act of recognition, judging a new event to be equivalent to some earlier event or model, does not involve re-cognizing or re-generating the entire original event—as an image theory may imply—but, rather, the choosing from some set of alternatives an event which may, for some purpose, be considered equivalent. This choice would presumably be based on some cues or features that had been selected or attended in the original event and not a copy of the total original event. This position has been clearly developed by Neisser (1967) and by Gibson (1969).

Construction and Visual Search

The important effects of the set of alternatives on recognition that have been discussed above would necessitate some revision of the relation between recognition and production, or perceiving and performing. There would be no one single thing as recognition; rather, it would be a function of its set of alternatives in each case. And, as we shall see in the final chapter, these differing sets of alternatives are implicated in construction of a pattern as well.

The extent and precision of the visual search before Ss knew what the alternatives were did show some consistencies. Ss tended to search somewhat more when the task was construction than when the task was recognition. The degree of visual search as a function of the subsequent use to be made of the information is summarized in Fig. 8–12. This is compatible with the hypothesis that the set of alternatives is greater; that is, more features are required for reconstruction than for recognition (Maccoby and Bee, 1965).

More important, however, is the fact that in the construction task, Ss could make some inferences as to what the alternatives were, the alternatives being specified by the empty holes. In the recognition task, on the other hand, Ss had no basis whatsoever on which to infer what the alternatives were. This may be the most reasonable way to interpret the fact that more looking, at least more precise looking, at the model was related to success in reconstruction of the X pattern. Ss with the necessary compe-

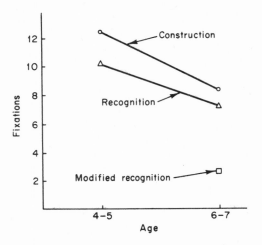

Fig. 8–12. Visual search as a function of the subsequent use to be made of the information.

tence could examine the model, noting the positions of the checkers or components relative to alternative positions that the checkers could be in. That is, they would know what to look for; hence, successful Ss examined the model more appropriately. On the other hand, Ss in the recognition task, regardless of their competence, would not know what to look for; they have no notion of what the alternatives may be. Merely more looking turned out to be irrelevant. The lot of these children in looking at the model is similar to that of a naive expiricist looking at the world: "the chance is negligible that you will [observe and] measure the right things accidentally" (Miller, 1962).

This interpretation is also compatible with the suggestion made previously as to the nature of developmental changes. It is in knowing what to look for and in utilizing the information so obtained that accounts for the younger childrens' poorer performance, not the visual search per se.

CONCLUSIONS

It may be concluded that the older children saw more in their limited visual search of the diagonal than the younger children saw in their more elaborate search. But what they saw that the younger children did not see is very difficult to state. In line with the conclusions of the earlier chapters, it may be suggested that both groups note the general configuration but the older Ss, recognizing it as the diagonal, notice how the components, the checkers, give rise to the general effect of the diagonal; the younger, not knowing the concept of the diagonal, do not see it in terms of the specific components. Yet one of those components is crucial to the subsequent recognition. The difference, then, is not in the visual search but in the information drawn from it.

It was also the case that older Ss obtained this greater amount of information in less time than younger Ss. The finding that young children had larger fixation times has been previously reported by Mackworth and Bruner (1969) and by Zaporozhets (1965).

The pattern of visual search in both the recognition and construction conditions was extremely unpredictable, except in the modified recognition task, and hence provided very little information. It was expected that the actual pattern of visual search would vary dramatically between age levels, levels of competence in constructing the patterns, and in terms of the requirements of the task. For example, in extensive testing of childrens' ability to copy the X pattern it was repeatedly noticed by E that when the child was asked to run his finger over the pattern, as was regularly done to assure the child's attention, different pointing strategies were employed.

Older Ss tended to run their fingers over the two diagonals crossing in the middle. Younger children, however, tended to point out the pattern by beginning with the center of the X and tracing the 4 radii separately from the center to the corners. The visual search of the X was not so sytematically conducted. Very few of the records show any systematic outlining of the figures by the series of fixations, or, for that matter, any other comprehensible pattern. This finding may be contrasted with that reported by Zaporozhets (1965) who found an increasing tendency for older children to "outline the figure" with their visual search. Our finding however is compatible with the conclusion drawn earlier, that the visual search is a function of the child's expectations of what the subsequent alternatives are likely to be. As these alternatives were not controlled on the first exposure, each child was free to make up his own. As Zaporozhets (1965) does not report what the alternatives to the model being explored were, nor whether the child had previous experience with them, it is difficult to guess what regulated his Ss' visual exploration of the model.

Finally, consider how the pattern of visual search on the houses is related to that on geometric patterns. Recall that the houses stimuli were chosen because they possessed a clear feature list; window, door, chimney, gable window; on the other hand, the geometric patterns involved form features which may be apprehended as a configuration. Especially for the younger children the early phases of the visual search of the houses did not reflect the use of such a feature list. Rather, because the search was general and unsystematic, it appeared that they look for general color and form properties. This general search was reflected also in the tendency of these Ss to accept all the variants as cases of "my house." Similarly, in the search patterns of the geometric arrays the search appeared to be directed to general form and position properties, not to specific features. For this reason Ss could easily recognize the X pattern because the alternative differed by such a general form feature as orientation; but this was not true of the diagonal because the alternative differed by a specific feature, the dislocation of a single checker.

For both types of stimuli then, the original search tended to be conducted for general features; presumably those that would be relevant to the most probable differentiations and recognitions. Moreover, for both types of stimuli, once the Ss grasped the nature of the alternatives among which they were to choose, the visual search was readily adapted to those specific features that they thought would be informative; Ss began to examine specific features of the houses and the specific location of the critical checker. In line with the theory of selective attention (Neisser, 1967), it may be suggested that the examination of a stimulus is never done naively; it always reflects the assumptions of the viewer as to what cues are likely to be informative for subsequent purposes. Other evidence for this position has been provided by Yarbus (1967) who has shown how questions direct the visual search conducted by a viewer. The effect has been shown more generally in Sokolov's (1969) demonstration of the role of expectancies in the orienting response.

What happens with development, then, is that the older children make a more accurate estimate of the alternatives that are likely to occur and they anticipate the potential relevance of a set of features for choosing among this larger set of alternatives. This view is generally compatible with Mackworth and Bruner's (1969) conclusion that development is a matter of acquiring skill in selecting informative visual features. However, they imply that the informative areas of a photograph are objectively given and it is then a matter of the child coming to know how to search for them. Rather it is that any area of a photograph is informative depending on the alternatives between which the viewer thinks he must choose. Hence it is not that young children cannot quickly find the informative areas, it is that they don't know which areas are likely to be informative, that is, they are unable to infer a large or appropriate set of alternatives. For this reason the quality of the search is so easily improved when the child actually knows what the set of alternatives and the corresponding critical features are likely to be. Hence, it is what the child knows, both of the present context of alternatives and of the expected context of alternatives that determines what a child looks for and what he sees.

The ease with which children were alerted to the cues or features of the houses that would differentiate them may be somewhat misleading. It should be recalled that it is not an easy matter for either our young children or our unschooled Kenyan children to look back at the diagonal model and apprehend the required information. It is as if a long exposure to the requirements of our culture is involved in shaping up an awareness of what features are critical. We shall return to this point in the last chapter of this book.

9

THE EFFECTS OF AN EDUCATIONAL TOY ON
INTELLECTUAL DEVELOPMENT

> . . . in which the effects of a year-long exposure to a toy de-
> signed to teach the child to construct the diagnoal were assessed,
> . . . and in which it was found that the toy itself, without the
> diadactic instruction of the teacher, could promote at least this
> aspect of intellectual development,
> . . . and in which the prototype for a more elaborate toy that
> could be used for this purpose and for many others is developed.

It is merely an overstatement, not a falsehood, to say that a child is learning to be an architect by playing with his blocks. Yet, precisely what the child learns or how he learns from that play is a largely uncharted domain. In the preceding chapters we have shown how the development of conceptual operations can be produced through appropriately organized experience. While this experience is usually organized through the language of instruction, other forms of nonlinguistic experience have been shown to be equivalent in developing the knowledge underlying the child's construction of the diagonal.

This being the case, it should be possible to construct a nonverbal toy which would teach the child how to conceptualize or articulate the diagonal in order to construct it.

An educational toy may be considered as an aspect of the culture that has been simplified and organized in such a way as to enable a child to apprehend it more directly than he would through his ordinary experience. Perhaps all school curriculum may be so viewed.

Although there is, at present, no general theory of educational toys, three general considerations may be stated.

First, although the only requirement of a toy is that the child voluntarily plays with it, an educational toy should make a measurable contribution to some educational objective. Those objectives are selected on the basis of their appropriateness to the child's present level of development, to the relevance of that knowledge to other tasks likely to be faced by the child, and the general relevance of the discipline in question to the aims of a general education (Bloom, *et al.*, 1956). There is some evidence that spatial knowledge plays a substantial role in logical thinking. To cite an earlier conclusion:

> The most promising hypothesis regarding the relation between spatial and linguistic knowledge is that spatial knowledge provides a framework upon which at least some aspects of language may be built. This suggestion is compatible with the findings of DeSoto, London, and Handel (1965), that syllogisms are solved on a mental spatial grid and also with the fact that so much of verbal description involves a spatial metaphor. Some obvious and frequent examples follow: up, above, beside, enclosed, near, outcast, upper class, underdog. It seems highly likely that good spatial intuition is a necessary condition for the development of at least such concepts. It is also the case that the "unseeable" is frequently translated into a spatial image to facilitate understanding; this is clearly shown in the Watson-Crick model of an organic molecule. (Olson and Baker, 1969, p. 280)

Moreover, Huttenlocher (1968) has recently provided evidence that the rearrangements one can imagine oneself carrying out in space are closely related to what one can intellectually rearrange in solving verbal logical problems. As the ability to construct the diagonal is an aspect of spatial knowledge, it may be defended as relevant to an educational objective. This relation between spatial knowledge and reasoning ability may provide a reason for the inclusion of the study of Geometry in a general education. That reason is somewhat overstated by Plato in the *Republic*.

> [Geometry] . . . is pursued for the sake of the knowledge of what eternally exists, and not what comes for a moment into existence and then perishes . . . [and it] must tend to draw the soul toward truth and give the finishing touches to the philosophic spirit.

Second, general experience underlies the ability to profit from more formal instruction, although in a presently unspecified way. It was the older children in our samples who benefited from instruction (Chapter 6), and it was the more experienced boys of the Logoli who appeared to benefit most from the minimal amounts of instruction provided during the first year of schooling (Chapter 7). It would thus seem reasonable to provide more systematically for that experience through the provision of an educational toy.

Third, the provision of this experience may be more relevant to some groups of children than others. In a culture or a subculture, such as the Logoli and Kipsigis considered in the previous chapter, where both the physical environment and the language of the culture are biased against the spatial differentiations that underlie the construction of the diagonal, constructed or directed experiences provided by such a toy may be more critical. Or on an individual basis, children described as "low spatial ability" may be in greater need of and hence may benefit more from such experience than some other children; for the latter, the toy may be simply redundant.

In the preceding chapters, evidence has been provided that the knowledge underlying the diagonal is conceptual, that it is developmental, and that it is based on experience and/or instruction. The problem then is to design a toy that provides the child with a form of experience that produces an increase in conceptual development. Specifically, an attempt was made to design a toy that could be added to the toys in the nursery school, with which children could, and would, play independently, and which would produce an increase in their ability to construct a diagonal.

Two attempts were made to develop an effective educational toy. In both cases the methodology was to take two similar nursery schools, put the toy into one but not the other for some period of time, and then compare the children in the two schools on their ability to construct the diagonal. After the first experimental test, the toy was redesigned and evaluated in a second experiment.

Educational Toy I

The Toy

This toy was constructed in a way similar to the standard checkerboards employed in our experiments. The only difference was that the holes forming both diagonals were drilled 1/16 inch larger than the remaining holes. Special checkers, selected so as to fit snugly into only these holes were painted white. The toy was completed by putting black checkers into the remaining holes. The toy was therefore a puzzle; when assembled the white X clearly stood out against the black checkers in the background. When the checkers were taken out of the holes, the slight size differences were not noticeable and the child has to reassemble the pattern by recalling the pattern, or by trial and error.

Method

Subjects. This toy was tested twice. The first employed two urban Toronto nursery schools,[1] one serving as experimental, the other as control. The second employed the morning and the afternoon classes of a nursery school in St. Catharines, Ontario. Only those children from each group who were unable to construct the diagonal were used in assessing the effect of the toy.

Procedures. In both tests of this toy children were pretested on the top row, middle column, both diagonals, and the X pattern prior to the provision of the toy. Only those children who failed in their attempts to copy the diagonal were considered as critical to the test of the effects of the toy.

Upon completion of the pretests, the toy was placed in the room of the morning class which was arbitrarily chosen to be the experimental group; the afternoon class served as the control. Teachers were instructed to keep the toy in a prominent place but to provide no instruction on how to perform with it. If necessary, they could return the checkers to the correct holes if a child asked for help, or before replacing it on the shelf. Teachers were asked to keep a record of who played with the toy.

After the toy had been in the room for a set period of time, children who had failed on the diagonal on the pretest were given posttests consisting of two attempts at each the left-oriented diagonal, the right-oriented diagonal, and the X pattern. The pretest posttest interval for the Toronto groups was one month, for the St. Catharines' groups it was five months.

Results. As is shown in Table 9-1, in neither case did the toy have a significant effect.

TABLE 9-1

THE EFFECTS OF THE FIRST EDUCATIONAL TOY IN TWO FIELD TESTS

	Total	Subject Nondiagonal	Length of exposure	Posttest Pass	Fail	X^2
First field test						
Experimental	28	10	1 month	4	6	.38
Control	21	9	—	4	5	
Second field test						
Experimental	39	15	5 months	6	9	.68
Control	29	12	—	3	9	

[1] I am indebted to the staff and students of Bloor Street Nursery School and Sacred Heart Nursery School, Toronto, and Glendale Nursery School and Queen Elizabeth Nursery School, St. Catharines, Ontario. I am also indebted to Nancy Johnson, Susan Pagliuso, and Donna Crosson for their help in conducting the experiments reported in this chapter.

Discussion. Observations by the teachers and by E provided several possible accounts of why the toy had little or no effect. First, it appeared that children who could already construct the diagonal were the only ones who actually succeeded in getting the checkers into the correct holes. When the children who did not already know how to do it played with it, they usually failed, returning the toy with the checkers simply piled on top of it. This was traced to the fact that younger children did not appear to notice that the larger white checkers did not fit into the smaller holes, the slight resulting tilt of the white checkers being ignored. This problem could be remedied by using deeper holes and thicker checkers that would make the poor fit more salient. The task also appeared to be too difficult—involving the entire X rather than a single diagonal.

Second, the toy was not very attractive; hence, it was somewhat ignored. One teacher noted, "It isn't the most popular toy in the school."

Third, it appeared that the children who could already solve the puzzle were the ones who played with it.

EDUCATIONAL TOY II

The Toy

In order to circumvent some of the limitations of the first toy, a new toy was constructed that was improved in appearance and feedback properties. The new toy was constructed with a bright yellow plastic base checkerboard. The larger blue checkers to fit into the diagonal holes were $1\frac{1}{8}$ inch in diameter and $\frac{3}{4}$ inch thick, while the smaller red checkers for the remaining holes were 1 inch in diameter and $\frac{3}{4}$ inch thick.

Second, the checkers were made with such precision that, given their thickness, there could be no doubt that the larger checkers for the diagonal holes would not fit into the alternative holes. Two forms of this toy were made, one with larger holes for only one diagonal, the other with larger holes for both diagonals (i.e., an X pattern).

As with the first toy, the size difference of neither the holes nor the blocks was readily discriminable. Every hole was filled with an appropriate checker and the toy was then set on the toy shelf of the nursery school. Normally, the children dump out all the checkers and then attempt to replace them. While it is possible but unlikely that the puzzle be solved by trial and error, the economical solution is to note that the blue ones go in the diagonal holes and the remainder go elsewhere. This improved educational toy is shown in Fig. 9–1.

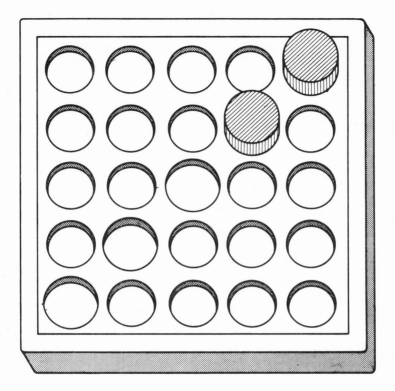

Fig. 9–1. The improved educational toy with two of the larger, diagonal checkers in place.

Method

Subjects. The *S*s in this experiment were taken from two nursery schools in middle-class areas of St. Catharines, Ontario. In Glendale Nursery School which was arbitrarily chosen to be the experimental group, and so had the educational toy, there were 37 boys and 30 girls ranging in age from 3–8 to 5–3, with a median age of 4–8. The Queen Elizabeth Nursery School, which was the control group, had 27 boys and 31 girls ranging in age from 3 to 5–11, with a median age of 4–7, (See Table 9–2).

Procedures. Unlike the preceeding study, no pretest was employed. However, the apparent similarity of the schools, the similar ages of the children, the equivalence of the groups in the preceeding study, and the relatively large sample size provide some assurance of the comparability of the groups.

Both toys were placed in the experimental school in September, 1968, and the testing was given in May, 1969. As before, teachers were requested not to provide any instruction on how to make the patterns, but simply to keep the toys, properly assembled, on the shelf, and let the children play with them as with any other toy in the school.

On the basis of some observations made about mid year by one of the Es,[2] two alterations were made in the procedure. First, it was clear that, as in the first study, children who had mastered the diagonal tended to repeat their play patterns, while many of the younger children chose not to play with the toy at all. To help remedy this, E, in the course of carrying out another experiment, had each child in the group play with the toy for about five minutes. Generally encouraging comments were made such as, "Do you like to play with that toy?" but no interference or instruction on how to construct the patterns was provided.

Second, E noticed that the problem was still too difficult for many of the children. While they no longer put the larger checkers into the smaller holes, they did the opposite. Once a small checker was in the larger diagonal hole, the younger children were frequently unable to correct the error. Hence, the smaller checkers were removed from the toy, only the larger checkers that could fit into the critical holes, those composing the diagonal or the X, were left. This appeared to make the problems considerably more soluble, although it increased the chances of solving it through trial and error.

Approximately 7 months after the toy had been placed in the experimental school all the children from both schools were tested individually on their ability to copy patterns on the checkerboard. As in other sections of this study, E constructed a pattern on his board, showed it to S who was asked to run his finger over the pattern; E's pattern was then removed, and S attempted to reconstruct it.

Each S was tested once on five different patterns in the following order: top row, middle row, left and right oriented diagonals, and the X pattern. If it was obvious to E that S did not understand the object of the game from his performance on the first pattern, E showed the original pattern to S and encouraged S to rearrange the checkers on his board until both boards looked the same. Then E proceeded to test S on the remaining four patterns.

As S attempted to make the patterns, E indicated on a scoring sheet the position of each checker. The patterns were first scored as follows: for each of the first 4 patterns, S received 1 point if all 5 checkers were correctly placed; otherwise his score was zero. Reversals were noted but considered

---

[2] Nancy Johnson diagnosed these problems and suggested these remedies.

incorrect. For the X patterns, S received 3 points if he reproduced the pattern correctly, 2 points if only one branch of the X was missing, 1 point if 2 branches of the X were absent, and zero points for any other configuration.

Results. Since the educational toy was designed to teach the concept of diagonality, only the scores on the diagonal and X patterns were analyzed.

To compare the groups' abilities to reproduce the diagonal from memory, each S's total score on both diagonals was obtained (a maximum of 2) and then at t-test was performed on these summed scores. It was found that the experimental group (Glendale—mean score of 1.19) performed significantly better on the diagonal patterns than did the control group (Queen Elizabeth School—mean score of .79; $t = 2.56$, $df = 123$; p. $<.02$). Similarly, the experimental group performed significantly better on the X pattern than the control group (mean scores, out of a maximum 3, of 1.42 and .81; $t = 2.53$, $df = 123$; $p<.02$). In the experimental class there were exactly the same number of correct copies of the right-oriented diagonal (40) as there were of the left-oriented diagonal. However, there were 14 reversals of the diagonal, that is, a construction of the left-oriented diagonal when shown the right-oriented one in the experimental group, and only 3 reversals in the control group. If these reversals are considered cor-

TABLE 9-2

THE EFFECTS OF THE SECOND EDUCATIONAL TOY

	N	Age range	Median age	% Succeeding on diagonal after exposure	% Succeeding on the X after exposure
Experimental					
Boys	37				
Girls	30				
Total	67	3–8 to 5–3	4–8	64.1	41.7
Control					
Boys	27				
Girls	31				
Total	58	3–0 to 5–11	4–7	39.6	24.2
				$z = 2.73$**	$z = 2.07$*

** $p < .01$
* $p < .05$

rect, as we have done in most of the other experiments, the difference between the experimental and control groups is even more striking; 64.1% of the experimental group received maximum scores on the diagonal as compared to 39.6% of the control group. The differences between groups in the percentage of Ss succeeding in their attempted reconstructions are shown in Table 9–2.

Discussion. In view of the comparability of the groups it may be concluded that the redesigned educational toy had an effect on the child's ability to reconstruct or copy the geometric patterns. As the toy then makes a contribution to the child's ability to deal with spatial or geometric forms, and as this latter may be defended as an objective of education, the diagonal toy may tentatively be considered as a legitimate educational toy.

In the course of carrying out the testing, several other observations were made. Children in the experimental group in the course of constructing the diagonal commented to the effect that "You got to put the little ones in the little holes 'cause if you put them in the wrong place they won't go." That is, several thought there were still size differences in the test checkerboard holes when in fact they were now identical. In one case this led to poor construction; the child apparently still had no mental model but pushed them around until they hit an appropriate hole. He used an inappropriate cue, size, to construct the pattern. In other cases, children believed there to be size differences, but put the checkers into the correct holes, one child remarking "It has to go in the right holes, like stairs. They won't fit in there, will they?" In this case the child did have the requisite knowledge of the pattern, the size cues now being incidental, and the memory of the form being critical. On the basis of the first observation it may be inferred that some children were constructing the pattern in a trial and error fashion, depending on the size differences to select the correct moves rather than their own internal plan. It also indicates that the children could not actually see the size differences in the toy itself.

Of even greater interest was the observation that not only did the experimental Ss succeed on more of their constructions than the control Ss, but even the unsuccessful children appeared to go about their attempts with noticeably superior strategies. Experimental Ss, for example, tended to put the first two checkers into the opposite corners, the next in the center hole, and then attempted to fill in the remaining spaces. The attempts at copying the X pattern tended to be articulated in a similar way. The occurrences of these strategies was too limited to warrant further analysis. It is possible, however, that these strategies provide a basis for the transfer effects of instruction—the child has some notion of how to proceed with a novel problem. This problem merits further more specific research.

Some tentative conclusions about the factors relevant to the effectiveness of this toy in particular and toys in general may be made.

1. The intellectual demands of the toy must be somewhat beyond the beginning abilities of the children. This lead must not be too great, as our task was before the smaller checkers were removed. For this game specifically it would appear to be wisest to set the game out with only the larger diagonal checkers. Once they mastered this task, the entire set could be utilized. Similarly, the toy with the single diagonal should be mastered before the one with the X is set out. The adult supervision required in pacing a child through these variations must be considered as one of the limitations of the toy.

2. A toy should be sufficiently visually attractive and intellectually challenging to provide its own motivation. The children left our toy on the shelf too much of the time for it to be considered completely successful. Simplifying the task as we did for the last month appeared to help somewhat. Alternatively a task having more options than a single correct solution may have had some advantage. Perhaps even more important is the teacher's apparent interest or disinterest in the toy. It was observed that after *E* had personally observed them play with that specific toy, children appeared to select it more often. We perhaps over-estimated the pure intellectual motives involved in toys of this sort. The toy may have had considerably more effect if we had informed the teachers as to which children particularly needed the experience and asked them to encourage these children to play with the toy occasionally. In the year following the experiment we found that the toy was judged by the teachers to be a valuable resource in the class; they showed considerable opposition to our repossessing the toy. We subsequently donated the toy to the school.

3. For an educational toy to produce learning or intellectual development, it must provide information, what, in other contexts, may be called reinforcement. As long as our toy was ambiguous, when it was not clear that the checker did or did not fit into a specific hole, no learning could occur. This is, in part, the one thing the toy does automatically; it tells or informs him if he is making an appropriate reconstruction of the pattern.

4. The knowledge acquired by means of the toy should have transfer value to related problems. We have presented some indirect evidence that the learning was not specific. The more basic question that is left unanswered is, "Does this learning through experience with an educational toy increase the child's subsequent ability to benefit from instruction?" As was suggested above it may have this effect either through developing general strategies for use in attacking such problems or through the acquisition of specific concepts which may be utilized in new contexts such as corner,

diagonal, square, etc. The question is all the more difficult in that there is no theory, at least to my knowledge, that specifies how what one learns from experience is related to what one learns from instruction. Bruner (1966) and Vygotsky (1962) have shown how they are different; in the concluding chapter an attempt will be made to show how they are related.

In general, the effects of toys and games on intellectual development and their potential role in education continue to be matters of speculation. There seems to be no limitation in principle to what could be learned through games, yet playing with a toy seems altogether too lighthearted an activity to be equated with education.

EDUCATIONAL TOY III

On the basis of the previous finding with the educational toy, a third toy was designed incorporating the successful features of the second toy and adding some new ones that increase the range of learning activities that may be accomplished by it and increase the motivational properties of the toy. While further field testing may be required, this last toy would appear to be most appropriate for actual production and marketing. The toy would be useful for both research purposes and as a functional toy for preschool and particular children, or even whole subcultures whose spatial or geometric knowledge is relatively undifferentiated.

The Toy

This toy is designed to teach children not only to copy or reconstruct the model of the diagonal, but also to copy a large set of spatial models. The models which are provided with the toy include single rows, columns, diagonals, X patterns, a square, rectangle, and some geometric patterns frequently used in such psycho-motor tests as the Bender-Gestalt. There is no limit in principle to the forms that may be taught by the toy.

Second, the toy may be used to teach strategies for locating and using information in problem solving. In an earlier study (Olson, 1966) it was found that strategies for information processing change with age, and that younger children made relatively poor use of the information in problem solving. This new toy is sufficiently versatile that these strategy problems could be carried out with the same toy. Again these strategy problems could be used either for research or instruction purposes.

Third, the provision of unspecified or free forms means that a researcher or teacher could easily add problems that they considered as having educational or research merit without altering the structure of the toy.

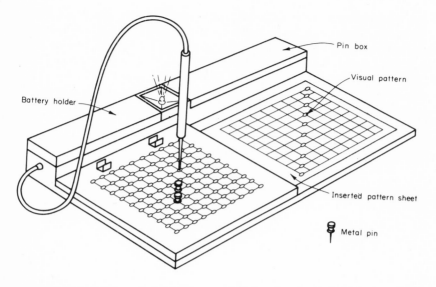

Fig. 9–2. Model of an electrically circuited version of the educational toy.

Both the versatility of the toy and its enhanced motivational value are due to the added electrical circuitry. A model of the toy is presented in Fig. 9–2. Basically, if the stylus is inserted into one of the perforations that corresponds to one of the positions indicated on the model, the light will come on; if it is entered into an inappropriate hole, the light will not come on. This control is achieved by the insertion of one of the interchangeable pattern sheets; part of this plastic sheet is inserted under the perforated grid and part of it remains in view to serve as a model. One series of the visual patterns corresponds in size to the copy that is to be made. The series differs in the form or pattern that is to be copied as was suggested above; as the studies of this book affirm, some patterns are more difficult to copy than others. A second series involves visual patterns that are reduced in scale; it is presumably more difficult to copy from a small model than from one of the same size as the copy. A third series consists of line-drawn models rather than point-by-point models. The fourth series consists of patterns set at various orientations to the copy. It is well known that it is more difficult to copy a model rotated 90° from the copy than one that is not rotated. This skill presumably underlies some conventional spatial ability tests.[3]

---

[3] I am indebted to Roland Olaon for his assistance in designing this toy.

The opposite task of pattern copying is map drawing. These alternative problems are created by inserting the pattern sheets upside down, thereby removing the patterns from view. In this case, the child would have to explore the perforations with the stylus and on the basis of his direct experience draw or construct a visual model. It is presumably more difficult to draw a map than to follow a map, but that relationship requires further research (Kershner, in press; Feldman, 1968).

Another feature of the toy is its optional "memory." It may be recalled that it was more difficult to copy a pattern on the bulbboard than it was on a checkerboard—a difference that was attributed to the fact that the checkers remained in view as an aid to memory, whereas the lights on the bulbboard went out. In this educational toy, this option was incorporated by providing a set of blunted metallic pins that could be inserted into the holes that the child had found to be a part of the pattern. This pattern of pins would then act as the "memory." Further, the child could confirm that he had positioned the pins correctly by touching them with the stylus; if they were correctly placed, the light would come on. Older children, further from the need for immediate confirmation, could reconstruct the entire pattern with these pins and, only when the pattern was complete, verify that they were appropriately placed by touching all of them with the stylus. Ordinarily, the use of the pins as a memory aid would be recommended for younger subjects as a means of simplifying the pattern copying tasks.

The strategy problems differ from those described above in that the visible part of the pattern sheet would contain two or more models, reduced in size, only one of which would in fact correspond to the perforations in the remainder of the insert. The child's task is, then, in as few moves as possible, to determine which of the visible patterns corresponds to the pattern in the toy. In an earlier study, Olson (1966) found that even nine-year-olds had difficulty developing a highly informational strategy that would minimize the number of necessary moves. Donaldson (1969) has used a similar task to study the beginnings of logical inference in children.

While this device should have considerable utility as a research instrument for investigating various aspects of the relation between what a child perceives and how he represents what he sees, or more simply, between perception and intelligence, the device has immediate utility as an educational toy. The principle of the toy bears an obvious correspondence to the concept of intelligence that has been developed by Dewey, Piaget, and Bruner, and that has been elaborated here, namely, that intelligence develops through the practical activity of the child, or, as we shall say in the concluding chapter, through the performatory attempts in various cultural media, not simply through looking or being told. The portability, durability, versatility, and economy of the toy make it a reasonable addition to the armamentarium of nursery, kindergarten, and primary-school toys that are used to facilitate the development of that aspect of intelligence involving the child's conception of space.[4]

[4] Information about purchasing this toy may be obtained from the author at the Department of Applied Psychology, Ontario Institute for Studies in Education, 252 Bloor Street West, Toronto 5, Canada.

10

CONCLUSIONS: SOME ASPECTS OF A THEORY OF COGNITIVE DEVELOPMENT

... in which it is postulated that cognitive development results from the elaboration of perceptual knowledge about the world that occurs in the context of such performatory activities as locomotion, prehension, drawing, making, and speaking,

... and in which it is shown that such a postulation provides an alternative account to that implied by the old dichotomies of stimulus/response, perceiving/performing, and perception/intelligence,

... and in which some aspects of the nature of instruction, its possibilities, and its limitations are considered

It may be argued that the primary reason for doing five years of research on a problem is to postpone the drawing of conclusions. The longer the delay before arriving at closure, the greater the likelihood of seeing the relation between the beginning point of view, the primary observations, recalcitrant facts, and distantly related ideas. This chapter is devoted to an exposition of what I now think I know about this problem that I did not know when these studies began. The plan of the chapter is to present an analysis of what is involved in this aspect of cognitive development beginning with what are assumed to be the simpler processes of perception and working toward the more complex ones of intelligence. En route, we shall consider the related aspects of language, perceiving and performing, representation, symbolization, and instruction.

PERCEPTION

Although the studies in this book were not focused on the problem of the perception of the diagonal, it is necessary to examine some aspects of this process because it turns out to be basic to my account of the more complex problems of representation and intelligence.

172

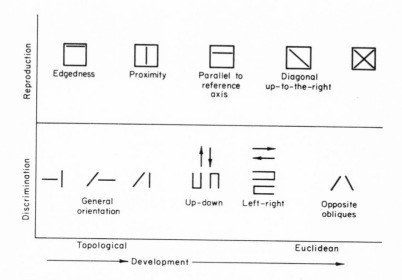

Fig. 10–1. Proposed ordering for difficulty as a function of the nature of the perceptual cues or features utilized.

In Chapter 2 the evidence was reviewed that certain orientations of line are more difficult to discriminate than others. A rough and tentative ordering is presented on the left side of Fig. 10–1. The discrimination of lines which are oppositely oriented obliques are the most difficult of those considered, followed by those differing in left-right orientation, then up-down orientation, with horizontal-vertical alternatives being somewhat easier. In general, this ordering for difficulty may be due to the difficulty children and other animals have in discriminating mirror images (Sutherland, 1960; Rudel and Teuber, 1963; Huttenlocher, 1967b). The fact that there are more alternative mirror images for an oblique line than for a vertical or horizontal line (see Chapter 2, Fig. 2–1), would appear to account for the greater difficulty of perceiving or discriminating a diagonal. But mirror-images, confusions in themselves, scarcely provide an explanation for the difficulty. For example, mirror-image confusions occur only if we imagine the mirrors set on the horizontal and vertical axes—if the mirror were set at an oblique, a horizontal line would be the mirror image of a vertical line. Thus, an account based on mirror images seems to assume the very thing to be explained.

Consider this problem in the light of two of the currently most plausible theoretical accounts of the nature of perception. An iconic or template-matching theory would assume that the perceiver had a model or picture or copy of the pattern in his head against which he matched the new stimulus. But if this was the case it should be no more difficult to discriminate the horizontal from the vertical line than to discriminate the two obliques. In both cases the alternatives differ from each other by 90°. If the viewer had a picture of the first of the pair of stimuli in his head, the second of the two pairs should be equally easily discriminated. For similar reasons, both Neisser (1967) and Gibson (1969) have found this theory inadequate.

Rather, it seems necessary to say that the viewer does not have a copy or an image that preserves all the information in the pattern, but rather that certain cues are selected from the pattern; a pattern is perceived in terms of a set of features. This feature theory of perception which has been developed by Gibson (1969) suggests that objects are perceived by means of certain features or cues which distinguish that object from all other objects. Objects viewed over time are perceived by means of detected invariants in the stimulus pattern. Perceptual development is primarily a matter of perceiving objects and events in terms of larger sets and higher-order sets or bundles of features. In any specific situation, the onset of a search for distinguishing features is the awareness of uncertainty; features are sought which will reduce that uncertainty, and the search terminates when the uncertainty is reduced.

Even with this theory we soon run into serious obstacles. For example, since features are primitive elements of perception, and since oppositely-oriented lines differ in at least one distinguishing feature, why are the latter more difficult to discriminate than horizontal and vertical lines?

One possibility is that because of the usefulness of some cues relative to others, the structure of the nervous system may have come to reflect these priorities. For example, the number and organization of various feature analyzers in the visual system may account for the differential lack of sensitivity to oblique orientation. Hubel and Wiesel (1959) and Spinelli and Barrett (1969), in their studies of the visual system of the cat, found that about 20% of the cells in the visual cortex had elongated receptive fields which were differentially sensitive to orientation. Thus some cells would be fired primarily by horizontal stimuli, some by vertical stimuli, some by one oblique, and some by the opposite oblique. There is, therefore, differential receptivity to opposite obliques. However, there is a tendency in the population of cells studied for there to be more cells concerned with horizontal and vertical than those concerned with oblique orientation. If the visual system of man is similar to that of a cat, there is no reason to expect that some orientation cues are scrambled or undetectable; there is, however, reason to suspect that the nervous system has a bias towards some types of orientation.

Even if perception occurs by means of cues or features, it seems necessary to argue that these features are not elementary in the sense of bits of lines and bits of angles. Rather, these first features are more general and may be roughly classed as topological as opposed to Euclidean ones. This conjecture is based on the fact that the most salient aspects of the patterns we have studied are those pertaining to such general properties as edgedness, proximity, and configuration, and not to elementary features such as corners (Chapter 3). Recall, too, the work of Piaget and Inhelder (1956), Abravanel (1968), and Zaphorozhets (1965) on tactile recognition of objects. In these cases the features detected by young children were those pertaining to such general topological properties as open-closed, adjacency, and, only later, to more specific Euclidean features. The same character was obvious in our eye-movement studies (Chapter 9). Viewers appeared to search for the most general cues that would differentiate the alternatives with which they were faced. There was little evidence of the complete elaboration of a visual object on the basis of careful scrutiny.

The ordering of cues utilized in the higher mental processes of construction appears to correspond roughly to the ordering of cues in perception. This relation is also indicated in Fig. 10–1. As Piaget and Inhelder (1956) pointed out, and as we have found in the present study, performatory acts such as copying a model are guided first by such general topological features as edgedness and proximity, and only later by such specific properties as corner.

There is other evidence for this point. Huttenlocher (1967a, p. 1175) observed that when children were attempting to set a second "horseshoe" into a frame to correspond to the one already placed, they "compare sample and copy, starting at the point where these are closest to one another." I would interpret this to mean that the child is basing his performatory decision on a topological cue, proximity, when, in fact, to make a correct reproduction, he requires Euclidean ones. A similar effect was noted in our observation of children copying the model on the bulb-board when the model was set just above the bulb-board: "The result can be a reversal; a red mark at the bottom of a model over the board may lead a young child to press the nearest bulb at the top of the board" (Olson, 1966, p. 150). Again it would appear that the topological property of proximity is the most salient feature in regulating the young child's performance.

To this developmental priority of topological features must be added another constraint. Garner (1966) pointed out that what one perceives in a stimulus is a function of the perceived and inferred set of alternatives, that is, the contrast set. He pointed out that a single stimulus, say two dots arrayed horizontally, would in one case be perceived as "a horizontal array" if it was embedded in a set of alternatives including a vertical and an oblique array, and in another case be perceived as "two" if it was embedded in a set of alternatives including arrays of one and three dots. Hence, the feature that one detects is always a function of the set of alternatives. The clearest evidence we have on this point is from the eye-movement experiment in which it was clear that the visual search of the model was a function of the alternatives between which the child had to choose. Similarly, in our recognition experiments, the alternatives between which the children had to choose were always differentiable on the basis of rather general, or configurational, cues; hence a more intensive visual search was irrelevant. While the role of the set of alternatives is implicit in the concept of "distinguishing" features, it makes explicit the fact that a feature that is distinguishing in one context may be less distinguishing in, or totally irrelevant to, some other context. To tie this point to the topological-Euclidean distinction, it appears that a young child perceives an event, such as an oriented line, as if it were drawn from a small set of alternatives which differ in terms of such topological features as general configuration, including open-closed, straight-curved, and so on. One of the primary changes that occurs with development is that the child comes to perceive an event in terms of a much larger set of alternatives, that is, on the basis of many more, or different, features including such subtle ones as direction of line, size and number of angles, and so on.

But why does the child attend to these types of cues in the first place and why does this developmental change occur? As a tentative answer to this question we may begin with a proposal made by Rudel and Teuber:

> Whatever the actual mechanism might be, the biologic utility of some of the features here described is obvious. In child and octopus, vertically-oriented contours in the visual environment may play a special role, reflecting their importance for the maintenance of upright posture . . . up-down reversals (which are correlated with loss of posture) would be of greater significance than right-left reversals. Similarly, as Sutherland has noted (1960), the equivalence of right-left mirror images may be related to the fact that one is converted into the other whenever the organism moves around and behind a given shape (1963, p. 897).

This statement may be taken as equivalent to that implied by the ecological validity of cues, but it adds an important constituent. Cues selected are not those that simply differentiate objects in the environment, but those cues are selected which differentiate alternatives in the contexts of performatory acts. That is, cues are not noticed simply because they are objective differences between stimuli, but because they provide information for the guidance of a performatory act such as locomotion or reading. It is obvious that one requires different information about a ball to catch it than to discriminate it from a cup. For the types of performatory activities in which octopus, rats and young children excel, such as locomotion and grasping, certain types of cues will be ecologically valid while others will not. Cues pertaining to orientation will be attended to or selected if they are invariant in the context of locomotive activity. Oblique lines are not invariant given locomotive activity in a horizontal plane; left-right differences are similarly low in invariance given such activity, while up-down differences are relatively invariant. Hence, some features, primarily topological ones, being invariant for these basic performatory acts, tend to be more easily handled than others. In general, it appears that while topological features are particularly appropriate for the performatory acts of locomotion, they are particularly inappropriate for performatory acts in such cultural media as printing and drawing.

This proposition will be more easily defended in the context of a general theoretical statement of the effects of various types of performatory activities or media on perception, to which we shall return.

LANGUAGE: PERCEPTUAL AND SEMANTIC STRUCTURE OF THE ORIENTATION OF LINE

What we perceive as inferred from the relative difficulties in the discrimination of these line segments bears a striking resemblance to the semantic structure of language.

Whorf (1956) was among the first to point out that we "dissect nature along lines laid down by our native language." The most familiar example of this process is the fact that Eskimos and skiiers make much finer distinctions between types of snow and have a correspondingly differentiated vocabulary compared to most of the rest of us. As people speak languages that differ not only in their semantic boundaries but also in their grammatical structures, we may infer that their pictures of reality are also different. One could predict that the distinctions that could be most easily apprehended would be those corresponding to the distinctions drawn in the language.[1]

Consider the relation between the ease of discrimination and the structure of the lexicon in English, some aspects of which were noted in Chapter 2. A possible hierarchical system for the differentiation of orientation of a

---

[1] Discrimination tasks are the wrong medium to assess the Whorfian hypothesis; description tasks would provide an appropriate medium.

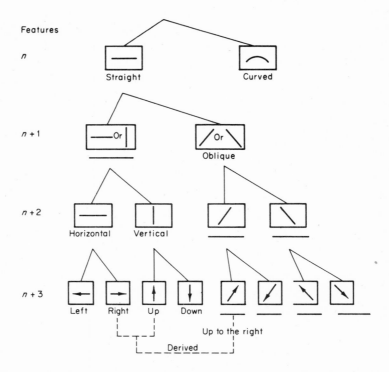

Fig. 10–2. A proposed relationship between the perceptual and semantic system for the orientation of line.

line is presented in Fig. 10–2. The words in English that mark these differentiations at each point in the hierarchy are also indicated in the diagram. Notice particularly that all perceptual differentiations are not marked by a corresponding lexical item. There is, for example, no word for the opposition (contrast set) for oblique—the word orthogonal perhaps comes the closest, and we shall use the word orthogonal in this sense for the remainder of the discussion. More important is the fact that there are no lexical items corresponding to the differentiations made between the oblique lines at either of the lower two levels in the hierarchy. Moreover, these are the differentiations that we find difficult in perceptually discriminating and in reconstructing or copying a model. Why?

The Whorfian hypothesis accounts nicely for the observations, but unfortunately it accounts for too much. Rats and octupi also have the same difficulty. Why does the structure of English predict the octupus' difficulty? The answer to this question presumably lies in the opposite of the Whorfian hypothesis, namely that the structure of the language reflects the information value or the ecological validity of the perceptual cues in differentiating among alternatives. At this point, it is impossible to know if the difficulty of using oblique orientation cues is because most organisms learn to pay attention to some cues and to ignore others, or if the difficulty is to be found in the structure of the nervous system—the nervous system could be expected to evolve to be receptive to cues that were important, and not receptive to cues that are irrelevant or misleading. Two arguments may be suggested in support of the latter.

First, for a relatively simple invertebrate, the octupus, Sutherland (1969) reports that even when direction of orientation is made to have ecological validity (one orientation of the line indicating food), the octupus is unable to make the discrimination. That is, for the octupus it is not just a difficult problem; it appears that it simply does not pick up the information.

Second, there is some evidence that when humans do deal with oblique orientation, it is not in terms of primitive distinguishing features at all. This evidence is indirect and is based on the analysis presented in Fig. 10–2. Notice that oblique lines have a name—the name differentiates oblique lines from both horizontal and vertical lines. Perceptually, oblique lines can be differentiated into two orientations. The question now is why are those alternatives, if they are perceptually primitive, not named? Moreover, when we do use language for those alternatives, we use a language derived via the orthogonal system, not via the oblique system at all. We would, for example, designate the $\nearrow$ as "up to the right." That is, the language system normally differentiates as the perceptual alternative differentiates, as in the orthogonal component. Yet in the oblique component, no such differentiation occurs; the perceptual alternatives are handled via a system derived from the orthogonal component. This derived component is indicated by the broken lines in Fig. 10–2. Hence, we may conjecture that those oblique alternatives are not processed as primitive perceptual alternatives which are differentiated by perceptual experience with oblique lines, but oblique lines are differentiated by means of coordinating features derived from the orthogonal component.

This suggestion would account for Rudel and Teuber's finding that children did not solve the problem of discriminating oblique lines until age 6 or 7, about the time they first began to generate coordinate descriptions of the forms "top-left" and "tall and narrow" (Sinclair-de Zwart, 1967).

It may be necessary to temper the preceeding conjecture of the derived nature of the cues for orientation of oblique lines by admitting that it may be only humans that process oblique cues via the orthogonal sytems, and then perhaps only by preference, because there is evidence that rats can learn such a discrimination and cats, at least, are differentially receptive to oppositely oriented oblique lines.

Another implication of Fig. 10–2 may be mentioned. If perceptual and linguistic differentiation follow the path suggested here, then discriminations higher in the hierarchy should be made more easily than those lower in the hierarchy. As far as evidence is available, it seems generally to conform to this model. It does not necessarily follow that language proceeds in the same hierarchical fashion. Once appropriate perceptual differentiation has occurred, e.g., vertical is differentiated into up and down, a lexical item may be learned that signals, or corresponds to, or means only the terminal perceptual partitioning. Thus the word up is in simple contrast to the perceptual contrast of down. The word meaning may imply the perceptual knowledge higher in the hierarchy; e.g., up is necessarily vertical, but none of this knowledge need be explicitly marked in the language. One of the tasks of semantics is to specify what perceptual information is implied by the word as it is rarely obvious or explicit. This is further indicated by the fact that the word up is learned before the word vertical, presumably because of its utility in human communication, even if the perceptual differentiation occurred in the reverse order. That these perceptual differentiations are implicit is indicated by the difficulty young children have in generating a superordinate (Donaldson, 1963).

Another implication of the hierarchical model presented in Fig. 10–2 is that it suggests that the higher in the hierarchy the alternatives are, the more easily they are discriminated; also the higher the node between two alternatives, the more easily they should be discriminated. Thus horizontal-vertical alternatives are more easily discriminated than left-right alternatives (Rudel and Teuber, 1963), and oblique-horizontal alternatives could be expected to be more easily discriminated than horizontal-vertical alternatives. There is some evidence that this latter may not be true (Rudel and Teuber, 1963). It may be necessary to revise the model as in Fig. 10–3. Considerable further research is necessary to choose between these alternatives or even to determine if this is the appropriate way to construe the problem.

The models presented in Figs. 10–2 and 10–3 would, in addition, be compatible with a theory of word meanings in terms of perceptual alternatives which I have discussed elsewhere (Olson, 1970). Specifically, the meaning of any word in the hierarchy is the information it conveys to partition the alternatives at the same level in the hierarchy. That is, left is defined in terms of right, horizontal in terms of vertical, and oblique relative to orthogonal. Fig. 10–3 suggests that it may be more appropriate to define oblique relative to horizontal and vertical.

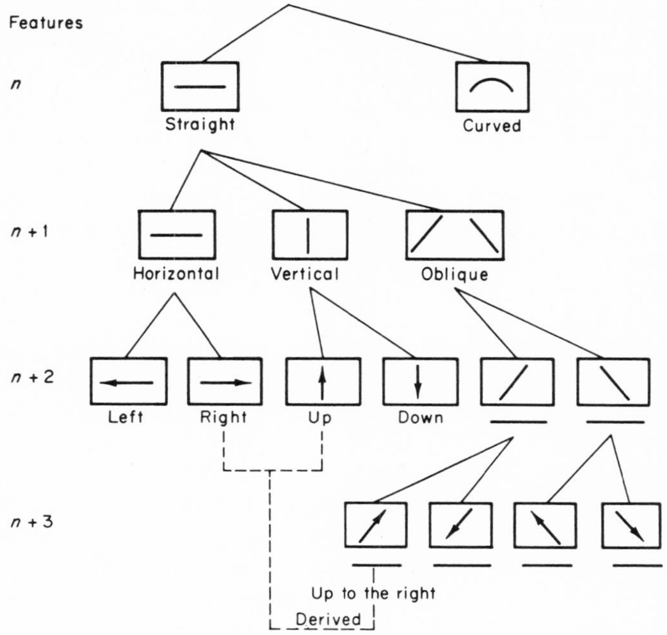

Fig. 10–3. An alternative proposal for the structure of the perceptual and semantic system for the orientation of line.

Such a model should, in addition, predict word associations at least to a limited extent. It would, for example, predict that one would obtain the following associations to "up" in diminishing proportions: down, vertical, horizontal, left, right, oblique. Entwistle's (1966) word association norms confirm that down is the dominant response to up, but the other terms do not appear with sufficient frequency to examine the remainder of the hypothesis. It may be suggested that such associations are not an account of anything; rather they are a terminal performance for which an account is required. (Clark, in press.)

PERCEIVING AND PERFORMING

When these studies began it seemed necessary to adopt Cassirer's and Piaget's distinction between perceptual knowledge and representational knowledge. The distinction implies that they are of a different substance. Cassirer's statement that the transition marked a "genuine crisis of spatial consciousness" was considered indicative of the transition. Even if that were true it would still be necessary to specify the conditions for the development of this new level of symbolic representation. What is this relationship?

Perceiving is usually taken as synonymous with recognition. But as I attempted to show in Chapter 9, the term recognition is misleading. Recognition is never complete; it is always a function of the alternatives being considered. In the early studies it was argued that the child recognized the diagonal because he could pick it out of a set of grossly different alternatives. It soon became clear, however, that this task could be accomplished by means of a few features such as obliqueness and straightness. It is possible to imagine that if the differences were subtle, the diagonal would not be recognized. Most of our subjects, for example, failed to differentiate the two opposite orientations of the diagonal. Recall that in the rod positioning 40% of the diagonal repositionings were reversals. In the eye-movement study it became even plainer that students did not see all the features of the pattern they examined; for both the pictures of houses and the pictures of the geometric patterns Ss looked at the model in terms of the features or cues they thought relevant to the subsequent discriminations. Hence, in perceiving the pattern, we must conclude that the child has only some information about the pattern, not a total ability for recognizing the pattern in all possible contexts.

This fact of the partial information involved in perception as recognition is also the key to the problem of reconstruction or copying of a pattern; but it is important to a radically greater degree. The child in looking at the diagonal picks up enough information to select the pattern from most alternatives, but he does not pick up enough information to reproduce the pattern. Consider how this could be the case.

Any performance is a sequential act. As such, it involves a continuous set of decisions at each point in time as to how to begin, how to continue, and how to terminate. Each of these decision points requires information. The young child simply does not have the information necessary for each of these decisions because of the unelaborated or undifferentiated state of his perceptual knowledge. Moreover, looking at the completed pattern provides little or no information for the performance. That is, the features which the child involves in his perception of the completed pattern will be appropriate to the alternatives between which he assumes he must select —those features may be irrelevant to the features or featural information required for his production. The child may perceive the pattern only in terms of its orientation or its regularity (Chapter 3), yet neither of these features may be relevant to his performatory act. This was repeatedly

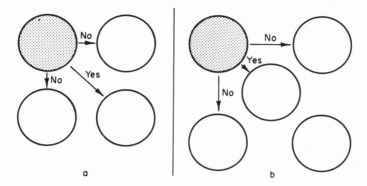

Fig. 10–4. Alternatives for which the child requires further information on (a) the original checkerboard and (b) the modified checkerboard.

shown in our studies. After seeing the pattern, the children often did not know where to begin; others knew where to place the first checker and that the next checker should be adjacent, but they did not know how to select among the alternatives facing them—they lacked the information.

This, then, is the critical point in the relation between perceiving and performing. Performing an act such as copying, making, or speaking, requires different perceptual information than the act of perceiving or recognizing an event amongst a set of simple alternatives. There are, however, several other pieces to this puzzle.

Which features did they perceive when they simply looked at the models? A tentative answer to this was formulated in Chapter 3. The most accessible to the child were such features as edgedness; next was proximity, or adjacency of the checkers, and next was parallel to a reference axis, such as the frame of the board. All of these features are, roughly, "topological". They were sufficient for the reconstruction of some of the patterns. Again assuming some aspects of a sequential act, such as initiating and terminating, this information would be sufficient for the production or reconstruction of a pattern such as the top row, as we found in Chapter 3. The knowledge of these features is not, however, sufficient for the reconstruction of the diagonal. When the child has, say, one checker correctly placed, he may have the information that the next checker is to be adjacent—but he cannot choose between the three relatively adjacent holes. As Fig. 10–4a shows, in this case the adjacency or proximity cue and the orientation due are in conflict. Free to choose, the child utilizes the adjacency cue, the topological cue, and continues his production in a vertical or a horizontal direction. When these cues are not in conflict, as in Fig. 10–4b, the child has no difficulty with his production.

Nor is it simply a matter of quantity. This is where the work of Gombrich (1960) and Arnheim (1954) again becomes critical. They insist on adding the phrase "in the medium you are working" (Arnheim, 1954, p. 97). Each medium will require somewhat different information. Drawing and making a checker diagonal may share many of the same features; that is, require some of the same information, but not the identical information. In choosing how to continue a diagonal line, the alternatives at any point in time on the uniform medium of paper are somewhat different from those of selecting among three relatively adjacent holes in the medium of the checkerboard. For this reason, it is no longer inexplicable that our students trained to draw diagonals in Chapter 6 often failed to reconstruct one with checkers. This same point is true in regard to the medium of language. The choices indicated by the language are nonidentical with those of performatory acts in different media. To the extent they overlap and only to that extent, skill in articulating the diagonal in language will have transfer value to performing it on the checkerboard.

To summarize to this point: the difference between "perceiving" or recognizing the diagonal and performing or copying it is that different perceptual information is involved in the two cases. To recognize a diagonal in the context of a set of static forms it is necessary only to detect the feature or features which will partition that set of alternatives. Performatory activity such as drawing or making on the checkerboard requires perceptual information for the guidance of each component of the act, that is, for selecting between all possible alternatives at each point in the performatory act. The alternatives confronted at each point in time are to some extent unique to the performatory medium—to draw a diagonal does not require the same information as to define in words the concept of the diagonal. In both cases, however, the information is perceptual, and in both cases the information must be appropriate to the alternatives with which the child is faced if he is to succeed. They differ primarily in the fact that each activity: discriminating, drawing, constructing on the checkerboard, and defining, involves somewhat different sets of alternatives for which different cues, features, or information must be selected from the model.

Now let us examine the general implications of this account on the effects of various performatory domains or media on perception. The term media requires clarification. By medium I mean a range or a domain of performatory activity. The media with which we are mainly concerned are those of which are evolved and transmitted by the culture such as drawing, speaking, counting, making. However, I also wish to include in the term media such other performatory domains as locomotion and grasping, even if these latter are more difficult to classify.

In line with the preceding argument, the information selected from an event is a function of the inferred or perceived alternatives between which one is to choose; as each medium involves different alternatives, each medium requires different perceptual information. For this reason, perceptual theories are necessarily inadequate until they begin to specify the ways that performatory attempts in various media determine which information will be picked up perceptually. To show that this is a currently unsolved problem would take us too far off the track, but the current psychological gap between perceptual and performatory activity is well illustrated by J. J. Gibson (1966), from whom the latter term is borrowed. Although Gibson has gone far in showing the forms of information extracted from perceptual activity, he simply treats perceptual activity and performatory activity as two discrete forms of activity in his model joined by a line with unspecified function. E.J. Gibson (1969) goes only so far as to say that both types of systems presumably rely on distinguishing features. Miller, Galanter and Pribram (1960), who explicitly attack the problem of the relation between knowledge and performance, get only so far as to show that stimuli are better construed as image, and responses are better construed as plans, and then to show that images control plans. They overlook the fact that images do not control plans any more than plans control images. Images are the information accumulated in the course of various performatory attempts in various media. This will become clear presently.

My hypothesis is that each type of performatory activity requires, for its guidance, different perceptual information. Just as learning to differentiate an object from a larger set of alternatives leads one to know more distinguishing features of that object, so learning to carry out new kinds of performatory activities in relation to that object leads one to know more or different features of that object. To extend my earlier example, one requires different information to catch a ball (will it take one hand or two?) than to discriminate it from a cup, or to draw it, or to name it.

A consideration of the performatory acts of locomotion and prehension brings us back to the difficulty various animals, including children, have in discriminating some orientations of line. The information selected from a visual world by a moving, grasping animal will be features, primarily topological, that permit the guidance of those movements. Cues which are not invariant, such as oblique and left-right orientation, provide little or no information for those performatory acts. Hence they will not be selected. Moreover, animals who specialize in such performatory acts should be biased toward cues which are invariant for the guidance of such activities. It is presumably for this reason that Bower (1966) finds that young human infants conditioned to respond to a wooden board set at a 45° angle responded to the same board set in a new vertical orientation; they had great difficulty however, in responding to the orientation cue itself. That is, early perception appears to be attuned primarily to features which are invariant in the performatory acts of locomotion and grasping. Perhaps this is true for children only at this stage of development.

The effect of the performatory act of locomotion on the development of perception has been shown even more convincingly in Held and Hein's (1963) famous experiment with the active and passive cats. The cat which had actually walked around the path performed successfully in such tasks as paw placement, while the cat which rode in a gondola over the same path could not. The inference that perceptual learning was therefore dependent on self-produced movement has been suspect in the light of the evidence that dogs totally immobilized by the drug curare could still learn a conditional stumulus to which they would respond after the drug wore off (Solomon and Turner, 1962). In terms of the argument presented here, these findings are not incompatible. The performatory act of walking requires for its guidance some visual cues which the cat presumably picked up from looking at the floor. The riding cat did not pick up that information because he was not confronted with the alternatives generated by that performatory act. Hence, the active cat has the information necessary to guide its subsequent paw placement. Other kinds of performatory acts, such as avoiding a shock, also require information for their guidance, but that information may be provided in very different ways, including a UCS, as in Solomon's study, or even by language.

To restate this point, it is not response information, if there is any such thing, that the experience has provided. Rather, it is perceptual information that has been picked up about the world; the attempted performatory act merely provided the occasion for picking up the new cues. At least one part of the information one has about the world is therefore a function of one's performatory attempts at walking and grasping. To make a very general speculation, locomotion may have been the occasion for the development of animal intelligence in the same way that tool using may have been the occasion for the development of human intelligence—but that is to get ahead of our story.

The performatory domains or media of more relevance to the perceptual development of children are those concerned with performance in various cultural media such as drawing, speaking, and counting.[2]

---

[2] I admit a difficulty in finding a place in my conception of performatory domains into which discrimination learning can be fitted. It may be a process in the service of other performatory acts in many media, or it may be a medium in its own right.

In this light, let us reconsider Piaget's insistence on the role of internalized activity on the development of representation. Piaget and Inhelder (1956) have argued that the performatory acts of copying forms and haptically perceiving objects require for their execution a form of knowledge different from that involved in perceptual recognition. The former depends on representational knowledge and it is presumed to be formed by internalized activity. These internalized activities, when they achieve a logical, reversible form, are called concrete operations. In my estimation Piaget and Inhelder have confused the means, the activity, with the effect produced. In line with the earlier position, it is the performatory attempts in various media which provide the occasion for apprehending further information from the perceptual world. But it is incorrect to say that it is the activity per se which has been internalized. Although Piaget has not commented, to my knowledge, on the effects of various media, it may be speculated that it is such performatory acts as drawing, constructing, and speaking that provide these occasions for elaborating and revising one's perceptual information. Hence, there are, in my view, not two independent systems, perceptual and representational, as Piaget has argued, but rather one system, a perceptual one, which is altered substantially by performatory acts in different media. Piaget is correct about the role of the child's activity; he is wrong about the nature of the effects of this activity.

We have considered the types of cues required for the performance of such acts as locomotion and prehension. It should be clear from that discussion that one knows not only much more but also different things about a ball or a city after one has attempted to perform some act on it such as handle it or walk around it, than one did when it was simply discriminated. But we have only considered indirectly the impact of media that are evolved in the culture, such as drawing and language.

Consider drawing. In representational drawing it has been clearly shown in the work of Arnheim (1954) and Gombrich (1960) that some portrayals true to natural life depended on information that was not given in naive perception. If it was given simply by more looking why didn't someone before Massacio see how drapery fell? It is in the context of performatory attempts in the medium of drawing and painting that the alternatives arise for which additional information is then sought. In drawing a house or a diagonal or a square, information is required to guide each component of the performatory attempt that is unique to the medium. That is, you must pick up new cues from the stimulus event. At the simplest level, drawing a ball requires the selection of form cues. You draw a round, empty circle. With the paint medium the ball is accomplished by means of a solid color patch. To quote Arnheim (1954, p. 162), "Representation never produces a replica of the object but its structural equivalent in a given medium."

But there is another aspect to drawing that is more closely related to making—the development of space and geometry that apparently had its origins in Greek drawing. Ivins (1946) has pointed out this fact:

> Whatever else the story, as I have pieced it together, may tell,
> it brings out the fact that Greek art and Greek geometry were
> based on the same tactile-muscular sensuous intuitions, that
> in many ways their developments went along similar lines, and
> that their limitations were implicit in those intuitions (p. 59).

Geometric notions, including such Euclidean features as square, corner, bisect, 90°, have their origins in performatory attempts at drawing and making. That is, these cues, like those conveying the gentle fall of drapery, were not given to naive perception by simply looking at nature. Rather, they are cues which have been selected in the course of performatory attempts at drawing and making. In this sense, squares were not detected in nature until they were made necessary in the pre-Socratics' attempts at geometric drawings. It is extremely difficult for all of us who have mastered these media at an early age to have any feeling that geometric features including diagonality are anything other than primitive. The following quotation from McLuhan (1964) shows that our comfort with Euclidean features is cultural.

> An anthropological film showed a Melanesian carver cutting
> out a decorated drum with such skill, coordination, and ease
> that the audience several times broke into applause—it became
> a song, a ballet. But when the anthropologist asked the tribe to
> build crates to ship these carvings in, they struggled unsuc-
> cessfully for three days to make two planks intersect at a 90
> degree angle, then gave up in frustration. They couldn't crate
> what they had created (p. 150).

In the same way many of our Kenyan children did not know how to isolate the corner as a critical feature of our pattern or how to isolate the other information relevant to its reproduction.

In a similar way it is performatory attempts in the medium of number systems that makes it necessary for us to pick up certain other invariants from the perceptual world—invariant cues that would, and do, go undetected except for the attempts at mastery of the medium of number. Thus, fiveness is not a simple objective cue given in naive perception, but a cue that is singled out as invariant in the performatory domain, or medium, of number.

Similarly, linguistic decisions require information. To be able to decide whether to use the present or past tense of a verb, or to understand the differential usage of other speakers, requires information of a kind that had not previously been selected, or attended, or perceived, because there was no occasion to look for it. In this way, language as a medium provides the occasion for obtaining not only more information, but different types of information from one's perceptual world than would be necessary if the medium did not exist. In this sense Brown and Bellugi (1964) are quite correct in noting the cognitive effects of acquiring the grammatical class of functor words.

> The meanings that are added by functors seem to be nothing less than the basic terms in which we construe reality: the time of an action, whether it is ongoing or completed, whether it is presently relevant or not; the concept of possession and such relational concepts as are coded by *in, on, up, down,* and the like; the difference between a particular instance of a class ("Has anybody seen *the* paper?") and any instance of a class ("Has anybody seen *a* paper?"); the difference between extended substances given shape and size by an "accidental" container (*sand, water, syrup,* etc.) and countable "things" having a characteristic fixed shape and size (*a cup, a man, a tree,* etc.). It seems to us that a mother in expanding speech may be teaching more than grammar; she may be teaching something like a world-view (p. 142–143).

As an aside, it may be noted that it follows from the proposition that information is at least to some extent unique to a medium, that concepts are cognitive events specified by the linguistic medium just as certain patterns of guided movements may be considered as units in the medium of representational drawing. As such, both types of units involve perceptual information, but information primarily suited to the demands of that medium. This may account for the frequent but frustrated attempt to provide a fundamental psychological account of concepts.

Three qualifications must be made here as to the nature of the effects of performatory attempts in various media on perceptual development. First, to return to a point made earlier, although performatory activity in a medium is necessary for the picking up of this information, it is not the medium itself which is internalized. I have already shown this in relation to the performatory act of locomotion; it is not the motor act that is internalized; it is not a response that is learned; rather it is that the performance of the motor act requires information for its guidance. The information that is picked up to permit the choice between these alternatives is perceptual information. Similar reasons could be given to show that other performatory acts do not result in the internalizing of these performatory acts themselves whether in the form of internalized speech (Vygotsky, 1962;

Bruner, 1966), internalized actions (Piaget, 1960), or internalized pictures or images (Paivio, 1969). Rather, the media provide the occasion for picking up more or different perceptual information. To say that the resulting knowledge is therefore linguistic, artistic, or mathematic, is only half true; it is perceptual knowledge that has been acquired and refined in the context of these different media.

The second qualification stems from the first—the fact that the information picked up in the context of various media is not media specific. As it is all perceptual information, it is to be expected that there is considerable overlap between the information picked up in the context of different media. It is not surprising, for example, that Descartes, after whom cartesian coordinates are named, found a way to show the equivalence between the two great and previously separate media of number and geometry. The information common to decisions in different media such as speaking and drawing is indicated by the degree to which transfer occurs from one to the other. While our experiments indicated there was considerable transfer, the information was not identical. Thus, in Chapter 6 we found children who could define the diagonal but still not construct it on the checkerboard.

The third qualification is that even in the context of performatory acts in various media, the critical information is not always, and perhaps only rarely, immediately attended. If it is simply that making the diagonal requires information that was not previously relevant to recognizing it, why didn't children see the necessary cues by looking back at the model? This is the same question that we have previously encountered in Gombrich (1960, p. 12). "What difficulty could there have been in this simple portrayal which prevented artists before Massacio from looking at drapery for themselves?" Why did microscopists drawing the cell prior to the "discovery" of chromosomes not include chromosomes, while after their discovery, drawings based on the same slides included chromosomes (Boring, 1963). E. J. Gibson's (1969) suggestion seems inadequate on this point. She argues that perception is a process of extracting the invariants in stimulus information. Since, in her view, information is in the environment, obtaining more of it is simply a function of more looking at the environment—more looking leads to "chunking," which frees the brain to "handle more of the total input, or . . . get more of the external available information (p. 129 and p. 142)." All of the above examples show that it is not a simple matter of more looking.

My answer to this question is a simple extension of my view that performatory attempts in various media create or provide the occasion for apprehending further information from the visual world. Information is selected to choose between alternatives, and each new medium presents new sets of alternatives. Aside from the use of that medium, one would not have been led to detect that new feature. It seems to me that this view makes the concept of information credible. Information is defined as the ability to reduce uncertainty; that is, to specify alternatives. If someone is not aware of the alternatives, there is by definition no information. Hence it is inappropriate to speak of all that information being in the stimulus to begin with.

But there are still two aspects to this occasion for picking up new information. The first is the sensitivity to the alternatives for which information must be sought; the second is the search for the cue that will permit the choice between the alternatives. The second of these is relatively simple. Once the child knows what the alternatives are he looks directly for the cues that will permit the choice. The eye-movement studies (Chapter 8) provided considerable evidence that this was so. Also, when we faced the child with the alternatives by a question ("Where does the criss-cross start?"), he immediately picked up the critical information. Sokolov (1969) has provided similar evidence. It is the first aspect, the sensitivity to alternatives, that is most difficult. My guess is that in a performatory act it is not immediately apparent what the alternatives or choice points are for which information must be sought. Not knowing, one can only guess or invent, try this and try that, and then see if the guess was a good one.

What I have in mind may be clarified by an analogous experiment. Many years ago Herbert and Harsh (1944) conducted an experiment on modeling in which two groups of cats learned to perform such acts as string pulling and door opening by observing the performances of other cats. One group of cats saw only the final errorless performances. The other group saw the early trials and so saw the mistakes as well as the correct responses. The latter group learned the performance most readily.[3] The reason for this may be described in the same terms we have developed here for describing perceiving and performing. The latter group of cats saw more of the alternatives between which their predecessors were choosing; they saw, moreover, which alternatives led to success and which led to failure. In the process they picked up the information necessary to choose between the alternatives at each of the choice points. The first group got less information; that is they did not see the alternatives between which their models were choosing.

Similarly, a child seeing an errorless performance or the result of such a performance in a finished product may not detect what the choices or

[3] This experimental finding is somewhat limited in that the cats who saw the error-filled performance saw more trials than the cats who saw the errorless preformance.

the sets of alternatives were. On the other hand our Montessori teacher was so successful because he modeled the alternatives as well as the correct solution. In carrying out a performatory act the child at first does not know what the alternatives are for his decisions at each point in time. Not knowing the alternatives, he does not know how to look back at the model in order to get the required information. As he becomes sensitive to the alternatives, either through observing his own productions and the consequences of each component of his act, or through instruction (to which we shall return presently), he comes to know how to view the model to obtain the required information. In the course of becoming sensitive to these decision points, and by gathering further information from the model, his perceptual knowledge of the model is elaborated. It is this back-acting effect of performance on perception that artists, for example, are so insistent upon.

I have been proposing that it is the beginning of performatory attempts in such media as language and drawing that require for their execution the selection of new cues or information. In the contexts of these performatory attempts, the child's perceptual world becomes elaborated. Nor are these effects of media, particularly cultural media, small effects. They are the most likely candidates for accounting for man's humanness in an evolutionary sense. The development of stone tools has been proposed as an early medium in human evolution. It has been supplemented by the more recent media of language, science, and art. It is reasonable to suggest that it is his development and mastery of more recent media of language, number, and art, that account for his continuing evolution. At the level of individual development it is the acquisition of skills in these media that may be proposed as an account of the development of intelligence and, hence, to the substantial cognitive changes that occur about the time of the onset of schooling (White, 1965). Similar suggestions have, in fact, been made by Bruner (1965) and Zaphorozhets (1965, p. 100–101) who argued that:

> . . . the development of the child's perception is not spontaneous; it takes place under the influence of practice and learning, in the course of which the child assimilates social sensory experiences and joins the sensory culture created by mankind. The adults give the child methods of learning the environment by acquainting him with the systems of musical sounds—speech phonemes, geometrical forms, etc.—that have been developed my man. They also teach him to designate the particulars of his environment, by means of language. As a result, the child assimilates a certain system of generally accepted sensory measures, sensory standards that he uses later in his perceptive activity to analyze the reality and reflect it in synthetic images.

INTELLIGENCE—SKILL IN A MEDIUM

It is the elaboration of the perceptual world that occurs in the context of acquiring cultural media that may be called the development of intelligence. Contrary to the usual distinction between perceptual processes and intellectual processes, the proposition will be defended that perception and intelligence are not different levels or different types of mental activities, but rather reflect the context in which new types of information are taken into the system. What is called perception is usually constructed as the process of differentiating alternatives in the course of practical acts, a development that occurs in most animal species and is less dependent on the culture. On the other hand what is called intelligence is developed through mastering a cultural medium, a development that is more exclusively human, and is therefore considered to involve higher level mental activity. This leads to the hypothesis that intelligence is skill in a medium, or, more precisely, skill in a cultural medium.

Although writers dealing with the psychology of art, notably Gombrich (1960) and Arnheim (1954), were the first to insist on the variable effects of different media, it was McLuhan (1962, 1964) who first showed, in a general way, the importance of the medium, apart from its specific content, on the structure of the perceptual world. He argued that the print medium tended to fragment and differentiate our perceptual world (1962), whereas electric media tend to synthesize our perceptual world (1964). McLuhan's discovery has tended to be used only for polemic purposes in psychology because it has not been possible to make any conjectures as to how media may have this effect. The account on the preceding pages shows how different effects of media are possible; information is selected to choose between alternatives; different media involve different sets of alternatives; therefore, mastery of a new medium requires selection of new information.

McLuhan (1964) points out both that media extend and modify our perceptual world, and that our society is blind to the nature and the extent of this modification. As a result, we tend to confuse the skill in the medium which happens to be ascendant in our own culture with a presumed universal structure of intelligence. Written language is one of the dominant media in our own culture, or subculture, and skill in it has been taken as the hallmark of intelligence. McLuhan (1964) states

> "Rational," of course, has for the west long meant "uniform and continuous and sequential." In other words we have confused reason with literacy, and rationalism with a single technology. . . . literate man is quite inclined to see others who cannot conform as somewhat pathetic". . . . It is in our IQ testing

that we have produced the greatest flood of misbegotten stand-
ards. Unaware of our typographic cultural bias, our testers
assume that uniform and continuous habit are a sign of intelligence, thus eliminating the ear man and the tactile man (pp. 30–
32).

The various media evolved in different cultures can be expected to
radically alter the information members of the culture select from the
perceptual world. It is hence no longer surprising that the Kenyan children
perform poorly on our tasks. We tested them on a task requiring excellence
in a medium foreign to their culture, even if it was not a verbal test.

I would go further: intelligence tests are not culturally biased, as a
limiting factor; they are reflections of skills in certain media that the culture currently finds useful and measurable. A list of intellectual factors
makes obvious the extent to which intelligence is a simple reflection of skills
in our various dominant cultural media: verbal ability, number ability,
spatial ability, etc.

McLuhan's evidence of the psychological effects of various media are
gathered from literary and historical sources; hence, a psychologist would
remain suspicious. Since a means for showing how such media would have
their effects has been suggested here, it may now be possible to examine
their effects more systematically. That is, the specific question of language
and thought should now be generalized to media and thought if we want to
develop a general account of the development of human intelligence.

In this book we have examined the acquisition of the child's ability
to construct the diagonal. It is an ability which could be on any intelligence
test, and sooner or later probably will be. We have presented considerable
evidence that the child comes to perform this task because he gradually
learns to make the appropriate decision at each point in the performatory
act. This information is not given by the original perception of the model
which was presumably made for simple discriminatory purposes. Rather,
new information is extracted from the model, information that will permit
the child to choose between the alternatives that arise in his performatory
attempts in the medium. In the process, the perceptual schema is both
elaborated and modified. The child knows both more of the features, and
different sets of features, when he can make a diagonal in some medium,
than when he could discriminate one. The features are to a large extent appropriate to the medium. Hence, making one is not quite the same as
drawing one or as describing one in the language.

It is to be expected that there is considerable overlap in the information
acquired in the course of mastery of various media. In our studies this was
indicated by the usefulness of one medium such as language for purposes of

instruction in another medium, that of space or geometry. This relationship is also shown by Descartes' discovery of the equivalence between number and geometry, and by the more recent findings of the use of a "spatial paralogic" in the solution of verbal reasoning problems (DeSoto, London and Handel 1965; Huttenlocher, 1969).

Performatory acts are skill in a medium, and the spatial medium involved in our diagonality tasks are somewhat specific to our culture. The spatial medium involved in the diagonality tasks is presumably that of Euclidean geometry that had its beginning in the culture with the Greeks. It is likely that the child's acquisition of skill in this medium has its beginning in such things as representational and geometric drawing, and building with blocks. As these skills are specific to our culture, people in other cultures or subcultures not sharing this medium can be expected to perform more poorly, as do, in fact, our Kenyan children.

To argue that their poor performance is restricted to performance in our media, it is necessary to show that their skills in their own media exceed our own. If one offers such evidence in the form of their carefully documented skills in tracking, herding, and identifying their own cattle (Dyson-Hudson & Dyson-Hudson, 1969; Munroe, Munroe & Daniels, 1969) and in such activities as sensitivity to kinship patterns (Baldwin, personal communication) or their assumed superiority in hunting, it is frequently objected that these are not conceptual or intellectual skills. But to do so is to fall into the trap we have earlier identified; it is to define intelligence in terms of skills in our own media. If we construe intelligence as skill in a medium, we are skilled in some—they are skilled in others. We are, however, skilled in media that make an advanced technology possible.

I have postulated that it is the elaboration of one's perceptual world under the influence of various media that accounts individually for man's intelligence, and collectively for man's culture. It is therefore not surprising that scholars examining specific media are led by their analyses to postulate that the description of their media provides a model for the functioning of the human mind. Humboldt was quoted earlier:

> By the same spiritual act through which man spins language out of himself he spins himself into it: so that in the end he communicates and lives with intuitive objects in no other manner than shown him by the medium of language (cited by Cassirer, 1957, p. 15).

But it is only recently that the structure of the medium has been projected into the nervous system in the form of innate structures. Chomsky (1968) says:

> . . . it seems that knowledge of a language—a grammar—can
> be acquired only by an organism that is "preset" with a severe
> restriction on the form of grammar. This innate restriction is a
> precondition . . . for linguistic experience, and it appears to be
> the critical factor in determining the course and result of lan-
> guage learning (p. 78).

Arnheim (1954), a scholar studying another medium, representational art,
makes a similar claim for the structure of the nervous system:

> The development of pictorial form relies on basic properties of
> the nervous system, whose functioning is not greatly modified
> by cultural and individual differences (p. 201).

From the viewpoint developed here, they are all correct so far as the
media, either language or art, are closely related to the structure of the
mind. While they may be correct in stating that the structure of the mind
makes certain media possible for some species, they fail to recognize that
it is the experience with the cultural media that gives mind its characteristic properties. These properties develop, not through internalizing the
medium in the form of inner speech, or mental pictures, or internalized
activity, but through requiring additional information to guide the performatory acts in those media.

The transition from perception to intelligence is then simply the beginnings of the acquisition of cultural media and its resulting elaboration of the
perceptual world. The change is no less dramatic, but we must look for
an account of the change in quite different terms than those previously
offered. The transition is not a function of developing a new type of mental
process, but of looking at the perceptual world in terms of new tasks or
requirements imposed by new media.

In the initial review of the development of conceptual representation,
it was pointed out that the term representation was employed somewhat
differently by both Gombrich (1960) and Arnheim (1954, who used it in
terms of a performatory act such as "using a circle to represent a man's
head") than it was employed by Piaget, Cassirer, Bruner, and Gibson. The
latter use representation to refer to imaginal processes, processes that occur
in the head, not on canvas or paper. In terms of the account we have developed in this chapter, the former usage is more psychologically defen-
sible. It is redundant to speak of representations in the head. Rather, attempts at the performatory acts of representation in art, and in language
and other media, provide the occasion for obtaining much more information

from the perceptual world. As I suggested earlier, internalized activity is a similar misconstrual. It is not the activity that is internalized, but the activity provides the occasion for gaining new information from the perceptual world. For this reason the activity may be replaced by appropriate means of instruction, such as observing or listening. How this occurs is the final topic of this exposition.

INSTRUCTION

It has been implied that it is through the child's performatory acts themselves that the child encountered the choice points that led him to look for or select further information. The evidence provided by Held and Hein (1963) on the effects of "re-afferentation," by Piaget (1960) on the role of internalized actions in the formation of operations, by Arnheim (1954) on effect of scribbling in the development of representational drawing, and our own on the Ligoli and Kipsigis lack of experience with the media for constructing spatial or geometric patterns, has all been cited in this context.

In this section it will be argued that this is usually but not necessarily so; the role of activity or experience on some occasions may be replaced by instruction. Recall that we have argued that the activity is the means for encountering the new alternatives and need for further information. It is not the activity per se that is internalized. The alternative means for encountering the alternatives and selecting the further information comes from various forms of instruction.

In the experiments reported in this book, we have only begun to assess the range of possibilities of instruction. We have, however, examined three. The first, as typified by the educational toy, involved a rearrangement of the environment so as to increase the likelihood that the child would encounter the critical choice-points or alternatives in his attempted reconstruction, and that he would receive information (reinforcement) as to the appropriate choice among those alternatives. This means of instruction is a variation of ordinary direct experience in that it leaves somewhat to chance the problem of the child's actually detecting the choice points, that is, the child's actually considering the appropriate set of alternatives. To be more specific, if the child is to place the first checker in the diagonal array, one child may note or select the topological cue of edgedness, and then simply slide the checker over all the edge holes until he hits the corner hole, which, being larger, admits the checker. The next checker may be positioned using the topological cue of adjacency. That is, he tries all the holes adjacent to the positioned checker and the size factor alone determines which of the three adjacent holes receives the checker. As we noted in Chapter 8, such performance did not lead to success. If, on the other hand, a child actually considers the appropriate set of alternatives, the alternatives among which he must select in the performatory act, he can select further information to choose among these alternatives. That information may be provided by looking at the model or by the reinforcement, but only if he has actually noticed the alternatives. That is, a reinforcement may or may not be informative depending on whether or not the child was considering the appropriate set of alternatives. Nonreinforcement may serve as an occasion for looking back at nature, but young children do not always, or even often, take the occasion (Chapter 4). Because the child is expected to encounter these alternatives on his own, such a procedure may better be described as directed experience than instruction.

Language provides a more powerful means of instruction. I have argued elsewhere (Olson, 1970b) that language provides information, not to the speaker but to the listener. The speaker, in this case E or the teacher, knows something that the child does not. Linguistic information is of the form that, in principle, permits the selection between alternatives. This point is frequently missed because of the erroneous belief that things have names. However, each thing has many names, and every name has many things. Rather than name things, a word partitions an object or event from some set of alternatives. Thus a cat may be called or designated as a cat, a white cat, an animal, or Felix, depending on the alternatives from which it is to be differentiated.

But this is precisely how language is so useful for instruction; it indicates to the listener what the alternatives are. For example, if you say "Triangles have three corners," you may violate some conventions in the linguistic medium, but you indicate to the listener that the figures from which you want him to differentiate triangles differ in the aspect of corners. This role of language in instruction is a critical one. Language can be used to indicate to a comprehending listener what the alternatives are that he is likely to have to deal with, as well as how to choose between these alternatives. Language presumably does this by means of directing one's attention to those choice points and to the critical features of an event which permit the choice between these alternatives. In so doing one reduces enormously the amount of information a child may have to deal with in order to arrive on his own at a knowledge of these alternatives and the features that permit a choice between them.

Consider a child learning which types of mushrooms are edible. Aside from the fact that he may die while finding out if the round, orange ones are edible, he would have to try out a multitude of hypotheses about which features in which combinations permit the choice among those alternatives.

His performance may be expected to resemble that of an experimental subject trying to learn a concept in a concept formation experiment. Some instruction by means of language may completely alter this process. An utterance of the form, "Poisonous mushrooms have brown spots and a gray undersurface," indicates what the range of alternatives will be and how he is to choose among them. The provision of information in verbal instruction of the form, "A diagonal begins and ends in a corner" had well documented effects on young children's productions in our experiments.

Four limitations of verbal instruction may be noted. First, it assumes that the teacher, the one providing the instruction, actually knows what the alternatives are; that is, he actually possesses the relevant information. Given the current ferment in such disciplines as psychology and education, that assumption must be tentative. More important, the teacher-speaker must assume that the alternatives for which he is providing information are in fact the alternative being entertained by the children. We have frequently found that statements we have considered informative contain no information for the listener because he is entertaining different alternatives.

One can easily see the difference between the alternatives being considered by the teacher and those being entertained by the child in exchanges such as the following one provided, as I recall, by Piaget:

> Science Teacher: Why does a boat float?
> Child: Because, if it sank, all the people would drown.

For an utterance, that is, for verbal instruction, to contain information, it must permit the listener to choose between the alternatives he is considering. For this reason perhaps it is pedagogically sound to ask the child some questions before attempting to teach him something.

A third limitation in language as a means of instruction is the limitation in the child's comprehension both of the meaning or use of the words themselves and of the implication of various logical propositions (Wason, 1959; Wason and Johnson-Laird, 1969). Again, words and propositions may convey no information if the child has not mastered that aspect of the medium.

Fourth, language as a medium is limited in what information it can convey. To quote McLuhan:

> All the words in the world cannot describe an object like a bucket, although it is possible to tell in a few words how to *make* a bucket. This inadequacy of words to convey visual in-

formation about objects was an effectual block to development
of the Greek and Roman sciences. Pliny the Elder reported
the inability of the Greek and Latin botanists to devise a means
of transmitting information about plants and flowers.

Hence it is that other writers have confined themselves to a
verbal description of the plants; indeed, some of them have
not so much as described them even, but have contented themselves for the most part with a bare recital of their names. . . .
(1964, p. 146).

The limitations of the medium are shown in our attempts to give a complete
verbal description for guiding or instructing performance in a medium such
as drawing or reconstructing. In that case, the use of language failed to
differentiate all the alternatives found by the child in his attempted reconstruction; hence language was not a completely successful means of instruction (Chapter 6). This point simply reflects the fact that different
media involve different sets of alternatives, and therefore require different
information.

In retrospect, it may be seen that we never even attempted a form of
instruction that was exclusively verbal. All of the instruction was done
in the context of the board or drawings and the verbal instruction was then
used to differentiate alternatives that occurred in the context of those
media.

In general, verbal description appears never to be equivalent to a motor
performatory act. A description of a curved line may help a person draw
one but it could never be so fully informative as to guide a skilled performance. The same point is frequently made in such other motor activities
as golf. Verbal instructions help specify some of the initial alternatives and
how to choose among them, but they are never fully adequate or exhaustive.

The third means of instruction that has been employed in the studies
reported in this book may be construed as modeling. Although no adequate
experiments were performed it was pointed out that a Montessori teacher
taught a young child, aged 3–2, to construct the diagonal by demonstration
only. He did so not by putting the checkers directly into the correct holes,
but by indicating the wrong moves in conjunction with making the correct
moves. This procedure was carried out completely nonverbally. Although
I considered that observation as completely anomalous at the time (I
was stuck on a verbal theory of thought), that observation has been repeated several times and, while it should be replicated, it seems to me to be
reliable. From the point of view developed in this chapter it is completely
reasonable that it should have that effect. The demonstration modeling

indicated to the child what the choice points were, what his alternatives were, and how he was to choose among them.

The training used in our experiments was a combination of verbal instruction and modeling, but to designate it as verbal modeling (Bandura, 1969) is just as much a misconstrual of the process as to designate it as verbal instruction with concrete props (Ausubel, 1968). It is rather a matter of providing information that will be critical to the child's subsequent performance, and at least some parts of that information may be provided by more than one means.

It is obvious that we have not exhaused the range of effects or the alternative means of instruction. It should, for example, be possible to conduct the instruction by means of animated film, or television. An exhaustive list of these media, an assessment of their effects in different types of performatory acts, and a theory of their interrelationships would be a suitable goal for a theory of instruction.

SUMMARY

I have tried to show that the basic cognitive process is a perceptual one—the detecting of features that will serve to differentiate an event from a set of alternatives as Gibson (1969) and Garner (1966) have proposed. The primary way in which I have modified this theory is by showing that it is the performatory acts in various media that confront the individual with the alternatives for which he then select further information. It is this performatory activity, therefore, that provides the occasions for the radical elaboration of the perceptual world.

Although each preformatory domain, or medium, may be expected to specify a somewhat unique set of cues as invariant and, hence, to have a somewhat unique effect on the type of perceptual information selected or attended, no attempt has been made to exhaustively list these performatory domains or their effects or their interrelation. Rather, I have selected two types: one that may be roughly described as locomotion and prehension, and the other as the cultural media, including language and geometry.

Locomotion and prehension, performatory acts that characterize many animals including man, required, for their guidance, information based primarily on topological cues such as direction, distance, and adjacency. To repeat, it is obvious that you require different cues to catch a ball than to discriminate if from a cup. Mirror-image alternatives such as oppositely oriented diagonals ordinarily provide no information, that is, are not invariant, to use J. J. Gibson's term, for locomotion; hence they are not easily apprehended by species which specialize in locomotion (Sutherland, 1969). Organisms deprived of the performatory attempts can pick up no relevant information because they have not been confronted with the alternatives (Held and Hein, 1963; Kohler, 1962). It is analogous to hearing the answer "Yes" when you did not hear the question. The bias of young children towards the performatory acts of locomotion and prehension may account for the fact that their early development is described in terms of sensory-motor intelligence (Piaget, 1960) or enactive representation (Bruner *et al.*, 1966).

The elaboration of the perceptual world that occurs under the mastery of performatory acts in various cultural media is responsible for the development of what is usually called intelligence. Both the acts of speaking and comprehending an utterance require for their mastery information based on the selection of cues that were otherwise irrelevant and hence undetected. I have reinterpreted the evidence for the existence of "internalized speech" (Vygotsky, 1962; Whorf, 1956; Bruner *et al.*, 1966) in this context. The language is not internalized; rather the perceptual world is elaborated in the context of mastering performatory skill in the medium of language. Similarly, performatory attempts in representational art, geometric drawing, and constructing, require, for their guidance, perceptual information that is somewhat unique to that medium. To state this point in the form of an aphorism: "Squares did not have equal sides and equal angles until one attempted to draw them." The information picked up in the course of the mastery of this medium is hypothesized to be responsible for what has been described, in my view, mistakenly, as "internalized actions" (Piaget and Inhelder, 1956) and "representation" (Cassirer, 1957; Bruner *et al.*, 1966; Gibson, 1969).

Although it is peripheral to my purpose it must be clear how far we have moved from a response-reinforcement theory of psychology. In my view, a person is not learning a response at all; he is elaborating his perceptual knowledge in the course of his performatory attempts in a medium. But it should also be noted how far this account is from perceptual theories that ignore the role of performatory acts in the elaboration of perceptual knowledge.

Finally, I have discussed instruction in terms of the provision of the critical information both of the decision points and the appropriate choice of alternatives to the uninformed by someone who has prior knowledge of what this critical information is likely to be. The successfulness of the instruction is determined by the accuracy with which the teacher anticipates the alternatives being considered by the student and thereby provides the critical information. The information systematically provided by the culture through the schools is relevant primarily to the alternatives encountered in the use of such cultural media as language, mathematics, and art.

It becomes obvious that we are now equipped with a whole new set of conjectures about the nature of intellectual development, conjectures that would probably serve better to introduce a volume than to conclude one.

REFERENCES

Aronfreed, Justin. The problem of imitation. In L. P. Lipsitt and H. W. Reese (Eds.), *Advances in Child Development and Behavior*, Vol. 4. New York: Academic Press, 1969. Pp. 209–319.

Abravanel, E. The development of intersensory patterning with regard to selected spatial dimensions. *Monographs of the society for research in child development*, 1968, **33**, (2, Whole No. 118).

Allen, W. S. *The Nazi seizure of power: The experience of a single German town, 1930–1935*. Chicago: Quadrangle Books, 1965.

Arnheim, R. *Art and visual perception*. Berkeley: University of California Press, 1954.

Arnheim, R. Comments and discussion. In D. R. Olson and S. Pagliuso (Eds.), From perceiving to performing: An aspect of cognitive growth. Special Issue: *Ontario Journal of Educational Research*, 1968, **10** (3), 203–207.

Austin, J. L. *How to do things with words*. New York: Oxford University Press, 1962.

Ausubel, D. P. *The psychology of meaningful verbal learning*. New York: Grune and Stratton, 1963.

Ausubel, D. P. *Educational psychology: A cognitive view*. Toronto: Holt, Rinehart and Winston, 1968.

Bandura, Albert. Social-learning theory of identificatory processes. In D. A. Goslin (Ed.), *Handbook of socialization theory and research*. Chicago: Rand McNally, 1969.

Benton, A. L. *Right-left discrimination and finger localization*. New York: Haber–Harper, 1959.

Bloom, B. S., Engelhart, M. D., Furst, E. J., Hill, W. H., & Krathwohl, D. R. *Taxonomy of educational objectives*. New York: David McKay, 1956.

Boring, E. G. *History, psychology, and science: Selected papers*. New York: Wiley, 1963.

Bower, T. G. R. Slant perception and shape constancy in infants. *Science*, 1966, **151**, 832–834.

Brown, R. W. *Words and things*. Glencoe, Illinois: The Free Press, 1958.

Brown, R. W., & Bellugi, U. Three processes in the child's acquistion of syntax. *Harvard Educational Review*, 1964, **34**, 133–151.

Brown, R. W., & Lenneberg, E. H. A study in language and cognition. *Journal of Abnormal and Social Psychology*, 1954, **49**, 454–462.

Bruner, J. S. On perceptual readiness. *Psychological Review*, 1957, **64**, 123–152.

Bruner, J. S. *The process of education*. Cambridge, Mass.: Harvard University Press, 1960.

Bruner, J. S. The growth of mind. *American Psychologist*, 1965, **20**, 1007–1017.

Bruner, J. S. *Toward a theory of instruction*. Cambridge, Mass.: Harvard University Press, 1966.

Bruner, J. S., Greenfield, P. M. and Olver, R. R. *Studies in cognitive growth*. New York: Wiley, 1966.

Burke, K. *A grammar of motives and a rhetoric of motives*. Cleveland: World Publishing, 1962.

Cassirer, E. *Substance and function*. Chicago: Open Court, 1923.

Cassirer, E. *Language and myth.* New York: Dover Publications, Inc., 1946.

Cassirer, E. *The philosophy of symbolic forms.* Vol. 3. *The phenomenology of knowledge.* New Haven: Yale University Press, 1957.

Chomsky, N. *Language and mind.* New York: Harcourt, Brace, 1968.

Christensen, C. M. Review of D. R. Olson and S. M. Pagliuso (Eds.), From perceiving to performing: An aspect of cognitive growth. *Canadian Psychologist,* 1969, **10,** 157–159.

Clark, H. H. Word associations and linguistic theory. In J. Lyons (Ed.) *New horizons in linguistics.* In press.

Cole, M., Gay, J., Glick, J., & Sharp, D. Linguistic structure and transposition. *Science,* 1969, **164,** 90–91.

Conklin, Harold C. Hanunoe color categories. *Southwestern Journal of Anthropology,* 1955, **2,** 339–344.

Daehler, M. W., Horowitz, A. B., Wynns, F. D., & Flavell, J. H. Verbal and nonverbal rehersal in children's recall. Unpublished manuscript, Institute of Child Development, University of Minnesota, 1969.

D'Andrade, R. G. Sex differences and cultural institutions. In E. Maccoby (Ed.), *The development of sex differences.* Stanford, California: Stanford University Press, 1966. Pp. 174–204.

Desoto, C., London, M., & Handel, S. Social reasoning and spatial paralogic. *Journal of Personality and Social Psychology,* 1965, **2,** 513–521.

DeVore, I. *Primate behavior: Field studies of monkeys and apes.* New York: Holt, Rinehart and Winston, 1965.

Dewey, J. *Democracy and education.* New York: Macmillan, 1916.

Donaldson, M. *A study of Children's thinking.* London: Tavistock, 1963.

Donaldson, M. The origins of logical inference in children's thinking. Paper presented at the International Congress of Psychology, London, July, 1969.

Dyson-Hudson, R., & Dyson-Hudson, N. Subsistence herding in Uganda. *Scientific American,* 1969, **220,** 76–89.

Entwisle, D. R. *Word associations of young children.* Baltimore: Johns Hopkins Press, 1966.

Evans, J. *Children in Africa: A review of psychological research.* New York: Teachers College Press, in press.

Feldman, D. H., A study of a fixed sequence of skill and concept acquisition requisite to performance of a common school task: Map drawing. Stanford: Stanford Center for Research and Development in Teaching, Research Memorandum No. 38, Sept. 1968.

Flavell, J. H. *The developmental psychology of Jean Piaget.* Princeton, N.J.: D. Van Nostrand, 1963.

Francis, E. D. *Highway arithmetic, the teachers' guide to Book One, picture number book.* Revised by D. Kirk. Nairobi: Longman's of Kenya, 1965.

Gage, N. L. Paradigms for research on teaching. In N. L. Gage (Ed.), *Handbook of research on teaching.* Chicago: Rand McNally, 1963. Pp. 94–141.

Gagné, R. M. The acquisition of knowledge. *Psychological Review,* 1962, **69,** 355–365.

Garai, J. E., & Scheinfeld, A. Sex differences in mental and behavioral traits. *Genetic Psychology Monographs,* 1968, **77** (2), 169–299.

Garner, W. R. To perceive is to know. *American Psychologist,* 1966, **21,** 11–19.

Gibson, E. J. Learning to read. *Science,* 1965, **148,** 1066–1072.

Gibson, E. J. *Principles of perceptual learning and development.* New York: Appleton-Century-Crofts, 1969.

Gibson, J. J. *The senses considered as perceptual systems.* Boston: Houghton Mifflin, 1966.

Gombrich, E. H. *Art and illusion.* (2nd ed.). New York: Bollingen Foundation, 1960.

Greenfield, P. M. On culture and conservation. In J. S. Bruner, *et al.*, *Studies in cognitive growth.* New York: Wiley, 1966. Pp. 225–256.

Greenfield, P. M., & Bruner, J. S. Culture and cognitive growth. *International Journal of Psychology,* 1966, **1**, 89–107.

Greenfield, P. M., Reich, L. C. & Olver, R. R. On culture and equivalence: II. In J. S. Bruner, *et al.*, *Studies in cognitive growth.* New York: Wiley, 1966. Pp. 270–318.

Held, R., & Hein, A. Movement-produced stimulation in the development of visually guided behavior. *Journal of Comparative and Physiolgical Psychology,* 1963, **56**, 872–876.

Herbert, J. J., & Harsh, C. M. Observational learning by cat. *Journal of Comparative Psychology,* 1944, **37**, 81–95.

Herman, D. T., Lawless, R. H., & Marshall, R. W. Variables in the effect of language on the reproduction of visually perceived forms. *Perceptual and Motor Skills,* 1957, **7** (Monogr. Suppl. 2), 171–186.

Hertz, Heinrich. *The principles of mechanics presented in a new form.* Preface by H. von Helmholtz. Translated by D. E. Jones and J. T. Walley. New York: Dover Publications, 1956.

Hubel, D. H., & Weisel, T. N. Receptive fields of single neurones in the cat's striate cortex. *Journal of Physiology,* 1959, **148**, 574–591.

Humboldt, W. *Einleitung zum Kawi-Werk.* In Königliche Preussische Akademic der Wissenschaften, *Gesammelte Schriften* (Berlin, 1903–1922). Cited by E. Cassirer, *The philosophy of symbolic forms.* Vol. 3. *The phenomenology of knowledge.* New Haven, Conn.: Yale University Press, 1957. P. 15.

Huttenlocher, J. Children's ability to order and orient objects. *Child Development,* 1967, **38**, 1169–1176, (a).

Huttenlocher, J. Discrimination of figure orientation: Effects of relative position. *Journal of Comparative and Physiological Psychology,* 1967, **63**, 359–361, (b).

Huttenlocher, J. Constructing spatial images: A strategy in reasoning. *Psychological Review,* 1968, **75**, 550–560.

Ivins, W. M. *Art and geometry: A study in space intuitions.* Cambridge, Mass.: Harvard University Press, 1946.

Johnson, S. C. Hierarchical clustering schemes. *Psychometrica,* 1967, **32**, 241–254.

Kahneman, D., Beatty, J., & Pollack, I. Perceptual deficit during a mental task. *Science,* 1967, **157**, 218–219.

Kendler, T. S. Concept formation. *Annual Review of Psychology,* 1961, **12**, 447–472.

Kershner, J. Children's spatial representations and horizontal directionality. *Journal of Genetic Psychology,* in press.

Kinsbourne, M., & Hartley, D. Distinctive feature analysis in children's perception of simple shapes. Paper presented at SRCD, Santa Monica, 1969.

Klein, F. Vergleichende Betrachtungen uber neuere geometrische Forschungen. *Mathematische Annalen,* 1893, **43**, 63–100. Cited by E. Cassirer, *The philosophy of symbolic forms.* Vol. 3. *The phenomenology of knowledge.* New Haven, Conn.: Yale University Press, 1957. P. 157.

Klima, M. *Mathematics in Western culture.* Oxford: Oxford University Press, 1953.

Koestler, Arthur. *The sleepwalkers: A history of man's changing vision of the universe.* New York: Macmillan, 1959.

Kohler, I. Experiments with goggles. *Scientific American,* 1962, **206**, 62–72.

Kohler, W. *Gestalt psychology.* New York: Liveright, 1929.

Kuhn, T. S. *The structure of scientific revolutions.* Chicago: University of Chicago Press, 1962.

Külpe, O. Versuche über Abstraction. *Ber. I. Kongr. exp. Psychol.* 1904, 56–68.

Lashley, K. S. The mechanism of vision: XV. Preliminary studies of the rats' capacity for detail vision. *Journal of General Psychology*, 1938, **18**, 123–193.

Lashley, K. S. The problem of serial order in behavior. In L. A. Jeffress (Ed.), *Cerebral mechanisms in behavior: The Hixon symposium.* New York: Wiley 1951. Pp. 112–136.

Levi-Strauss, C. *Structural anthropology.* New York: Basic Books, 1963.

Levy-Bruhl, L. *La mentalité primitive.* Paris: Librairie Félix Alcan, 1922.

Luria, A. R. *Speech and the regulation of normal and abnormal behavior.* New York: Liveright, 1961.

Maccoby, E. E. Sex differences in intellectual functioning. In Eleanor E. Maccoby (Ed.), *The development of sex differences.* Stanford, California: Stanford University Press, 1966. Pp. 25–55.

Maccoby, E. E. What copying requires. In D. R. Olson and S. Pagliuso (Eds.), *From perceiving to performing: An aspect of cognitive growth.* Special Issue: *Ontario Journal of Educational Research*, 1968, **10** (3), 163–170.

Maccoby, E. E. & Bee, H. L. Some speculations concerning the lag between perceiving and performing. *Child Development*, 1965, **36**, 367–377.

Mackworth, N. H. The wide-angle reflection camera for visual choice and pupil size. *Perception and Psychophysics*, 1968, **3**, 32–34.

Mackworth, N. H. and Bruner, J. S. Measuring how adults and children search and recognize pictures. Submitted to Monographs of the Society for Research on Child Development, 1969.

Mandler, G. From association to structure. *Psychological Review*, 1962, **69**, 415–426.

Mandler, G. Verbal learning. In T. M. Newcomb (Ed.), *New directions in psychology.* Vol. III. New York: Holt, Rinehart & Winston, 1967. Pp. 1–46.

Manners, R. The Kipsigis of Kenya: Culture change in a "model" East African tribe. In J. H. Steward (Ed.), *Contemporary change in traditional societies.* Vol. I. Urbana, Ill.: University of Illinois Press, 1967. Pp. 205–360.

McLaughlin, G. H. Psychologic: A possible alternative to Piaget's formulation. *British Journal of Educational Psychology*, 1963, **33**, 61–67.

McLuhan, M. *The Gutenberg galaxy.* Toronto: University of Toronto Press, 1962.

McLuhan, M. *Understanding media: The extensions of man.* Toronto: McGraw-Hill, 1964.

McNeill, D. The development of language. In P. A. Mussen (Ed.), *Carmichael's manual of child psychology.* (Rev. ed.). New York: Wiley, in press.

Miller, G. A. *Psychology, the science of mental life.* New York: Harper and Row, 1962.

Miller, G. A., Galanter, E., & Pribram, K. H. *Plans and the structure of behavior.* New York: Henry Holt, 1960.

Modupe, Prince. *I was a savage.* New York: Harcourt, Brace & World, 1957.

Montessori, M. *Dr. Montessori's own handbook.* New York: Schocken Books, 1914.

Munroe, R. L. & Munroe, R. H. Maintenance-system determinants of child development among the Logoli of Kenya. Paper presented at the meeting of the American Psychological Association, Washington, D.C., 1967.

Munroe, R. L. & Munroe, R. H. Space and numbers: Some ecological factors in culture and behavior. Paper presented at the workshop of the Makerere Institute of Social Research, New York, December, 1968.

Munroe, R. L., Munroe, R. H., & Daniels, R. E. Effect of status and values on estimation of coin size in two East African societies. *Journal of Social Psychology*, 1969, **77**, 25–34.

Neisser, U. *Cognitive psychology*. New York: Appleton-Century-Crofts, 1967.

Olson, D. R. On conceptual strategies. In J. S. Bruner, *et al*, *Studies in cognitive growth*. New York: Wiley, 1966. Pp. 135–153.

Olson, D. R. From perceiving to performing the diagonal. In D. R. Olson and S. Pagliuso (Eds.), From perceiving to performing: An aspect of cognitive growth. Special Issue: *Ontario Journal of Educational Research*, 1968, **10** (3), 171–180.

Olson, D. R. Language acquisition and cognitive development. In C. Haywood (Ed.), *Social-cultural aspects of mental retardation*. New York: Appleton-Century-Crofts, in press, 1970(a).

Olson, D. R. Language and thought: Aspects of a cognitive theory of semantics. *Psychological Review*, in press, 1970(b).

Olson, D. R., & Baker, N. E. Children's recall of spatial orientation of objects. *Journal of Genetic Psychology*, 1969, **114**, 273–281.

Paivio, A. Mental imagery in associative learning and memory. *Psychological Review*, 1969, **76**, 241–263.

Pascual-Leone, J. A mathematical model for the transition rule in Piaget's developmental stages. Unpublished manuscript, University of British Columbia, Vancouver, 1967.

Pascual-Leone, J., & Smith J. The encoding and decoding of symbols by children. *Journal of Experimental Child Psychology*, in press.

Peristiany, J. G. *The social institutions of the Kipsigis*. London: Routledge & Kegan Paul, 1939.

Piaget, J. *The construction of reality in the child*. New York: Basic Books, 1954.

Piaget, J. *The psychology of intelligence*. Paterson, N.J.: Littlefield, Adams, 1960.

Piaget, J. and Inhelder, B. *The child's conception of space*. London: Routledge & Kegan Paul, 1956.

Polanyi, M. Logic and psychology. *American Psychologist*, 1968, **23**, 27–43.

Popper, K. *Conjectures & refutations: The growth of scientific knowledge*. New York: Basic Books, 1962.

Premack, D. & Schwartz, A. Preparations for discussing behaviorism with chimpanzee. In F. Smith & G. A. Miller (Eds.), *The genesis of language: A psycholinguistic approach*. Cambridge, Mass.: M.I.T. Press, 1966. Pp. 295–336.

Price-Williams, D. R. A study concerning concepts of conservation of quantities among primitive children. *Acta Psychologia*, 1961, **18**, 297–305.

Price-Williams, D. R. Abstract and concrete modes of classification in a primitive society. *British Journal of Educational Psychology*, 1962, **32**, 50–61.

Reudel, R. G. & Teuber, H. L. Discrimination of direction of line in children. *Journal of Comparative and Physiological Psychology*, 1963, **56**, 892–898.

Ryle, G. Thinking. *Acta Psychologia*, 1953, **9**, 189–196.

Sapir, E. *Language*. New York: Harcourt, Brace & World, 1921.

Scheffler, I. *Conditions of knowledge*. Chicago: Scott, Foresman, 1965.

Schmidt, W. H. O. School and intelligence. *International Review of Education*, 1960, **4**, 416–432.

Segall, M. H., Campbell, D. T., & Herskovits, M. J. *The influence of culture on visual perception*. New York: Bobbs-Merrill, 1966.

Seigel, S. *Nonparametric statistics*. New York: McGraw-Hill, 1956.

Sinclair-De Zwart, H. *Acquisition du langage et developpement de la pensee*. Paris: Dunod, 1967.

Skinner, B. F. *The behavior of organisms*. New York: Appleton-Century-Crofts, 1938.

Snell, B. *The discovery of the mind*. New York: Harper & Row, 1960.

Sokolov, E. N. The modeling properties of the nervous system. In M. Cole and I. Maltzman (Eds.), *A handbook of contemporary Soviet psychology.* New York: Basic Books, 1969. Pp. 671–704.

Solomon, R. L., & Turner, L. H. Discriminative classical conditioning in dogs paralyzed by curare can later control discriminative avoidance responses in the normal state. *Psychological Review*, 1962, **69**, 202–219.

Sperling, G. The information available in brief visual presentations. *Psychological Monographs*, 1960, **74**, (11, Whole No. 498).

Spinelli, D. N., & Barrett, T. W. Visual receptive field organization of single units in the cat's visual cortex. *Experimental Neurology*, 1969, **24**, 76–98.

Spring, Carlton. Same-different reaction time to letters in dyslexic and normal children. Unpublished doctoral dissertation. Stanford University, 1970.

Staats, A. W. Categories and underlying mental processes, or representative behavior samples and S–R analyses: Opposing heuristic strategies. In D. R. Olson and S. Pagliuso (Eds.), *From perceiving to performing: An aspect of cognitive growth.* Special Issue: *Ontario Journal of Educational Research*, 1968, **10** (3), 187–202, (a).

Staats, A. W. *Learning, language and cognition.* New York: Holt, Rinehart and Winston, 1968(b).

Sutherland, N. S. Visual discrimination of orientation by octupus: Mirror images. *British Journal of Psychology*, 1960, **51**, 9–18.

Sutherland, N. S. Shape discrimination in the rat, octupus, and goldfish. *Journal of Comparative and Physiological Psychology*, 1969, **67**, 160–176.

Thorndike, E. L. *The fundamental of learning.* New York: Teachers College, Columbia University, 1932.

Vurpillot, E. The development of scanning strategies and their relation to visual differentiation. *Journal of Experimental Child Psychology.* 1968, **6**, 622–650.

Vygotsky, L. S. *Thought and language.* Cambridge: The M.I.T. Press, 1962.

Wagner, G. *The Bantu of North Kavirondo.* Vol. 1. London: Oxford University Press, 1949.

Wason, P. C. The processing of positive and negative information. *Quarterly Journal of Experimental Psychology*, 1959, **11**, 92–107.

Wason, P. C., & Johnson-Laird, P. N. Proving a disjunctive rule. *Quarterly Journal of Experimental Psychology*, 1969, **21**, 14–20.

Werner, H. *Comparative psychology of mental development.* New York: Science Editions, 1948.

White, S. H. Evidence for the hierarchical arrangement of learning processes. In L. P. Lipsitt & C. C. Spiker (Eds.), *Advances in child development and behavior*, Vol. 2. New York: Academic Press, 1965.

Whorf, B. L. *Language, thought and reality.* New York: Wiley, 1956.

Witkin, H. D., Dyk, R. B., Faterson, A. F., Goodenough, D. R., & Karp, S. A. *Psychological differentiation.* New York: Wiley, 1962.

Yarbus, A. L. *Eye movements and vision.* New York: Plenum Press, 1967.

Zaporozhets, A. V. The development of perception in the preschool child. In Mussen, P.H. (Ed.), European research in cognitive development. *Monographs of the Society for Research in Child Development*, 1965, **30** (No. 2), 82–101.

AUTHOR INDEX

Numbers in italics refer to the pages on which the complete references are listed.

211

SUBJECT INDEX

A

Activity, internalized, 17, 89, 187, 189–190, 196, 197, 202
Affluvia, 3
Age,
  intellectual development and, 97, 101, 120, 122–123
  visual search and, 132, 139, 155
    construction and, 150, 151
    distinguishing features and, 140–141, 156
    pattern of, 142–145, 146–149
Alternatives, *see under* Perception
Anomaly, 6
  discovery and, 2–3
    schema and, 3
  instruction and, 51
    nonverbal, 105–106
  in problem difficulty comparison, 36
  visual search and, 143
Art, *see* Representation in art
Associationist learning theory, 42–43, 53

B

Block designs, copying of, general experience and, 127
Bulb-board, 6, 25, 26, 44
  compared to checkerboard, 46–47
  effects of instruction and, procedure, 45
  misperception of model and, 57
  topological features and, 175

C

Card sorting, 79–80, 82–83, 85, 87, 102
  forming conceptual systems and, 59, 63–64, 66–67, 73
  lexicon and, 113
Cat,
  locomotion and development of perception and, 186

modeling and, 191
  visual system of, 174
Checkerboard, 25–27
  advantages of use of, 26, 61
  card sorting and construction on, 81
  compared to bulb-board, 46–47
  as educational toy, 160, 162
  limitations of, 104
  misperception of model and, 57
  performance of Kenyan children on, 119–122
    age and, 122–123
    general experience and, 126, 127–128, 129
    language and, 126–127, 129
    schooling and, 123–126, 127
    tribe and, 127
  recognition of configuration on, 64
Cognitive learning theory, 43, 53
Concept(s), 15–16, 53
  distinguished from percepts, 15–17
  distinguished from response, 54–55
  linguistic medium and, 189
  of mind, 110–111, 114
  origin of, 59
  scientific, 72
    in formal instruction, 88
  transfer of training and, 53
Concept formation, 1, 5, 72–75, 95, 159, 199
  theory of, 72
Conception, distinguished from perception, 14, 56, 70, 181–182, 196
Conceptual development, 17, 96
  language as basis of, 103–104, 105
Conceptual space, 16–17
  educational toy and, 171
Conceptual systems, 5, 16, 58, 59–60, 61–75, *see also* Structure, conceptual
  articulation by language and, 85–89, 102–104
    experience and, 89–101, 102
  culture and, 113, 114–116
    in Kenyan children, 110, 120–130
  development of, 126, 128–131

214

L

Language, 4, 59
  articulation of conceptions by, 77–78,
    84, 85–87, 102–104
    experience and, 89–101, 102
  concepts and, 15–16
  conceptual systems and, 126–127, 129–
    131
  cultural influence on, 111–112, 115
  effect on perception, 115–116
  in instruction, 76–78, 84, 85–87, 102–
    104, 198–200, 202
    articulation of experience and, 89–
      101, 102
    limitations of, 199–200
  internalized, 40, 77, 88, 96, see also
    Internalized speech
  Kenyan, 126–127, 129
  as a medium, 189
  nervous system and, 196
  performance and, 184
  serial tasks and, 68, 69, 71
  skill in, 193–194
  structure of, 10–11, 40
    influence of on perception, 112–113
    semantic, 111–112, 177–181
  transition to conceptual system and,
    73–74
Learning, see also Educational toy;
  Overlearning
  effects of instruction on, 48–55
  efficiency of, 43, 48
Learning theories, 42–43, 53, 54
  language in instruction and, 89, 103
Lexicon, 67, 75
  discrimination of orientation of line
    and, 177–181
  organization of experience and, 113
  problem difficulty and, 11
Linguistic decisions, 188–189, 190
  as a means of instruction, 103–104,
    198–200, 202
  limitations of, 199–200
Locomotion, 4
  perceptual information gained in, 172,
    185–186, 187, 189, 201–202
Logic, 130–131
Logical operations, 14–15, 115

M

Mediation, 66
  by representations, 22
Medium, 19–20, 24, 184–185
  cultural, 8, 21–22, 184, 192
    drawing, 187–188, 192
    effect of on perception, 184–186,
      187–197, 201–203
    intelligence as skill in, 193–197
    language, 189, 192, 194–196, 199–200
    number, 188, 192
    space, 195
Memory, 7, see also Recall; Recognition
  aid to, educational toy and, 170
  construction from, educational toy and,
    165, 166
  language and, 90, 116
  reproductive, 67
  short-term, visual, 115
  visual search and, 139, 140–141
Methodology,
  for assessment of effects of instruction,
    44–46, 78–82, 98–99, 102–103
  cultural effects on intellectual develop-
    ment and, 118
  educational toy and, 160, 161, 163–165
  of Montessori approach, 106, 108
  for problem difficulty comparison, 27–
    28, 29–30, 35–36
  temporal sequence for reproduction
    and, 68
  transition to conceptual system and,
    62–63
  verbal articulation of experience and,
    90–93
  visual search and, 133–139
Mind,
  concept of, 110–111, 114
  skill in media and, 195–196
Mirror images, 176
  discrimination of, 10–11, 173–174
  in locomotion, 201–202
Misperception, 57
Missing stimulus effect, 153
Model, 2, 43
  on checkerboard, 25, 26
  in cognitive development, 3
  copying of forms and, 6–7, 14, 15
  discrimination and, 10